CW01511297

'What does it mean to "judge fairly"? First, it should require us to shut our mouths and open our ears, our hearts and our minds. Then to examine our assumptions and biases as we stand as naked as possible before God desperately seeking the wisdom that can only come from that authority to help us understand the experience of another. That's what *Unmuted* forces an honest reader to do. In *Unmuted*, the reader is confronted with new ideas and people not like themselves in situations not like theirs and the rupturing experience invites transformation, if we take the time to listen deeply. *Unmuted* encourages us to "let the whole earth sing to the LORD" (Ps 96:1, NLT), with every voice contributing to the harmony unrestrainedly, even if to our ears it seems a little off pitch or out of sync. This book challenges us to deal with real relationships in groups rather than large disembodied systems. It is likely to be far more beneficial as a tool to help Christians understand how to create space for others to speak and be heard. To judge fairly is to participate in co-creating new creation and to be changed in the process, with unmuted voices making us the better for listening.'

**Dr Jay Matenga**, Executive Director, World Evangelical Alliance Mission Commission


'The irony that it falls to me, a white British able-bodied university-educated male in his late fifties, to write an endorsement for a book which gathers the perspectives of those whose voices have been muted, is not lost on me. Not to be heard, nor even allowed to speak, is one of the ultimate indignities, yet it is sadly very common, even in the Church and in Christian mission, as the book you have in your hands painfully recounts.

This book is, as the author confesses, an uncomfortable read. As we hear the unmuted voices of women, disabled people, the Roma, those from other cultures and many others, our discomfort stirs in us a desire to interject. Yet may I invite you, for just a moment, to mute that inner voice so that you can genuinely hear the voice of those who are rarely given a platform like this. As Jesus said, "Let those with ears use them and listen!" (NCV).'

**Jim Memory**, Co-Regional Director, Lausanne Movement in Europe

# UNMUTED

# UNMUTED

Speaking to be heard

Edited by
Usha Reifsnider

APOLLOS (an imprint of Inter-Varsity Press)
SPCK Group, Studio 101, The Record Hall, 16–16A Baldwin's Gardens,
London EC1N 7RJ, England
*Email: ivp@ivpbooks.com*
*Website: www.ivpbooks.com*

*First published 2025*

**British Library Cataloguing-in-Publication Data**
A catalogue record for this book is available from the British Library.

ISBN: 978–1–78974–553–5
eBook ISBN: 978–1–78974–551–1

Typeset by Fakenham Prepress Solutions, Fakenham, Norfolk NR21 8NL
Printed in Great Britain by Clays Ltd

Produced on paper from sustainable sources

માતા, પિતા, ગુરુ, દેવ (Gujarati)
Mata, Pita, Guru, Deva
Mother, Father, Teacher, God

'Speak up for those who cannot speak for themselves,
for the rights of all who are destitute.
Speak up and judge fairly; defend the rights of the poor and needy.'
Proverbs 31:8–9

# Contents

Contents

# Contributors

**Claire Tse Chien Chong** is Affiliate Assistant Professor of Global Leadership at Fuller Seminary in Pasadena. She holds a BSc from King's College, London, an MSc from the National University of Singapore and an MEd from the University of Western Australia. Claire Chong and her husband lived in Cambodia for fifteen years, establishing self-sustaining churches and businesses. She is a research and training associate with the Singapore Centre for Global Missions, an innovation catalyst with 'Christ in Theravada Worlds' of Frontier Ventures and serves in the leadership teams of Asia 2020 & Beyond and WEA Mission Commission. Chong is in the final stage of her PhD from the Oxford Centre for Mission Studies (OCMS), UK, exploring the use of a Buddhist epistemological approach in studying Cambodian ritual and religion.

**Elsa Correia Pereira** is a PhD candidate and researcher in Sociology of Religion at the University of Porto, Portugal, affiliated with ISUP-FCT. Married and a mother of two children, she is a worship music composer and author. She is responsible for the Support Network for Migrant and Refugee Citizens and Human Trafficking Prevention of the Portuguese Evangelical Alliance. An activist for women's ministries, her ongoing research focuses on the role of women in Evangelical Churches in Europe.

**Thomas Creedy** is the Publishing Director for Inter-Varsity Press (of which Apollos is an imprint), based in London. He is a member of the Tyndale Fellowship and the American Academy of Religion. He holds a BA in Theology and Religious Studies and an MA in Ministry and Mission. He blogs regularly on a range of topics at www.thomascreedy. co.uk and intends to pursue a PhD in Systematic Theology.

**Lemma Desta** is originally from Ethiopia and now lives in Oslo with his wife, Helen, and two young children. He holds an MA in Theology and another in comparative and international education. Having worked as an instructor in a theological seminary in Southern Ethiopia, he now serves as coordinator for the multicultural church network of the Christian Council of Norway and is a member of the Executive Committee for the Churches Commission for Migrants in Europe (CCME).

**Ashleigh Gibb** is a trauma-informed crossfit and weightlifting coach with a passion for the intersection of fitness, spirituality and trauma. Having worked with survivors of human trafficking for the past seven years, she has been on a journey of researching how to integrate spirituality and fitness as a catalyst for recovery from trauma. With a keen interest in attitudes to the body, she spent a year living in a safe house completing research for her masters. Ashleigh is a PhD candidate in the area of practical theology, clinical spiritual care and counselling at the Claremont School of Theology in Los Angeles.

**Donna Jennings** is passionate about equipping the Church to be both biblically faithful and culturally relevant as we stand at the interface between gospel and culture. She holds an MA in Missiology and has recently started doctoral work. She lives in Belfast with her husband, Nathaniel, and children, Micah and Tabitha.

**Dr Guichun Jun** serves as Research Tutor for Congregational Studies and Admissions Tutor, at OCMS. He is an ordained minister who has experienced various ministry contexts in both Korea and the UK. He holds a BTh from Seoul Theological University, an MDiv from Seoul Theological Seminary and a PhD in Congregational Studies from OCMS/Middlesex University.

**Dr Gigi Khanyezi**, founder of Jesus and Justice, is a certified historical trauma specialist. She integrates liberative theology, interpersonal neuroscience and collective healing to train leaders in co-creating faith communities that heal intergenerational trauma (especially racial) and mobilise towards a more just society. She earned a BA in Sociology and African and African American Studies from the University of California,

Davis; an MDiv in Intercultural Ministry from Denver Seminary, and a DMin in Healing Racial Trauma from Howard University School of Divinity. She is a Brown artist and activist of Amish and Afro-Brazilian descent and a proud adoptive mother who spent ten years serving in Soweto, South Africa.

**Dr Rafael Năstase** works in Public Relations for Operation Mobilization. He holds an undergraduate degree in Philosophy and Journalism from Spiru Haret University, as well as a Masters in Theological Studies and a Doctorate in Theology and Ecclesiology/Ethnography from the University of Bucharest. He is a husband and father to two teenage boys.

**Revd Dr Israel Oluwole Olofinjana** is the Director of the One People Commission at the Evangelical Alliance (UK). An ordained and Accredited Baptist Minister, he has led two multi-ethnic Baptist churches and an independent charismatic church. He is the founding director of the Centre for Missionaries from the Majority World, an honorary research fellow at the Queen's Foundation for Ecumenical Theological Education in Birmingham and is on the advisory group on Race and Theology at the Society for the Study of Theology (SST). He is a consultant to the executive team of Lausanne Europe and on a Christian Aid working group of Black majority church leaders exploring the intersection of climate justice and racial justice.

**Dr Usha Reifsnider** is a British Gujarati Christ-follower. She has served in cross-cultural mission since 1988 and holds an MA in Practical Theology and a PhD with a special focus on the intersection of cultural anthropology and practical theology. She is one of the two Lausanne Europe regional directors, serves on the board of the European Evangelical Alliance and is a director at the Centre of Missionaries from the Majority World. Usha received the Pioneers Award from the One People Commission and the Evangelical Alliance (UK) for her contribution to diaspora theology in the British Hindu context. Usha is married to Dr Matthew Reifsnider and has two married children and an increasing number of grandchildren.

**Dr Melody Wachsmuth** lives in Zagreb, Croatia, where she researches, writes and teaches on topics related to mission and creation care at the Evangelical Theological Seminary in Osijek and at the Roma Bible School. She holds a PhD from OCMS and is part of the newly formed 'Friends of A Rocha in Croatia'.

**Revd Dr David Wise** is a mentor/coach working with Christian leaders in churches, education and mission. He holds a BA in Theology and an MA in Biblical Interpretation from the London School of Theology, as well as a DTh from the University of Roehampton. He has formerly served as a Baptist pastor and a programme lead for the MA in Spiritual Formation at Waverly Abbey College.

**Dr Paul Woods** is an outward-facing Theological Educator at Large. He holds a PhD in Chinese Corpus Linguistics from Sheffield University, a PhD in Biblical Theology from the Asia Graduate School of Theology (AGST) Alliance and an MTh in Applied Theology from Spurgeon's College. Paul's wife, Nadine, is originally from China. She is an administrator at OCMS. They have three grown-up children.

# Acknowledgements

First of all, I would like to thank each of the contributors to this book. Not only did they trust me with their precious, personal and sometimes painful life experiences, but they agreed to make them public. This is possible because of the depth with which we individually and collectively acknowledge our commitment to the Lord Jesus Christ and our role as part of the worldwide body of Christ.

I honour my late parents Hirabhai Somabhai Patel and Kunverben Hirabhai Patel of Aat, Navsari District, Gujarat, India. As migrants in the 1950s, they silently and graciously lived the harsh realities of discrimination and isolation. They moved to England so that I would be born in a place where I encountered Jesus and thus fulfil my *dharma* – God-given spiritual destiny.

In 2017, as the idea for this book was conceived, Revd Dr Joel Edwards CBE mentored me until his death in 2021. He left me with precious words that still echo, 'Usha, enjoy your voice.'

Similarly, I am grateful to the late Dr George Meyers and Jason Benedict of Go To Nations who prompted me to trust my intellectual capacity and prayed that one day I would publish my ideas in print. I will always appreciate the Oxford Centre for Mission Studies for being the perfect place for my PhD and allowing me to present my ideas for this book in a series of Montague Barker Lectures.

Thanks to Cham Kaur and Kate Coleman of Next Leadership who have provided me with such invaluable personal advice and kindness and who inspire me to thrive.

My colleagues in the Lausanne Europe Regional Leadership team have patiently listened and carefully spoken words of encouragement. Ole Magnus Olafsrud unmuted my voice in Amsterdam in 2018. After more than twenty-five years in cross-cultural ministry, I felt heard for the first time. He walked alongside me as I unmuted myself within the Lausanne Movement.

## Acknowledgements

I'm so grateful to my son Kieron and daughter Tara who remind me often how proud they are that I am speaking to be heard. Thanks also to their wonderful spouses Megan and Joe who joined our family and listen and cheer me on from the sidelines. Last but not least, Matt, my husband, friend and helper who diligently takes care of the details and complexities of my life and graciously stands in the shadows. You are my gift.

# Introduction

This is a deliberately uncomfortable book. As the epigraph from Proverbs 31 might have given the reader a hint, this book seeks to offer a place in which some of those who cannot speak for themselves can speak. These pages are an opportunity for Evangelicals to hear from some of our own, albeit with a different life experience from that which is usually expected. As we seek to let the contributors to this volume 'speak up', we ask the reader to 'judge fairly', too. The voices that have contributed to this book come from wide ranges of cultures, places and perspectives. They are united by their shared faith in Christ – yet that faith is expressed in different registers and styles. Readers in the Anglosphere will be particularly challenged – perhaps made to be uncomfortable – we are all invited to hear and 'judge fairly'.

As well as a potentially uncomfortable and challenging book, this is also a book of three parts. The first unpacks a little of what Muted Group Theory (MGT) is – both historically and in terms of how it can be utilised as a tool in Christian theology. After the two introductory chapters, we begin to consider what it might mean to 'unmute' specific voices, with seven chapters seeking to take seriously the lived experience of, and theologically reflect with/on, disparate groups of image-bearers. The volume then concludes with four chapters that offer more specifically practical and missiological reflections, touching on challenges that are both personal (such as religious practices) and universal (such as climate change). Each author applies Muted Group Theory in a context as they understand it.

Dr Usha Reifsnider, the editor and compiler of this volume, introduces MTG, drawing on her own experience, and offers insight to the Evangelical Church. Later, she writes a deeply personal and wide-ranging chapter, 'Unmuting cultural practices in conversion'. She is surely right in observing that 'new believers from different cultures bring new ideas and experiences that become part of the body of Christ. Those within may experience changes of ideas and interaction with differences as an ongoing benefit in being a part of the body of Christ.' Other observations of note include the possibility of considering the challenge of our own cultures and how they interact with the cultures of others.

Dr Paul Woods, with an eye on his extensive experience of working with Chinese churches in the UK and Southeast Asia, continues our exploration by offering some theological insights into how MGT and Scripture might relate. Compelled by the Evangelical conviction of the authority of Scripture, Woods bookends his introduction with Genesis and Revelation. A short introduction to the theory sets the stage, before we are shown how the creation narrative of Genesis 2 contains elements of 'unmuting'. A particular focus is given to the words of Jesus and also the narratives around his birth. Woods shows us how MGT is one way of making sense of some of the movements of God's kingdom throughout Scripture, as we will see throughout this volume.

Elsa Correia Pereira offers a provocative chapter that in some way must be seen as seeking to unmute around half of Evangelicals – women. She avoids, in general, the questions that so often dominate the (predominantly historically Western) 'complementarian/egalitarian' debate,[1] instead seeking to *listen to the voices of women*, in what will ultimately be forty-five interviews among Portuguese Evangelicals as part of her doctoral work. What emerges is a complex picture – readers are given the opportunity to listen and to compare the experiences of some of our sisters in Christ to the words and teaching of Jesus. Taking seriously the vital differences between men and women, her chapter will not find agreement in every church, but it engages with vital questions.

Resilient hope is not easily seen in the harrowing opening of Ashleigh Gibb's chapter, which alludes to some of the most horrendous crimes extant in our fallen world – the sexual abuse and trafficking of women, including underage girls. She carefully uses the language of trauma – itself contested, but clearly describing something very real – drawing from a

---

1 For another example of an engagement with the experience and potential of women, from within evangelicalism, see Dawson (2024). As Mark Meynell, of the Langham Partnership, notes in his foreword, 'her correspondents hold a range of different views. But what they share is a sense of pain and confusion derived from their lives in churches over many years… Surely that is not a question of being complementarian or egalitarian. It is a matter of Christian love and service' (Dawson 2024:xiii–xiv).

wide range of theological and theoretical voices to speak meaningfully of the relationship between trauma and muting. In this there is an echo of the psychosomatic wholeness of the human being, damaged in trauma, that is a key theological theme of this volume. A particular contribution of this chapter is a fresh and moving perspective on Esther.

Donna Jennings offers a contribution that poignantly combines theological rigour with the lived reality of being the mother of a disabled child/child who lives with severe disabilities. From this, she rightly challenges bad theological anthropology – noting the rich biblical language (notably Genesis 1 and Psalm 139) that confronts hyper-cognitive or ability-based understandings of what it means to be made in the image of God. There is an invitation to hear, however that might sound, the voices of all, including those who are profoundly disabled. As Frances Young notes in her moving book, *Arthur's Call*, 'it's the broken, vulnerable, clay pots of our bodies which paradoxically bear testimony to God's power: God's glory, light, life and wisdom hidden in the ordinariness of fragile clay jars' (Young 2014:134) – Jennings offers us tools to consider how we might see that, in all image-bearers, as part of Christ's eschatological community.

Revd Dr David Wise opens his chapter by inviting us into a specific place (Greenford, in the London borough of Ealing) and a specific time period (1987–2015), and the fascinating journey of one local church. Under the providence of God, Wise's stewardship and leadership was one aspect of the coming into being of a significantly intercultural church. Wise comes across as an engaged and humble pastor – not least in his recognition that 'unmuting' relates not just to speech, but to practices such as dance and worship! This chapter offers one methodology of unmuting in devoting space to the voices of a culturally diverse church, introducing us as readers to brothers and sisters in Christ who we might otherwise not meet this side of the Eschaton. His chapter concludes the opening trio, preparing us to move on to specific voices.

Lemma Desta opens the final section of this volume with dry humour around how 'muting' and 'unmuting' have taken on a specific cultural meaning as a result of the digitalisation of society from the Covid-19 pandemic, before considering how his own personal story can contribute to both muting and unmuting. His chapter makes for hard reading for those of us living in comparatively comfortable contexts and will challenge us to consider what it might mean to truly be a brother and sister to the Church around the world. His personal story gives weight to his engagement with topics and questions that we might find uncomfortable – with his resilient hope offering another gift to the wider Church.

A powerful reflection from Dr Gigi Khanyezi opens with a simple yet painfully rich vignette, captured by the question, 'I'm a human, what are *you*?' As someone who bears multiple cultural and ethnic identities in her own self, Khanyezi invites us, from our different cultures, to consider the reality of the in-between. It is likely that for many readers this will be their first encounter of someone who is half-Brazilian and half-Amish! This chapter invites the reader to consider a wide range of stories and data, before rooting its theology in Genesis 1 and the radical goodness that God teaches us there. As Khanyezi closes, she reminds us that 'Jesus' life is an invitation and a call to follow his lead', pointing to a time yet to come.

The closing middle section of this volume considers a group of people who have often been misunderstood. Dr Melody Wachsmuth and Dr Rafael Năstase consider what it might mean to 'unmute' the Roma, who, as they observe, 'have been living as long-term subordinate groups to the majority cultures for centuries'. This chapter focusing on the Roma has a powerful challenge to ecclesial and Evangelical perceptions of 'being normal', with the possibility of readers applying that to other groups being roundly challenged by a sobering summary of Roma history in relation to Christian cultures. For Evangelicals used to Anglo-American-centred stories, Wachsmuth and Năstase's chapter is a profound testimony to the way in which the incarnation acts as both a centring reality and a hint of the eschatological future of the Church, which includes Roma disciples and non-Roma disciples alike.

Dr Claire Chong adds missiological, historical and cultural perspectives to the theological explorations of this volume. Building on Reifsnider and Woods's contribution, she examines 'the Ancestor Controversy', bringing MGT to bear. Her lively and interdisciplinary chapter raises important questions around how we relate to the Bible and the implications of that for global evangelicalism. Acts 15 is unpacked as a theoretical example of unmuting – Chong demonstrates the complex interplay between submission to Scripture and the Holy Spirit and a serious engagement with cultural issues. Her application of this to a Cambodian cultural practice is a careful and helpful demonstration of the importance of understanding what different things do and do not *actually mean*.

The Revd Dr Israel Oluwole Olofinjana contributes with a wide-angled view, considering a global challenge and how it disproportionately affects the Majority World. His careful parsing of different speech and linguistic norms in discussion of climate and creation theological topics represents a vital form of unmuting. Olofinjana's contribution carefully combines both the specific concerns of climate justice and some of the themes identified in this volume around reverse mission, World Christianity and the need for genuinely authentic unmuted expressions of theology and practice.

Dr Guichun Jun opens his chapter, the title of which might raise a wry smile for those of us who have experienced congregational conflict, with the shocking words 'Pastor, our church building is on fire.' He recounts a complex situation – different aspects of which will resonate with many– before suggesting some ways *through* the conflict, ultimately finding the key theological resource in Paul's teaching on unity in 1 Corinthians 12. Jun's contribution invites us to take inter-congregational conflict seriously, trusting God for the provision of resources to resolve it – primarily Scripture – but also important tools for conversation, connection and reconciliation.

The editors of and contributors to *Unmuted* represent a complex intersection of Jesus-followers, with different sexes, cultural backgrounds, ethnicities and denominational affiliations. A common thread that ties these chapters together is one of eschatology. In Revelation 7:9–14 (ESV), we are granted a glimpse of one aspect of the wedding supper of the Lamb:

After this I looked, and behold, a great multitude that no one could number, from every nation, from all tribes and peoples and languages, standing before the throne and before the Lamb, clothed in white robes, with palm branches in their hands, and crying out with a loud voice, 'Salvation belongs to our God who sits on the throne, and to the Lamb!' And all the angels were standing around the throne and around the elders and the four living creatures, and they fell on their faces before the throne and worshipped God, saying, 'Amen! Blessing and glory and wisdom and thanksgiving and honour and power and might be to our God forever and ever! Amen.' Then one of the elders addressed me, saying, 'Who are these, clothed in white robes, and from where have they come?' I said to him, 'Sir, you know.' And he said to me, 'These are the ones coming out of the great tribulation. They have washed their robes and made them white in the blood of the Lamb.'

Our prayer and hope for this volume is that these contributions might bring a little more light and help us understand a little better the 'who' that Jesus is drawing to himself.

Usha Reifsnider and Thomas Creedy

# 1

# Opening Muted Group Theory

## USHA REIFSNIDER

Titling a book *Unmuted* was probably the biggest step to allowing myself to speak with honesty about a huge part of my life. As a second-generation migrant and first-generation Christ-follower from a Hindu background, my life experiences don't always have the common overlaps with other Christians in the West. Instead, only the parts that are common to others or that spark a curiosity hold their interest for a moment. Many other marginalised individuals and smaller collectives are on the borders of social groups within the Christian contexts. When we attempt to voice ideas, we regularly find those with whom we speak have made assumptions about us before we have even spoken. This book is written for those who want to engage with the 'Other' from a posture of honest, open listening, without the subconscious prejudgements that are the shortcuts of assumptions.

While the challenges of social media are largely unprecedented, so are the opportunities to hear articulations that could not have been possible face to face. These, I believe, have led to encouraging minority and marginalised peoples to speak out with the hope of being heard. The voices of women, minority ethnic groups and many others have found ways to be noticed. In many instances, if Western Christians are honest, they are feeling censured, and are acutely aware of the privilege and responsibility of being White and/or male and/or being or holding Western Christian perspectives. Even Christians who reside in the Majority World are having their Western Christian theological practices questioned.

At the very least, the Church all over the world is deeply influenced by Majority Western Christian thinking by virtue of the fact that most

Christian writing is in English. Individuals have no choice in skin colour, birthplace, birth time or birth gender. Western Evangelical Christians didn't choose initially to consciously choose privilege. They didn't know about the certain amount of ease that they take for granted until they hear the unfiltered voices from those of us who have not just felt stung, slapped and shocked for our entire lives for not being White or Black enough, not being male, or not speaking English. They have felt the long-term impact of imposed identification by Western forms of Protestant Christian representation.

As I write, I can almost hear the questioning of my honesty followed by the sting of shame, guilt and then acceptance that those who have the authority have a powerful voice.

# Growing up muted

From my earliest memories, I listened to other people inform me about me. I am British by birth and Gujarati by heritage and I am a follower of Christ. I was 9 years old when I was taught in primary school that India was full of savages, that the people were all poor and lived in mud huts. After school, I told my father what I had learned. He corrected me and said India had fine palaces, the Taj Mahal and civilisations far before England. The next day in class, as we continued to learn about India, I raised my hand and asked Mrs Barton if she had heard of the Taj Mahal and repeated my father's depiction of India's rich past. I was told to leave the classroom and stand in the corridor until the headmaster, Mr Barton, disciplined me appropriately. I looked at my ugly dark skin and frizzy black hair. There was no hiding it. I was a type of savage or, in Gujarati, *jungli jaat*. Full of shame, I went back into the classroom with the absolute conviction that my father was an ignorant savage. Mr and Mrs Barton would ever represent the voices of authority. They had the real knowledge of India from a book and what they taught was true, because that is how I would pass my exams, succeed and have value.

The following year, my teacher, Mrs Baker, who had been taking me and my sisters to Sunday school for the last five years, asked what I wanted to be when I grew up. Boldly, I said I wanted to be a missionary doctor. I had seen a visiting missionary's slides of Asians in churches, perhaps in Taiwan. They were dressed in fine Western clothes and learning English. They were not of the *jungli jaat* like my Mum, who still dressed in her traditional sari and babbled in her backwards mother tongue. I spoke English and I was educated and I could be just like them if I converted to Christianity and left wicked heathen ways behind. No more annual chaotic cultural family events, no more attending noisy festivals at homes in the community or in the mandir (Hindu Temple), no more wearing a sari that was inappropriate and deemed by some Christians to be deliberately sensual.

Decades later, I still bear the imprint of Mrs Barton and the imposed savage identity. Trust me, the muting process once initiated is self-perpetuating. It is a shortcut to self-inflict the inevitable. As muted, marginalised minorities, we have often remained silent. We have 'put up' with rejection and humiliation and have anesthetised ourselves before those with power hurt us or anaesthetise us.

As an adult, I still remember the cultural inferiority set within me during my years at primary school. Decades later, as I was studying for my doctorate, I found myself in a lecture room in Oxford with nine other students; three of us with a Majority World background. I was the only woman. I spent six weeks of classes waiting for the college registrar to walk in the room and tell me I shouldn't be there, that the acceptance letter for my place on the course was due to an administration error.

So here I am, having served in cross-cultural mission with the Church in numerous countries and as a PhD, a kind of doctor. To a great degree, Usha is unmuted! My ministry peers like me live in the West. They initially show an overwhelming sympathy and even endeavour to empathise as they listen to my narratives. They genuinely want to 'give me a voice'. They are often disappointed and offended when, instead of being thankful for their consideration, I tell them perhaps a little objectionably, 'I don't need you to "Give me a voice." I have one. I have always had a voice of my own.' Then, with a level of unexpected audacity that shocks even my own ears, I ask them, 'If you give me a voice, who gives you your voice?'

When people speak for others, there is a missing dimension. The individual may be unaware of their patterns of articulation as they are lost among the voices in a community that are the same as their own. Arguably, if the individual has differing experiences from the majority, they find themselves silenced in a particular setting. Their articulations, their comments, their conversations come from their own lived experiences, but they are not understood nor perhaps even considered relevant or even true as they are not shared by the majority. The result is a symbolically violent extraction or silencing to fit into a particular Christian expressed dominant setting. The individual is systematically muted.

The outcome is a box, template or structure created by the dominant voice that decides how individual extraordinary experiences (although not limited to) – race, gender, ability – are cut away, extracted, diluted and deleted. The template becomes a tool that is offered back to the muted, marginalised, subordinate misfits, to make them fit for purpose.

There are cultural practices that have defined and deafened us as the muted group. The dominant culture's voice has an impact on the lives of those who are muted. However, the muted voices, as the subordinate cultural perspective, have little influence on the dominant culture. Once dominance is recognised, cultural routines must be deliberated out loud and challenged by all those who claim to be concerned for all human life and experience. The subordinate and marginalised should not suffer from the categorisation of others and have to brace themselves for the inevitable disappointment of not being understood, considered or valued. Unmuting is an opportunity for the erroneous patterns to become evident. *Unmuted* is a collection of life experiences that are often raw and vulnerable. The authors invite you to listen and walk alongside those who have aspects of their lives articulated and analysed by others. Often, their personal lived experiences are left unexpressed.

Allow me to share one of my own ethnocentric prejudice templates. Born and educated in Britain and married to an American, I, together with my husband, have humbly submitted to share the love of Jesus among Muslims. In 1992, we relocated overseas and attended an Arabic language programme and learned the local dialect. Sometime later, I was in Egypt in a local *dukkan*, a corner shop, about the size of a living room. When the *dukaanji* (shopkeeper) said to me, '*Biddik aeesh?*', with my limited grasp of Arabic, I interpreted '*Biddik aeesh*?' as 'Do you want life?' Immediately, I perceived an instant and violent threat to my life. Despite my declared God-given love for the Muslims to motivate me to a lifelong commitment to mission, in that moment, my latent prejudice burst forth and manifested itself. In that moment, I was operating with a perspective that Muslims and Islam were evil and that their goal was to kill me. I had grown up with Muslim school friends and neighbours. I had Muslim friends in the country that was my home at the time. I had shared in churches and small groups in numerous countries about making the love of Jesus known to Muslims. But in that moment, I operated from my own position of White privilege that I had no idea was imbedded within the dominant Western Christian framework. I made an enemy of an entire people group who used the Arabic word *aeesh* as the colloquial word for bread.

That dear, old wrinkled Egyptian *dukaanji* was offering me bread. The word for bread in Egyptian Arabic is from the root word for the word 'life'. The irony of the whole situation for me as a missionary called to share Jesus, the Bread of Life, with the Muslim world fills me with utter disgust at my own imbedded sinful nature. I implore you to hear me as I unmute my own shame and share with you how deeply the violence of silence needs to be constantly unmuted.

Listening to muted voices is an idea that arose from the research that occurred during my PhD thesis. In my investigation of the stories of those who had converted from Hinduism, Sikhism or Islam to Evangelical Christianity, I found there were two versions of their stories. One story was trimmed, tidied and tied into a five-minute testimony for the church service or for a short magazine article. The progression was virtually the same. And while my observation simplifies the formula, it is basically this: everything about my life was hell-bound. Through a simple prayer to Jesus, I am now heaven-bound. Nothing of my culture of origin, including my parents, siblings or the wider extended family has any relevance to my new life as a Christian. My real life only began when I converted. I am grateful to the Western Church.

I have the church-worthy versions of my own conversion story. The things that we as Christ-followers can't talk about is the pain, the isolation, the separation, not just our own, but that of our dear family and extraordinarily varied community. I soon recognised that muted voices were not limited to those of other religions alone. Muted voices are silenced and exist in every sphere of our structured Christian lives.

Without challenging and pushing against the outer edges of categories, we are in danger of such specialisation that our voices ring only in an echo chamber. Our connections with the 'Other' as part of the body of Christ are limited to the comfortable focus of only what we hold in common. I struggle to see this as a viable expression of being a community, the body of Christ.

Essentially, MGT is about living in community. For the purpose of this book, it is about living as the 'body of Christ' in Christian community. But perhaps I should challenge us to take a less fixed approach on who decides what validates the terms of 'community' and how the 'body of Christ' might function.

This book is a collection of the voices of people with whom I have had the deep pleasure of connecting by listening and being heard. Each chapter is a narrative and analysis from lived experiences along with the lens of MGT. Each contributor is aware of the different ideological and geographical locations where they would like to be heard, but feel as though they are outsiders or marginalised. The collection of voices serves as occasions for each reader to examine their own positions as subordinate voices in dominant structures. These are opportunities for us all to intentionally listen to those who speak and intentionally speak to those who desire to listen.

Many of the chapters begin from personal experiences that challenge traditional perspectives that have held particular beliefs in place. The result of fixed understanding severely limits interactions and inclusion from the margins and minorities. Often, the suffering or, at best, misunderstanding of the less heard or acknowledged group or individual is buried underneath well-meaning statements. Arguably, digging into stereotypes and commonly held views will make us squirm. After all, surely, we have moved on from the days when Christianity was steeped in the language of hierarchy of race, gender, able-bodied and Western culture. How does the body of Christ deal with issues of gender equality, racial disparity, climate justice and the general misunderstanding of the suffering of others? How much of our ordinary theology, our lived practice of the Christian faith deals with realities of individual, interpersonal and communal conflict?

A number of voices in this book will graciously encourage perspectives from those in the margins of ministry under defined labels such as: Roma, Migrant, Woman, Refugee, Mixed Ethnic, Disabled, Majority World. Their identities are generated most often by externally created categories that are habitually reinforced internally. The paradox is that of the dominant voice creating the category, based upon their value system above the subordinate groups and individuals. However, concurrently, the subordinate marginalised willingly compromise in the hope of being heard and accepted by the dominant culture. But their subordinate marginalised identity is often absorbed or diluted to the degree that their voices fade away and are left at worst under the cloud of insubordination or at best settling for vague mythical impressions of promises to do better.

If it were not for the times we live in where the victim might be the hero and the hero portrayed as the victim, then this book would perhaps have less interest. Dominant ideologies appear to cry out the shocking injustice as they sense a loss of their influence and rightful position within cultural hierarchies. However, I don't believe MGT is a clear line between the victim and the perpetrator. This false binary may invite everyone to claim victimhood. We may all spend times as subordinates; however, perhaps the measure of impact of subordinate status is where the individual is knowingly or unknowingly categorised most of the time and dependent upon on another with influence and position to represent them positively or label them as 'insubordinate'.

As a second-generation migrant, a woman of colour, a Christ-follower from another religious identity, there are still places where my privilege of having a British education and using English finds creative ways for my muted voice to unmute. However, when I try to explain the subordinate position to individuals within the dominant group, they begin by justifying their position. First, they often claim to be champions for all subordinates because no subordinate has ever challenged them. Second, they claim to be subordinates and victimised themselves, thus negating my attempt to speak from a different perspective. Perhaps instinctively, they simultaneously position themselves as dominant and subordinate, as if the very claim of subordination can also be dominated.

# Silencing as symbolic violence

To silence is to mute. It is to limit expression to what is valuable, acceptable and controllable, though not always consciously. To silence is to create an acceptable structural replicable template to save time, money, resources or to create profit. Symbolic violence is an imposition by dominance that may not necessarily be deliberate, but it becomes so habitual that it becomes impossible to acknowledge it as unethical or erroneous. To ignore or overlook cultural and historical patterns because they bear no relevance to the dominant group destroys personal identities. The violation of erasing aspects of lived experiences that bring meaning to life hides and denies the value of being a bearer of God's image in the subordinate and marginalised.

The subtlety of symbolic violence is that it is exercised upon those within our societies who have less agency. Thus, the victim perhaps unknowingly becomes complicit in the perpetuation and reproduction (Bourdieu and Wacquant 1992:167). The self-fulfilling prophecy becomes accepted as unavoidable; worst still, it may be considered to be in everyone's best interest. Symbolic violence can become part of the conventional acceptable behaviour, like asking non-English speakers to give up their birth name or no longer participate in cultural practices that are not within the confines of Western Christian culture. This deletion of a person's family history and culture by the dominant group erases the birth family role, but worse still, it leaves the subordinate isolated from the dominant and subordinate groups. Symbolic violence becomes part and parcel of a valuing of one cultural expression over another, unless some situation provides a challenge.

I use MGT in order to provide a theoretical background to unmuting. The theory was initially used in feminist studies in the 1970s by Edwin and Shirley Ardener. Discussions on MGT have been revisited and reapplied to address deliberate and perhaps less obvious forms of hierarchy. West and Turner developed the theory further by looking at how silencing is perpetuated and reinforced by ridicule, ritual, control and harassment (West and Turner 2017:493). The foundation of MGT is based on three assumptions. First, dominant and marginalised groups have different world views, hence they respond differently within similar roles. Second, the dominant group perpetuates their power and sometimes, even inadvertently, suppresses the subordinate groups; and third, the subordinate group must modify their unique ideas and experiences to be understood (West and Turner 2017:488).

In discussing ways that subordinate groups communicate with dominant groups, Stanback and Pearce argue that dominant group behaviours have higher agency than subordinate ones (1981:21). As an English speaker, when among speakers of other languages, it is very common that the language of the group shifts to English. Arguably, using the *lingua franca* is a handy shortcut. However, the long-term implication is that all too often, the shift in culture goes with the shift in language. This may carelessly create conventional practices that dominate and favour certain individuals, cultures and people groups.

Edwin and Shirley Ardener suggested that, within the concept of MGT, collectives that function at the top of the hierarchical structure may determine the communication of the entire society (Ardener 1978; Orbe 1998a:20). MGT can be thought of as, 'Aware[ness] of the dynamics between the powerful and the marginalised' (Barkman 2018:3).

So, what happens to those who fall outside the margins? A template by its very nature cuts away and discards what is deemed unnecessary. If English becomes the template for Christian expression, non-native speakers not only have their language discarded, but also their culture.

Orbe's development of co-cultural theory as a response to MGT applies to what he refers to as Standpoint Theory. All perception is limited, but those positionally disadvantaged by the size of representation may have a fuller understanding of the hierarchical structure of the dominant group.

Barkman (2018) acknowledges the 'subtle overlapping power issues' found in church and mission contexts. She offers three points of reference in assessing control:

1 dominance – upholds and reinforces a viewpoint and is privileged to define terms;
2 acceptance – where there is less acceptance, there is less respect;
3 subordination – points of reference flow from dominant communication and resist change (2018:3).

Unmuting is thus voicing unresolved articulations of identity denied the opportunity of expression. This is due to the control of the dominant's acceptable and even expected ways of thinking. However, thinking, speaking and being heard do not come necessarily as a result of being aware of dominant structures, but through repeated cycles of trusting, listening, experiencing, listening, speaking, listening, thinking, listening, researching, listening believing, speaking believing, listening acting, *ad infinitum*.

# Methodology

My use of MGT brings into play important factors of who speaks for whom. In an ideal world, we would have cultural capacity to influence the structures that dominate one group at the expense of another. By speaking with those whose experiences are global and who grapple with the frustration of not being heard, I organised a series of talks. Because the speakers are those with whom I have interacted primarily in the British context, this book has some contextual limitations. However, each author speaks through their experience of being muted by offering the rawness of their life narratives. The listeners must therefore attempt to attune their ears to the voices rather than have the voices adjust to the ears of the dominant. I feel incredibly honoured and humbled to be able to walk alongside those who unmute themselves to me, and equally, so to journey with those who willingly choose to actively listen.

# 2

# Muted Group Theory and Scripture: some theological insights

## PAUL WOODS

At the beginning of this chapter, I wish to introduce a few principal concepts of Muted Group Theory (MGT) by referring to some of the scholarship on the subject and then look at some of the implications of the theory for Christian theology. For reasons of space, I use theological reflection on sections of Genesis and Revelation as bookends for the human experience; individual and corporate. I bring Genesis into dialogue with MGT to gain a sense of where we have come from, and then I look for resonances between Revelation and MGT to look forward to a redeemed and restored future. Finally, I pick up a few themes from the rest of Scripture to see what MGT has to teach us in the here and now, the 'already, but not yet'.

## Muted Group Theory

It is only appropriate to begin with the Ardeners, the first scholars to articulate the theory in their research on women. Although we may think of spoken communication, Ardener reminds us that mutedness relates to all modes of communication because it is 'concerned ultimately with structural relationships' between groups (1993:13). Because mutedness results from the way in which groups relate to each other within existing structures, it is not necessarily the case that one group actually controls or dominates another. Indeed, the power relationships between groups and the structures that govern communication between them operate almost in the background. Mutedness is not necessarily something caused by one group actively seeking to restrict or constrain another, but it is often the result of how society works. One result of this is that muted groups find ways to deal with the existing structures; either they simply work around them or inhabit what Ardener calls the 'interstices' (1993:14).

Although the Ardeners' early work focused on women as a muted group, Meares claims that in any society there are 'cultural groups' who suffer muting (2017:1). Primary modes of expression are decided by dominant groups and subordinate, or muted, groups must learn and agree to express themselves in ways determined by the mainstream. This is related to 'structural relationships' within society, which are products of that society.

Ardener (1993) clarifies that mutedness does not refer to the inability to speak at all, but rather to the issue of how, where and when people can speak. Some muted groups feel that their utterances are not heard, because they are not constructed and voiced in the right way as defined by the dominant groups who specify how communication is done (Ardener 1993:9).

Meares (2017) helpfully summarises the four principal concepts of MGT:

- First, people who belong to different groups in society have different experiences and society has different expectations of them.
- Second, communication is the channel by which power is exercised and privilege displayed.
- Third, marginalised – muted – groups are forced by society to adopt the communication style and methods of the dominant culture and its group.
- Fourth, change is possible, through communication. Muted groups can challenge the *status quo* through creativity and by resisting cultural norms and expectations.

Barkman (2018) agrees that a vital element in MGT is that change is possible. The theory not only diagnoses and explains current mutedness, but also points to solutions.

The phenomenon of mutedness also requires a 'collective understanding' (Mahrukh et al. 2017:165) of who holds and exercises power. Because marginalised groups are forced to communicate in terms that represent the experiences of the dominant group rather than themselves, muted groups are forced to recast their experiences and narratives of them into terms established and maintained by others. People are effectively forced to speak in a foreign language.

# Genesis: humanity's origins and Muted Group Theory

Here, I apply certain ideas from MGT primarily to the first three chapters of Genesis. In Genesis 1, the whole creation can be seen as God communicating his purposes to the universe and its inhabitants. In that sense, he controls the narrative and the means by which it is communicated. The creation itself, moving from formlessness and emptiness into its myriad structures of environments and life forms, is a statement of authority and power. God who originally existed alone now brings into being entities other than himself and at this early stage in the history of creation, everything that is not God is muted. The content of the communication and its channels come from God himself, literally by *fiat*.

In the first chapter of Genesis no one speaks apart from God, whose speech creates, and is addressed to, physical and organic parts in the creation. The Creator determines the relationships between the various elements in creation as he lays out his agenda for the complex interactions in the physical and spiritual universe. This creation narrative is punctuated by God's repeated pronouncements of how what he has created fits with his plan and will. The climax of the creation is humankind, to whom God speaks sovereignly to pass on a commission of authority over and care for the creation and to confirm his provision for his image-bearers.

When the narrative shifts to the detailed account of the creation of humankind in Genesis 2, God continues as sole speaker, laying out the terms of reference for the man and the woman and the relationship between them. In chapter 2, God fleshes out the man's duties, giving him responsibility for the garden and his own well-being, but also specifying the first boundaries and restrictions on his behaviour. The infinite

Creator speaks not only to confirm his authority, but also to specify the subordinate relationship that the man is designed to have with him and establish power structures which, in theory, are capable of being violated. God is very clear in his communication to the man about the trees in the garden, particularly the tree of the knowledge of good and evil.

After setting out the basic ground rules for the man's existence in the garden, God calls the man to name each creature and next creates the woman. Only at the end of the chapter does God allow the man to comment on the woman. The man speaks about his environment, the world of animals and plants around him. At this early stage in human history and the relationship between God and human beings, the man is unmuted, in order that he speak about issues relevant to the stewardship framework that God has given him and which also reflect his status as a created being, albeit one who is an image-bearer. When the man speaks, is his unmuting a consequence of his being made in the image of God? No other animal speaks. Is the ability to engage in conversation with God proof of being made in his image? All other created entities are muted, but not the man. The unmuted man names all of the animals and in so doing realises that he is alone, spiritually and emotionally, on the horizontal plane. The man speaks to declare to the creation what God already knows: humanity is a communal species.

When God creates the woman by taking material from the man's side, the Almighty makes no pronouncement. It is left to the unmuted Adam to announce to the world that his companion is a 'bone of his bones and flesh of his flesh' (Gen. 2:23). Within the power structures ordained by God and using human language, itself a concession to the finiteness of the man and the woman, the man presents her as one who shares the very essence of his being. The unmuted declaration adds a horizontal dimension to a hitherto primarily vertical relationship. The man has authority only by virtue of the fact that he existed first and has a developing relationship with his Creator. With regard to the power dynamics at the heart of MGT, there is no sense that the woman is inferior to the man.

At the very end of chapter 2, where the man has spoken to the Creator and creation and has begun an egalitarian, horizontal relationship with someone who is like himself yet also different, the man is unmuted with regard to his Creator and, presumably, also in his relationship with the woman. The human power structures governing our appearance and self-perception have yet to exist; the two people were naked, yet they felt no shame. Such a comment is in itself anachronistic, both in the pre-Fall state and in the absence of other human beings. In other words, the controls on behaviour and associated narratives within human cultures and societies that have various forms of muting at their centre belong to the future. The Genesis account shows the beauty and purity of an unmuted existence when men and women communicate freely with each other and with God, without being subject to the human regulations that began immediately after the Fall. The man and the woman are still following a narrative decided by God and not by human beings. Acknowledging God's right not only to create the universe and the living creatures within it, but also to construct and deliver the narrative describing the process, means accepting a degree of muting. Insofar as MGT relates to the exercise of power, then the creation story is a demonstration and affirmation of God's authority.

The first two chapters of Genesis show the absolute power of God as Creator and as initiator of the relationships between the living creatures and the environment and specifically between human beings. However, this creation story is delivered to us in human language and employs complex literary devices. Although God is the ultimate power and initially the only unmuted party, in using human language he surrenders some of his rights to his human readers; God's condescension is a manifestation of self-muting. Yet a power dynamic remains. God communicates in this way in order to initiate a relationship of dependence and trust, a pre-Fall partnership of submission between humanity and himself. In creating us according to his image, he also requires that in our finite way we represent him and continue his work of creation. God does his part and we are supposed to do ours, within a power structure founded on his perfect love and knowledge. God's negotiated or relative muting is part of a theological distinction and relationship between an infinite and a finite party. However, because MGT emphasises the role of power structures, it is important to recognise that in this context, the more powerful player is not only infinite in authority and knowledge, but also in moral goodness. Our human existence, individual and corporate, shows us that power is almost always abused for the benefit of the stronger party; after all, the very word 'muted' suggests that someone has been denied an ability to speak and express an opinion, which we feel is an inherent human right. Here then, power is exercised with moral purity, for the glory of God and the well-being of the creation, with human beings at the centre.

God's relative self-muting has implications for him and the world he has created. In empowering the man in this way, God is entertaining the possibility that he may begin to craft his own narrative and make his own assessment of the trees in the garden and the appropriateness of eating of their fruit. The man has yet to speak, but God's instructions to him in Genesis 2:15–17 and the responsibility and trust extended to him mark the beginning of humanity's unmuting. The man now has the ability to make decisions, voice them and act upon them. When the man names each living creature in human language (Gen. 2:19), he is exercising his own power and authority under God and over the animals.

Having been invested with the power to administer the garden and create his own narratives, the man is now brought into a deep sleep, during which the woman is created from his side. On waking, the man speaks again, not about birds and animals, but about his equal before God: 'bone of my bones and flesh of my flesh' (Gen. 2:23). It is as if the process of naming the animals, an experience of unmuting, has prepared the man to speak about a new entity in the creation. The unmuted human being pronounces his initial assessment of his complementary equal in a way radically different from his interaction with any of the animals. Humanity here is exercising the right to communicate, not about his ontological inferiors, but about an equal in value and status. It is clearly only a matter of time before the woman speaks too.

At the beginning of chapter 3, the 'Fall chapter', the serpent appears without any introduction. So far, the only entities to speak and the only dialogue partners have been God and man; neither the animals named by the man nor the woman have spoken. In this chapter we see the unmuting of various created entities and the selective muting of the Creator. Completely unexpectedly, the serpent speaks. Does the sudden, manipulative intervention of the serpent suggest that existing power and communication structures are being violated? We do not at this stage know the identity or provenance of the serpent or why it is able to twist God's words. MGT tells us that those at the wrong end of power dynamics are compelled to use the language and communication forms of the powerful. Yet, given that the man and the woman are created in God's image and share the commission to rule and sustain the creation, for the serpent to speak ahead of the woman seems a violation of the God-ordained order of things and an example of how unmuting can be negative and destructive. If the man and the woman represent the pinnacle of the creation, then how does the serpent become unmuted? The text is not clear, but if God is omnipotent Creator, then the implication is that this was permitted by him.

The conversation between the serpent and the woman is something completely new. Both have been muted until now and their conversation implies challenges to existing authority structures and systems of power, both between Creator and created and between different created beings. The serpent knew and understood the instructions that God gave to the man. When the prohibition to eat from the tree of the knowledge of good and evil was given, the woman did not yet exist. It appears to me from Genesis 3:2 that the man must have reported his conversation with God to the woman, passing on God's commands explicitly and an understanding of the power structures governing the conversation between God and human beings implicitly. When the serpent speaks, it is not only no longer muted, but also acting to deceive the woman, a radical form of unmuting in which it violates the existing authority structures and forms of communication. After questioning and sowing doubt in Genesis 3:1, in Genesis 3:4 the serpent goes directly against what God has said and impugns his character. By suggesting that created entities can be like the Creator, the serpent is again altering the structures of power, a form of unmuting that empowers the marginalised, but also deceives and misleads. The serpent's impure motives make its unmuting negative and corrosive towards those who might expect to be liberated.

In response to the serpent's challenge to the established order, the woman takes unilateral action in offering fruit to the man. Because there is no inherent structural hierarchy in the man–woman relationship, we may not consider her action as unmuting in itself. She is as free to talk as the man is and they have a shared form of communication. However, in taking the fruit and eating it and then offering some to her husband, she is acting in opposition to the instructions that the man received from God. In effect, she is muting God, by rejecting what he said and speaking in a way inconsistent with his authority structures.

The man and woman realise that they are naked and hide in the trees from God when he comes, self-muting by avoiding interaction with God and their role as his image-bearing stewards and attempting to mute God by ignoring his instructions. God acts in accordance with established power structures by calling to the man, who reacts appropriately, giving an account of himself to God (Gen. 3:10). God enquires and man responds, and the original muting status of both is temporarily restored. However, the subsequent interaction between God and his people displays successive passing of responsibility. The man informs God that he was given the fruit by the woman whom God put there. In blaming the woman, the man is attempting to mute her. When God turns to the woman, she blames the serpent. Neither person mentions God's clear instruction to the man. The serpent's original unmuting allowed it to question God's character and communicate a falsehood to the woman in Genesis 3:4. However, in their interaction with God, although the two human beings do not try to deceive him, they are unwilling to accept responsibility for their actions. This is a new, negative form of unmuted communication. The consequences of eating of the fruit are a breakdown in relationships between God and people and between people also. God still controls the dialogue, asking the man and the woman in turn what they have done. There is a distinction between humanity's declaration of independence from God, which we call sin, and the unmuting of the woman and the man. Attempts by the marginalised to speak are not inherently wrong and in Genesis 3 it is not unmuting *per se* that is problematic, but the content and aims of the unmuted speech.

At the end of the chapter, we see God's provision for Adam and Eve, but this is accompanied by their exclusion from the garden and the direct presence of God. The physical, emotional and spiritual estrangement between God and humanity can be considered a form of muting.

We know from the rest of the Scripture, beginning in the very next chapter, that people begin to view the world, including their attitudes to each other and to God, in a way not consistent with God's character or desires. Cain's offering to God and subsequent murder of his brother;

Abraham's moral weakness; Jacob's stealing of the birthright; the golden calf; and the repeated ethical failures of the nation of Israel; all represent a relative unmuting of human beings and a relative muting of God. It has been said that at the creation God made people in his image and ever since we have been returning the compliment. Humanity's imposition of its own standards and attempts to interpret God and his plans for our own purposes are forms of muting.

## Revelation: humanity's destiny and Muted Group Theory

Having looked at the first three chapters of Genesis through the lens of MGT, it is time to look at the book of Revelation. The two bookends allow us to understand where we have come from and where we are going in terms of muting and unmuting.

In Revelation 4 and 5, we have the vision of the throne of God, the four living creatures and the twenty-four elders. The display of divine glory and the submission of created beings is a confirmation that God is no longer muted. As it was before the Fall, he now controls the content and form of communication, employing his sinless power for his own glory and the benefit of what he has created. The doxology of Revelation 4:11, which evokes the one in Romans 11, is redeemed humanity's willing act of self-muting.

The affirmation of linguistic and cultural diversity in Revelation 5:9 – 10:5 is significant for any consideration of muted groups. The same theme is found in the famous 'every nation, tribe, people and language' statement of Revelation 7:9). The future vision of God's people in the consummated kingdom is a statement of inclusion and a challenge to any current form of racial or cultural discrimination. This diverse group is present at the throne because of what Christ has done; no human group has any right to mute another and there will be no marginalised groups in the eternal future. At the same time, one of the tasks of the redeemed will be to serve the Lord, accepting his commission to reign and to praise him.

The large central section of the book, containing God's judgement of Satan and evil forces on earth, represents his muting of those opposed to him and his total control of the narrative. The end of Revelation (chapters 21 and 22) is marked in the NIV with the subtitle, 'A New Heaven and a New Earth'. The future vista that God has for us echoes his plan in Genesis. The focus of the narrative is God, as he makes his dwelling with his people. In this new order, with Jesus as the Alpha and the Omega, communication is fully restored between Creator and created and while no group is marginalised, finite, created humanity submits to infinite Creator, divinity as originally envisaged. We note that the presence of the incarnate God-man Christ on the throne, represents not only the unmuted sovereignty of God, but also the unmuting of perfect humanity. The Jesus of Revelation is an unmuted second Adam in the sense of Romans 5. In terms of MGT, redeemed humanity is partly muted in that it submits to a power purer and greater than itself and, at the same time, is liberated to serve and praise God.

In Revelation 21:22, John tells us, 'I did not see a temple in the city, because the Lord God Almighty and the Lamb are its temple.' In the future age of openness and holiness, there is no intermediary or priest between God and his people, a theme developed into a whole book by Beale (2004). For the purposes of this chapter, while the priestly system of the Old Testament constituted a partial muting of ordinary believers and the unmuting of human mediators between God and people, the full access of believers to God after Pentecost (Acts 2) is a spiritual and linguistic unmuting facilitated by the diffuse ministry of the Holy Spirit, as anticipated in the upper room discourse of John's Gospel, especially chapter 16.

The kings of the earth will bring their splendour into the holy city and the glory and the honour of the nations will also be taken into it (Rev. 21:24 and 26). This is an affirmation of human endeavour and creativity and an exhortation to celebrate what it means to be human, made in God's image. It is also a prohibition on any kind of muting; if any group of people is muted, marginalised and pushed out of the mainstream, they will not be able to contribute to the glory, honour and splendour of the nations, which God wishes to see in the city. Our future in God's kingdom will contain the results of hundreds and thousands of years of people employing the gifts that he has given them. At the same time, Revelation 21:27 reminds us that nothing impure will enter the city.

There will be a filtration of what is and what is not acceptable to God, so even as we seek to unmute and empower all human groups, this does not equate to a licence to sin and to produce and disseminate that which God detests.

This paradoxical combination of partial muting and unmuting can only exist in a relationship between humanity and a personal being holier and more complex, who has undergone mutings and unmutings of various kinds in his long relationship with what he created. As a whole, humanity is a group that undergoes partial muting before its Creator. At the same time, all muting within humanity and attempts to establish marginalised groups have come to an end in the fully consummated kingdom.

## The here and now: our witness and Muted Group Theory

Having looked at where we have come from and where we are heading, I wish to pick up a few small themes for our Christian lives and service in the 'already, but not yet' phase of God's kingdom and our role in it.

The Beatitudes of Matthew 5 can be considered a manifesto for life in God's kingdom in the here and now. The eight groups here represent either the vulnerable or those who critique the world and advocate a better way, consistent with the nature and heart of God. Such people can easily be marginalised, pushed to the sides and muted. They rarely control the discourse and in today's world may be misrepresented in media of various kinds. Indeed, in Matthew 5:11, Jesus tells these people, his people, that they will be blessed when people persecute them because of him and because they have a voice similar to the prophetic heroes of the Old Testament. James makes a similar exhortation to God's people in the second half of chapter 3 of his epistle. In this in-between age, between Genesis and Revelation, we are called to be salt and light in this same chapter of Matthew, as God asks us to stand with the muted and bless them, as God is a source of blessing to us. Indeed, the command to be salt and light is an instruction for us to unmute and bring change.

In Matthew 15, we see part of Jesus' broader disputation with the Pharisees and teachers of the law. The criticism of Jesus and his followers by the Pharisees and their intolerance of ordinary people are an attempt at muting. The Pharisees cannot understand Jesus' flexible and organic understanding of the law and emphasis on God's mercy and are also intimidated by his grace and popularity with the people. Their view of God and his purposes is a little different from that of Jesus and they would prefer it if he were quiet. They relate to the man in the street as someone who is not holy enough, ignorant or lacks understanding of the law and the external behavioural requirements that they believe God has for his people. They would like to force their understanding onto others and where they cannot, they view them with disdain. Religious legalism in whatever form emphasises the content and form of communication of a perceived mainstream and pushes those who do not agree to the sidelines. In an age of suspicion of and alienation from the Church, I believe we are called to undo muting and be as inclusive as our individual consciences allow under God. Such a spirit is also found in the parable of the wedding banquet (Matt. 22), when the kingdom of God welcomes those at the margins and unmutes them.

The various narratives around the birth of Christ also provide powerful and moving examples of unmuting. The appearance of the angel to Mary and the resulting Magnificat represent unmuting of the humble and faithful. Something similar occurs when the heavenly host appears to the shepherds, social outcasts looking after sheep on cold hillsides. They experience the acceptance of God and then, having seen the child, spread the word, amazing all those who heard what they said (Luke 2:17–18).

There is a lot of teaching in the epistles that we might identify as forms of unmuting and reconfiguring mainstream discourse. In 1 Corinthians, Paul upbraids the Corinthians for selectively following different Christian leaders. By emphasising any person apart from Christ, people will cause division in the body by muting those who do not see things in exactly the way that they do. In our age of persuasive preachers and superstar Christian leaders, we too can fall into muting and consequent divisions. As in Genesis and Revelation, humanity may be a partially muted group *vis-à-vis* God, but we can never allow one group of people to be muted by another. Paul's plea for empowering unity is found in 1 Corinthians 12 and he describes the spirit in which, and the resources by which, it is to be achieved in the next chapter. Love makes muting impossible. John gives us a similar exhortation in chapter 2 of his first epistle; after all, muting within the Christian community would amount to hating our brother or sister.

In Galatians 3, Paul affirms the law, but asks his Christian readers to go further and see that it was pointing to faith and served as a guardian until God's grace was made manifest in Christ. His summary that we can only be children of faith because of what Christ has done is the background to the remarkable unifying words in verse 28. Among those who belong to Christ there is no salvific division between Jew and Gentile, or free and enslaved, or male and female. Distinctions that allow human beings to discriminate against, marginalise and mute others have no influence on our status in Christ. As Volf reminds us: 'Baptism into Christ creates a people as the differentiated body of Christ. Bodily inscribed differences are brought together, not removed' (1996:48).

In human history how often have ethnicity, social status and gender been used to mute people and push them to the sidelines? Indeed, Crenshaw (1989) introduces us to intersectionality, when simple dichotomies overlap, resulting in even greater exclusion. In today's society, should we build on Paul's reasoning for the narrow, specific context of Galatians 3:28 and broaden our thinking about the problem of muting? Resident and migrant, straight and gay, politically left and right, disabled and able-bodied, and in the sense of Matthew 25, even Christian and non-Christian? There are echoes of the same spirit of inclusion and unmuting in the first few verses of Philemon 2 and James 2. Those who control the discourse have a responsibility to facilitate unmuting and give all a voice.

# Conclusion

This chapter has brought together a number of Scripture passages and elements of MGT. For reasons of time and practical theological emphasis, I have looked at Genesis 1 – 3 as a summary of where we have come from, and the last couple of chapters of Revelation to give us a sense of *telos*, where humanity is heading. I then identified and reflected on a very small number of Scripture portions that can help us apply the insights from MGT to work towards a more inclusive, irenic and relevant Christian presence in society.

Much more could be written, applying MGT to the whole of Scripture to produce an integrated theological response with a clearly practical focus. However, that is beyond my remit. In the forthcoming chapters, the other authors develop and share new insights and interpretations as they apply MGT to a variety of issues.

# 3

# Evangelical women: unmuting Portuguese women in leadership

## ELSA CORREIA PEREIRA

The writing of this chapter takes place during my PhD research, in the field of sociology of religion. The theme of my doctoral thesis is: 'The Role of Women in Evangelical Churches in Europe'. My aim is to bring the women to the centre of the narrative and research discourse, since the investigation on the sociology of religion has been during many years dedicated to the Church(es) and religion(s) as institutions, with all statistic and quantitative data, regarding the affiliation and religious attendance, almost forgetting the gendered experience of the lived faith. Gina Zurlo, in her book, *Women in World Christianity, Building and Sustaining a Global Movement* (2023), remembers Dana Roberts's question from 2006: 'What would the study of Christianity ... look like if scholars put women into the center of their research?' and Zurlo adds: 'World Christianity is a women 's movement' (Zurlo 2023:7).

The silencing of women over many decades, both as researchers and as the subject of research, is unavoidable. Nevertheless, the history of the Church proves that, although it is the journey we still have to make, Evangelical Christian communities globally will likely provide more opportunities for women to actively participate in faith communities. Albeit at different levels or degrees of leadership, women have assumed prominent roles and positions of distinction throughout history, from within the Bible to Evangelical Christianity as it is practised today.

The United Nations (United Nations Women 2017) highlights the role of religion in promoting gender equality and in empowering women. Gender equality is goal number 5 of the Sustainable Development

Goals within the scope of Agenda 2030.[1] Therefore, in line with the UN's statement, my research is based on the premise that actors in faith communities are critical to dismantling structures and practices that promote inequality.

Sociologist Max Weber, in his work, *Economy and Society* (published in English in 1968, repr. 2022), provides some important insights to support this perspective. He introduces the concept of charisma, an authority different from the authority derived from tradition or legal authority. Charisma is an authority whose legitimacy is attributed by followers to a particular person due to the extraordinary characteristics of their personality or recognition of special attributes given by the Divine.

On the other hand, Pierre Bourdieu speaks of 'symbolic capital' in his work, *Distinction* (2010). He introduced this concept to explain that some forms of power are not only economic, but also symbolic and cultural. Bourdieu argues that 'symbolic capital' is a form of prestige, recognition and status that operates in the cultural field. Symbolic capital is therefore related to the accumulation of symbols, signs and recognition that confer power and distinction on a person in a particular community. In the religious context, symbolic capital could be associated with spiritual recognition, moral authority and prestige that a leader acquires. The ability to influence and mobilise followers based on symbolic legitimacy is a manifestation of symbolic capital in the religious context.

Bourdieu argues that symbolic capital is closely linked to cultural and social capital, forming a complex system of power that permeates different spheres of social life. Thus, the legitimacy of the power of a religious leader can be understood as a specific form of symbolic capital, playing an important role in reproducing hierarchies and legitimising power in faith communities.

In this case, a leader of a faith community, through their 'charisma' or 'symbolic power', to use the concepts of the cited authors, sees their authority legitimised because believers believe that it is bestowed by God.

---

1 'Agenda 2030' refers to the United Nations 2030 Agenda for Sustainable Development. At the core of Agenda 2030 are the seventeen Sustainable Development Goals, which are an urgent call for action by all countries in a global partnership. The goals include: no poverty, zero hunger, good health and well-being, quality education, gender equality, clean water and sanitation, affordable and clean energy, decent work and economic growth, industry, innovation, and infrastructure, reduced inequalities, climate action, and more.

Yet that same leader may not provide opportunities for certain groups (namely, women) to participate, represent or intervene in decision-making and leadership circles in faith communities, or that leader may not provide moments and contexts where the voice of women is heard. This may be the starting point for the invalidation or disaffirmation of women, not only in that community, but in all satellite spheres where these women participate with the followers of that leader. Moreover, continuous compliance with rules, norms and traditions that keep these women away from prominent positions or silence their voice helps reinforce their self-image, as they internalise the dispositions of the dominant group (men) about themselves and reproduce them uncritically, thus perpetuating the unjustifiable and unequal relationship between the dominant group (men) and the dominated group (women).

The dialectic between 'charisma' or 'symbolic power' from the dominant group, and the dominated group creates the tension that can lead to change. Using the words of Mark P. Orbe, 'Muted Group status is not fixed; it is constantly reinforced, augmented, or challenged' (1998b:24). In some faith communities, where the topic of women's participation is still hard to speak about, the strategies that Orbe calls 'Nonassertive Accommodation' (1998a:16–17) could be a peaceful way to start this change. In practice, this means that women engage in activities that provide them with greater visibility and the opportunity to dispel stereotypes, especially with regard to the idea that 'this ministry is not for women'. They can do this by opening new paths for women in those ministries. In other words, this is a non-confrontational way of communicating to the dominant group the need to change.

The Bible contains a series of narratives, in both the Old and New Testaments, featuring women as pioneering, courageous and prominent social actors. However, throughout history, and in the vibrant and diverse tapestry of evangelicalism, women often find their voices are muted or relegated to the periphery. This chapter seeks to unravel the complex dynamics that have contributed to the suppression of these voices within the Evangelical community. By delving into the historical and cultural contexts, we aim to shed light on at least three of the challenges faced by Evangelical women in reclaiming their rightful place in theological discourse.

But before we delve into the three examples themselves, I offer a methodological note. In my doctoral thesis, instead of opting for a deductive approach, i.e., starting with the analysis of existing studies, research and theories regarding the roles of women in Evangelical Christian communities, I chose an inductive approach, namely grounded theory. This means beginning with data collection in the field to later constructing a typology of roles allowed for women, a conceptual framework and its interpretative theory. I did this for two reasons: the first is that there is no comparable qualitative study, as far as I know; and the second is that I wish to contribute to a true heuristic sociological approach at the intersection of gender studies and (the sociology of) religion.

In this chapter, we embark on a journey to unveil some of the intricate challenges faced by Portuguese Evangelical women in asserting their voices within theological discourse, drawing insights from Muted Group Theory (MGT). As we explore the societal structures, namely in the Portuguese Evangelical context, contributing to the muting of women's voices, we anchor our understanding in biblical principles that advocate for equality and inclusion: 'There is neither Jew nor Greek, there is neither slave nor free, there is no male and female, for you are all one in Christ Jesus' (Gal. 3:28 ESV).

# Do not open: closing the doors of dialogue

This section will explore the subtle yet pervasive ways in which dialogue is stifled within Portuguese Evangelical circles. When men intentionally or unintentionally obstruct the path for women to engage in theological discussions, a significant disservice is done to the community as a whole. This section will analyse instances where theological learning was, at least for many years, an exclusive domain for men, creating barriers that hinder the flourishing of diverse perspectives.

Inspired by real-life narratives, such as the poignant example of a woman desiring to pursue theological studies fifty years ago, but facing resistance from male counterparts, we explore how women's voices are deliberately stifled. By incorporating findings from interviews in countries where open dialogue on women's roles in biblical schools is encouraged, we unveil a correlation between dialogue and increased leadership roles for women, resonating with the biblical call for mutual edification.

In addition to the forty-five interviews that I have been conducting as part of my doctoral project, of which eighteen have been completed, I have also conducted interviews with Portuguese Evangelical women aged 70 or older. As at the writing of this chapter, I have completed eight interviews with these women. My goal is to understand the perception of these women who have at least five decades of conversion to Evangelical Christianity, regarding the evolution (or lack thereof) of the role of women in the Portuguese Evangelical communities to which they belong.

The first example is Maria[2] who converted at the age of 9 and who is now 70 years old. At 18, as she was preparing to enter a science course, she felt called by God to work in the Church. She then enrolled in a humanities course to complete what would be equivalent to secondary education today. Meanwhile, she also started attending the Theology course at the Theological Seminary. She and another colleague were the first female students to attend the Theological Seminary in 1972. Until then, the study of theology was exclusively undertaken by men who would enter ministry as pastors. Previously, the seminary would allow the wives of theology students at the seminary, and if they were already married, the women accompanying them would be enrolled in an educational programme specifically for women, the pastors' wives, called 'Christian Education', with a view to performing practical tasks in the church, such as teaching Sunday school, counselling other women, etc.

When Maria went to seminary to study theology, there were some voices against it. Some people directed her to join the other women on the Christian Education course, stating it was specifically designed for women. However, Maria was determined to study theology. The first opportunity for her to teach in her denomination was with the young people. She then became the second President of the Youth Department of her denomination. She organised activities more focused on biblical study and reflection, as according to her, youth activities, especially for

---

2  This is a pseudonym – please note that throughout the volume, some personal and institutional names have been changed for reasons of security and privacy.

boys, had previously focused more on recreational and sports activities. Along with her team, Maria organised the first youth congress of her denomination, shortly after the Portuguese Revolution of 25 April 1974. From this point onwards (1975), current affairs topics of the time began to be debated nationally, and sometimes motions were also proposed. The first congress, after 25 April, had the theme, 'The truth will set you free', associated with the freedom of the democratic regime, breaking decades of dictatorship.

According to Maria's account, in previous years, biblical studies for young people were available, but without direct application to real and current life problems. With the 25 April Revolution and the fall of the dictatorship, it was expected that greater freedom in society for behaviours previously not tolerated (at least according to the regime) could allow Evangelical youth to address the issues that, during oppression and censorship, could not be spoken about or even admitted to. Therefore, the debates on societal topics that interested young people started to make complete sense. At the end of the congress, if a motion was approved, it was a way of involving and getting young people to commit to certain actions. It gave them an active voice in their denomination – in the sense that something they had developed together was recorded in writing. Maria's leadership and her passion for theological studies and debates, as well as her persistence in studying theology, strongly contributed to these changes.

Maria was supported in her work in helping the youth through the creation of national activity plans and she began the publication of a magazine addressing current topics that involved various young people from throughout the country. Under Maria's direction, a historical survey of youth activities in the denomination since 1950 was published.

Later, Maria was funded by churches in the United States to work full-time with young people. With her team, they initiated contacts with churches in other countries and in the 1980s, began to be represented in Europe at congresses and conferences. They shared activities among churches. Maria was invited to speak about youth work in Portugal in churches in other European countries, about the dynamism of activities that were being developed in the country and whose vitality was beginning to be known in Europe.

She married very young and motherhood interrupted her academic studies. She returned years later to graduate in Philosophy. Later, she joined the Evangelical Education Commission in Public Schools (COMACEP), promoting this discipline from north to south of the country from 1990 onwards. If Maria had been prevented from pursuing enrolment in the study of theology, how much work would have been lost, not only in Portugal, but in the positive influence she brought to the Church in Europe during those years? Maria's initiative, combined with her organisational skills, team management and theological knowledge, made a difference that has lasted for many decades and had a positive impact on many generations.

The dominant group seemed to try to keep women away from the privileged place of dialogue and reflection that would influence churches, theology and the subsequent generation. In this example, that place is the theology course, that was exclusively intended, at that time, for men, the future pastors. Theological seminaries are an example of 'arenas where societal rewards are obtained' in the religious context (mutatis mutandis and recovering the concept of Ardener on Muted Groups – see Barkman 2018), from which men seemed (at that time, fifty years ago) to want to exclude women, a trend that, at least in some denominations, continues to this day.

Like many authors of MGT, sociologist Pierre Bourdieu in his article, 'The Economics of Linguistic Exchanges' (1977), explores the idea of linguistic capital and how language can be used to establish and maintain social hierarchies. Bourdieu argues that certain social groups have more access and ability to use the specific languages of their professional fields, giving them an advantage in social competition. This idea aligns with the notion that professional languages can function as hermetic codes, making it difficult for those outside the professional group to fully understand and participate in the communications and practices of that group.

Thus, this limiting of women's entry into the space of dialogue, learning and interpretation of 'theological language' is as if only a few experts will know how to use the Scriptures, thereby increasing the prestige and social recognition of men who can do so. However, this goes exactly against what the Scriptures teach, and what Jesus, in fact, did, by teaching women, contrary to Jewish tradition. Allowing women to learn directly from him, Jesus demonstrated that he considered them 'disciples' with full learning and the capability of disseminating Christianity to others, as he expected of any of the disciples (Luke 8:1–3; Luke 10:38–42; Matt. 28:9–10; John 20:11–18).

According to the interviews we have conducted, countries such as Sweden and Germany, where women are ordained as pastors more frequently, are also those that bring up the issue of women's role in ministry for debate, both in theological schools and in workers'/ leaders' meetings. There is, therefore, a directly proportional relationship between dialogue on this subject and the greater acceptance of women in ministry.

# Not me! The women who silence themselves

Despite the strides towards gender equality in opportunities to exercise their calling and ministry, some women choose to remain silent, adhering to traditional roles even when opportunities for leadership arise. By examining the factors that contribute to self-imposed silence, we uncover the internalised norms and societal expectations that restrain women from stepping into roles where their voices could make a transformative impact.

When presenting my ongoing reflections on my research on women's roles, even in academic settings, I have been asked the following question: 'If women do not feel that they are in a situation of inequality, should we (researchers) bring these issues to light?' The point here is to understand: do these women comprehend their situation of inequality? Over time, have they internalised the dispositions and rules of the dominant group to the extent that they mute themselves and other women who may wish to pursue a different and independent ministerial path?

Through the lens of MGT and biblical principles, we analyse instances where women voluntarily adhere to traditional roles. Using a case study of a woman invited to take on a leadership role, but declining in favour of her husband, we explore the internalisation of societal norms and expectations that lead to self-imposed muting among Evangelical women.

This introspective analysis is juxtaposed with the biblical encouragement for individuals to use their God-given gifts, as we read in 1 Corinthians 12:4–7 (ESV): 'Now there are varieties of gifts, but the same Spirit; and there are varieties of service, but the same Lord; and there are varieties of activities, but it is the same God who empowers them all in everyone.'

The example I quote here occurred in one of the interviews I conducted with church leaders, according to my study plan. In this case, it was a Portuguese pastor. At a certain point in the interview, the pastor (interviewee John) said the following:

> I believe that the Church has much to gain from women available to serve, without complexes … I have encountered some refusals to serve in some church ministries because this is a ministry that has always been for men … 'Pastor, no, because I am a woman.' … In this case, I invited her to coordinate the couple's ministry, and she said she preferred her husband to lead, and she could assist … In this case, I wouldn't say it was due to shyness; it was due to a concept rooted in the person herself that the leadership of these ministries should not be entrusted to a woman.

MGT helps us explain this type of attitude. It suggests that subordinate social groups, especially women, face linguistic and cultural barriers that prevent them from fully expressing their experiences and perspectives. This can result in a phenomenon where women internalise the dominant linguistic and cultural norms, contributing to their own silencing.

The idea is that, due to the structure of language and culture, certain groups encounter difficulties in expressing their experiences authentically and may silence themselves to conform to predominant norms. This not only implies external silencing, but also the adoption of linguistic and cultural patterns and perpetuated cycles that may not adequately reflect the richness and diversity of their abilities.

Between 1 September and 17 October 2023, we conducted a survey of young people in Portuguese Evangelical communities. In total, we obtained 664 responses, mostly from those aged between 18 and 40 (79%). The remaining 21% of respondents were over 40 years of age. Those who reported they felt called to pastoral ministry made up

11% of respondents. According to this survey, if churches prevent or, more implicitly, do not support the integration of all women who feel called to pastoral ministry, out of the 664 interviewed, 21 claimed they felt a pastoral call. There are also those women who responded, 'It's something I have been thinking about'; 'I would really like to, but I don't know if I have a calling from God in that direction'; 'I have been challenged, but I have resisted the idea.' They are possibly undecided, doubtful, fearful, because there are few or no female pastors in their denomination, or very few women work full-time in ministry. These represent 12% of respondents, or more than eighty women. Pastors, or workers, missionaries, whatever we want to call them, in our country where, according to the research from earlier this year, 50% of pastors are over 50 years old, and where many workers from other countries come to pastor, 101 women in ministry can make a significant difference. Perhaps more than 101 churches, more than 101 missions in other countries, or fewer than 101 pastors experiencing burnout.

In this same survey, there was an open-ended question in which a young woman made the following comment: 'In my denomination, there are no female pastors. What is the point of having academic preparation or feeling called to pastoral ministry?' This may be a question that is even muted within the minds of many young women. It reveals the need to work simultaneously with church leaders, reminding them that they should challenge men and women to realise their calling by entering Bible school or ministry. It also reinforces to young women that they should not give up on their calling and ministry just because of perceived restrictions to ordained ministry in the near future. Church history proves that God has used women tremendously, women who did not always see their ministry immediately recognised (such as Selina de Huntingdon, Sarah Crosby, Mary Bosanquet, Jarena Lee, Sarah Jane Lancaster, Aimee McPherson and many more).

The responses of women when asked to consider the possibility of attending Bible school are surprising (see Table 1).

When we look at the percentages corresponding to the responses, 'It's something I've been thinking about' or 'I would really like to', we see that the percentages of women are higher than those of men, indicating a greater gap between women who wish to study in a Bible school and

**Table 1 Survey responses of females considering possible Bible school attendance**

*Have you considered the possibility of studying at a Seminary/Bible Institute?*

|  | Gender | | Total |
|---|---|---|---|
|  | *Women* | *Man* |  |
| It's something I've been thinking about | **57.80%** | 42.20% | 100.00% |
| I hope to enrol in the near future | 39.50% | 60.50% | 100.00% |
| I would really like to | **61.70%** | 38.30% | 100.00% |
| I have studied or am currently studying at a Seminary/Bible Institute | 32.10% | 67.90% | 100.00% |
| I have been challenged to think about the subject, but I have resisted the idea | 37.90% | 62.10% | 100.00% |
| I have thought about it, but I don't consider it as a possibility | 49.30% | 50.70% | 100.00% |
| I have never considered that possibility | 59.10% | 40.90% | 100.00% |
| **Total** | **49.40%** | **50.60%** | **100.00%** |

better prepare for ministry than men, as they actually enter theological schools more frequently.

# My baby and me: is maternity silencing women?

This section shines a light on a subtle form of muting often veiled under the guise of concern for familial responsibilities. Leaders who assert that women can assume comparable roles to men, but only if they do not have young children, even if unintentionally, perpetuate a harmful narrative. We will explore how maternity should not be a barrier, but rather a source of strength, enriching the diverse perspectives brought to theological conversations. One of the pastors interviewed (let us call him Albert) referred to the role of women in ministry in this way:

> We have couples in this presbytery ... obviously due to issues of time, activity, availability, most presbytery meetings are conducted by men, by husbands, assuming that men, being there, have the agreement, the consent of their wives. But when wives can, they are. But what happens, as the church developed, the pastors' wives who were part of the presbytery were young women with children. They had many activities, and it was very difficult to reconcile the time for the husband and wife to be in these meetings. So, it became common for the presbytery meeting to be held with men, not in a discriminatory sense that women cannot participate, but for a practical and logistical reason.

Applying MGT, we unravel the subtle discrimination faced by women while performing maternal responsibilities. Examining instances where pastors seemingly endorse equal roles for women, but who maintain traditions that seem to impose limitations during the child-rearing phase, we critique the perpetuation of traditional gender norms. By highlighting the strength and wisdom that motherhood can bring to theological discussions, we challenge the notion that women's voices should be muted during this crucial life stage, aligning our discussion with biblical principles of valuing all seasons of life: 'For you formed my inward parts; you knitted me together in my mother's womb. I praise you, for I am fearfully and wonderfully made' (Ps. 139:13–16 ESV).

The woman of Proverbs 31:10–31 is perhaps the most multifaceted we will ever know. However, her motherhood did not prevent her from developing her business, caring for her husband and even caring for the poor. Motherhood should not be a factor excluding women from ministry; rather, it enriches a woman's perspective on the world around her, and the Church has much to gain from it.

If, in secular contexts, there are companies, organisations, universities that provide lactation rooms and/or caregivers for children while mothers work, why does the Church not offer the same services, allowing mothers to continue fulfilling their calling and ministry?

# Conclusions

In the concluding segment, we reflect on the multifaceted challenges Evangelical women face in reclaiming their voices. Drawing from the insights gained in the preceding sections, we offer practical tips and strategies to resurrect and amplify the voices of women within the Evangelical community. This chapter aims not only to diagnose the issues, but to provide a roadmap for fostering inclusivity and empowering Evangelical women to contribute meaningfully to theological discussions.

As we navigate through the complexities of gender dynamics within Evangelical communities, this chapter stands as a call to action, urging the community to embrace the richness that comes from diverse voices engaged in theological dialogue. The following provides some possible ways to begin the unmuting of women's potential within Church leadership.

- Promote spaces for women to discuss with men the role of women in ministry in Bible schools/institutes, leaders' meetings, conferences, symposiums, seminars, in churches, in small groups.
- Ensure that motherhood is not an impediment to women fulfilling their calling (encouraging churches to provide practical and emotional support for this to happen).
- Maintain sensitivity to the Holy Spirit. When leaders pray for the right person for a particular ministry, may their criteria not be defined by gender, but by a person committed to the gospel and filled with the Holy Spirit, as in the early Church.
- Senior leaders, both men and women, should encourage young women to continue on the path of preparing for their calling. Whether through theological education or service in their local church, young women should show flexibility, as some of them may

be pioneering a path that no one has taken before, and opening doors for other women to follow after them. This means that their service may not always be recognised with a title, or at least not immediately.

- Give women equal access to all platforms including decision-making and at every level of leadership.

In some Evangelical contexts, there have been and still are women who, with their tenacity, resilience, courage and persistence, continue to develop their ministry, even if silenced – not in the sense that they are prevented from doing what they want to do, but in the sense that they no longer have the institutional framework they were included in. Many continue on their own initiative, even opening different churches.

The fact that these women, who may be considered insubordinately obedient to their calling, do not have such a large institutional framework may reduce the amplification of the impact of their ministry. Their impact is only visible locally and among the communities they usually work with, which see and recognise their calling. Still, this voice is not amplified by institutional filtering or institutional framework. Male Evangelical leaders are much more likely to benefit from this 'institutional voice amplification'.

The voices of women in ministry, in my understanding, and from my observation of decades of ministry by men and women, are amplified by the following factors: financial resources that fund their own ministry and others, kinship with a man hierarchically well placed in ministry (for example, being wives or daughters of a pastor), or with a 'resounding' surname (familial connection with a highly regarded worker in the Evangelical community where they move). However, it is rare for women to be able to develop their ministry in prominent leadership roles, without any of these supports or any institutional framework, in some countries and some denominational contexts. Their tenacity should be honoured, acknowledged and celebrated.

Regardless of the obstacles, Ana, a woman pastor who is 89 years old, served in pastoral ministry for forty years, leaving her institutional framework because she felt a call to pastoral leadership to open a new church. However, God also continues to use those who remain acting according to their institutional 'norms'. Both situations are a testament to the manifold grace of God, as stated in 1 Peter 4:10, 'Each of you should use whatever gift you have received to serve others, as faithful stewards of God's grace in its various forms.'

May our voice always echo the biblical call for unity and shared ministry. May our commitment align with the call of Proverbs 31:8–9 (ESV), 'Open your mouth for the mute, for the rights of all who are destitute. Open your mouth, judge righteously, defend the rights of the poor and needy.'

# 4

# Unmuting her body: a reflection on trauma and healing

## ASHLEIGH GIBB

As a 10-year-old kid, I didn't receive much love or care from my parents as other kids did. Instead, I had to be like a parent to my mother. She would spend the night drinking and passing out. I remember wrapping her in a blanket while she lay in her drunken sleep. I don't even remember what my father looked like; he left when I was 4 years old. I don't think anyone knew what my homelife was like. If they did, nobody stepped in.

By the time I was 15, I met a local guy, Ben. He was 23. I liked older guys because it seemed as though they understood me. Ben made me feel special; it was as if he knew I was different and that I was the one person who understood him. I felt seen and cared for. He became my boyfriend, but a few months later, he said he was struggling financially and wanted us to make money together. I found myself giving my body to several men a day. Ben took control of my life. He set up different men for me to have sex with and he took the money. Even though I worked for it, I rarely saw the money I earned. During those times of selling my body I learned to shut my mind off; a way to escape just what was happening to me.

This story tells a similar narrative to those told by many other women who fall victim to sex trafficking. At the age of 22, Suzie exited her exploitation and began the long process of healing. Despite seeking healing in places where she thought she would be safe, the subtle muting of her body that had begun in the post-sexual trauma stage drove a profound need to fit in. Suzie attempted to find solace in the Church. However, the muting she had applied to her sexual abuse was deeply embedded within a subculture of the Evangelical church where the simplified messages of forgiveness, repentance and redemption had no language to understand her experiences. As part of her healing process, Suzie began to experiment with many modalities of treatment and decided to take agency over her body through physical fitness. A combination of spirituality and fitness led to the eventual unmuting of her body.

While the story presented rings true for a survivor of sex trafficking, fourteen years ago, I stood in front of a mirror in college with no recognition of who was staring back at me. I had experienced sexual trauma prior to and during college. Both my body and voice had been muted and years later, I was still seeking the tools to my own empowerment and unmuting. Before my healing process began, I sought to heal myself through adding new physical experiences of sexual intimacy and alcohol abuse to drown out the rage that plagued my body.

During the recovery from my sexual trauma, I took a multifaceted approach to healing, which encompassed body, mind and spirit, and discovered that physical fitness was the catalyst for my recovery. Upon starting a fitness routine, I experienced the ability to release trauma and to develop tools to heal the mind. Through the act of getting stronger, there was an appreciation for my body as my own. This contributed to my spiritual formation.

My formative years were spent in an Evangelical church. The language used to depict the image of God neglected to acknowledge the feminine attributes of God. This omission fostered a patriarchal perspective of God that gave rise to the presumption that God was ashamed of me due to the events my body had experienced. This, combined with preaching a narrative of a punitive God, resulted in a profoundly damaging impact upon my perception of God. Without trauma-informed church space, the healing of a survivor can be severely muted.

The pursuit of research that intersects trauma, fitness and spirituality is driven by a deep passion to empower survivors to reclaim their sense of self throughout their recovery. Muted Group Theory (MGT) (Ardener 1975) can serve as a catalyst for understanding how to empower survivors in claiming agency over their voice. When addressing the dehumanisation of survivors of sex trafficking and sexual violence, MGT can be applied as a way of understanding the dominance that is placed over survivors' bodies and voices both before, during and after their exploitation. This chapter will explore the different ways in which muting occurs, not only by the abusers and traffickers, but also by those who are considered 'safe' people, such as anti-trafficking organisations and churches.

The US Department of State (2020) explains sex trafficking as 'the range of activities involved when a trafficker uses force, fraud, or coercion to compel another person to engage in a commercial sex act or causes a child to engage in a commercial sex act'. Despite this definition, many are confused and misled about the ways in which trafficking occurs and base their knowledge upon movies and media. This ignorance can be damaging when identifying signs of sex trafficking. This crime can be much more subtle than many realise.

## Sex trafficking and my working contexts

While my personal experiences of abuse were not connected to sex trafficking, it became a lens through which I connected with those who had experienced abuse because of trafficking. In the contexts in which I have worked, primarily Thailand and the US, trafficking takes place in the form of familial trafficking and 'boyfriending'. According to the Polaris Project (2023), sex traffickers groom their victims through what is perceived as romantic love. This manipulates them into cooperating in their own exploitation. What can seem to the outside world as a choice is, in fact, a result of extreme grooming and the creation of a deep trauma bond. Of the many survivors I have worked with, most are shocked at how they found themselves in a web of exploitation. This is true for Suzie's story and how she was manipulated into selling her body; the attachment to her trafficker was deep, therefore the choice to leave became more difficult as the months went on.

When thinking back to my own trauma, over the years, I continued to ask myself, 'How did I get here?' Shame was a powerful tool that contributed to the belief that I was somehow complicit in my own exploitation. The purity-based messaging I had received from many faith-based teachings was that my flesh was a temptation to those around me.

Dubar (2021:Loc 173) states that sex trafficking thrives on silence, invisibility and the heightened vulnerability of the exploited. When the body is deemed merely a product, it is easy to dehumanise it and maintain its subordinate status, as a subordinate who is subdued, the idea is that the body is a product to serve the dominant who has physical and economic power.

When assisting survivors, it is crucial to adopt a trauma-informed approach that empowers, rather than make assumptions. I believe this is where the Church and those who serve survivors fall short. Using MGT allows an opportunity for humility and to gain a wider perspective on how to place the survivor at the centre of the conversation. Muting can manifest when key members of the survivor's care team make assumptions about their needs without giving the survivor the opportunity to express themselves. Assuming that the survivor needs to unquestioningly follow a pattern of repentance and forgiveness for their abusers can be damaging if not considered through a trauma-informed approach. All too quickly, the Church can enforce the need for forgiveness without understanding the extreme suffering that a survivor has endured.

A prominent part of the unmuting process is recognising that survivors are the experts on their own story. Growing up in the Church, I did not believe I had power over my life, leading to a distrust of my body and desires. This, coupled with a patriarchal message that I was to submit to men, led me to believe that I needed to shrink myself to be pleasing and acceptable. With hindsight, the path to trauma seemed inevitable, given my overwhelming belief that I was not enough. This indoctrination was already imbedded in me. Having my body violated only confirmed a message that I was already living by. It has taken years of healing to recognise that my desires and body are deemed good by the Creator of my soul. Making decisions for myself and my body empowers me to take up space in a world that has typically stated and reinforced that I do not belong and would never be equal.

MGT can provide a framework to explore ways in which the survivor's voices are diminished instead of elevated, thus creating an unhealthy power dynamic for those who are in the helping professions. On many occasions, churches and other institutions encourage a survivor to share her story for the purpose of fundraising and to ensure that others are aware of the Church/institution addressing the horrors of trafficking. Many fail to realise that this can cause re-traumatisation for the survivor and results in another form of exploitation when the motivation is to benefit the Church. This lack of perspective can lead to further muting of a survivor and contribute to the stagnation of the healing process. A trauma-informed approach allows the survivor to decide on how and when she shares her story, if at all.

## Those who mute

Shirley Ardener (1975) defines MGT as a communication theory that focuses on the muting of marginalised groups via the use of language and acceptable patterns of dominant behaviour. While muting occurs via the dominant group or culture, what happens is the marginalised group consequently aids in their own muting. Furthermore, this muting is rarely acknowledged by those who are muted.

Applying MGT allows us to acknowledge where muting is occurring. By using this approach, those who desire to help gain the understanding that the healing process can be better served through the alongside approach, rather than through the management or director approach, thus contributing to the healing process. As Suzie's story demonstrates, it was not only the perpetrators who were complicit in her muting, but also those who seek to replace the control of the sex trafficker by assuming a more moral form of protection and provision for the survivor, who is considered unable to care for themselves.

## Traffickers/perpetrators

The manipulation of survivors occurs prior to the crime of sexual violence or trafficking. For example, in 'boyfriending', the perpetrators will prey on a vulnerable victim, and the grooming process will begin. The use of affirming language or a level of undeserved attention through the giving of elaborate gifts, serve as forms of manipulation. The victim interprets this as love, as in Suzie's case. At this point, the trafficker deems the victim as property, a commodity to be bought and sold, thereby beginning the process of muting.

In the face of sexual violence, I distinctly remember the absence of my voice. Intoxication mixed with fear resulted in a muting of my body and voice. Walter Cannon's trauma response theories cited in *Simply Psychology* (Guy-Evans 2023) discuss theories of fight or flight, which explore how the body reacts in the face of a threat. Later, psychologists coined two more responses: freeze and fawn. My body decided to protect itself by using the method of freezing, but with that came shame and disgust at my sheer inability to fight back.

From my research and personal experience, muting that emanates from people that we assume to be safe can incur much more anger and confusion for the survivor once the muting has been acknowledged. Van der Kolk (2014:Loc 3608) states, 'The challenge of recovery is to re-establish ownership of your body, your mind and of yourself.' Often, the place, position and posture of rescuers inadvertently results in an alternative muting.

## Churches

O'Donnell and Cross (2020:3) question the purpose behind our own personal theologies, they ask, 'Does our theology have the capacity to touch pain, or does it bypass it, move about it or too readily sweep it up into overarching narratives of redemption and victory?' Pain is rarely linear, on most occasions suffering is akin to the emotional roller coaster, the constant battle of choosing between joy and weeping. It's sitting in 'Holy Saturday' instead of jumping into 'Resurrection Sunday'.

In his chapter, 'When God Is Unfaithful: Reclaiming a Theology of Lament', Enns (2016) explores the importance of lament using the Psalms as a powerful example throughout Scripture. Psalm 44:15 (NLT) states, 'We can't escape the constant humiliation; shame is written across our faces.' The psalmist is willing to express suffering and question God. These Psalms are paramount in allowing us to bring our pain to God without shame or the need to jump to celebration. For survivors, the ability to express raw pain as a part of their spirituality can allow the trauma to move through the body and unmute their relationship with God on their terms rather than those imposed, however well-meaning.

Churches that do not create spaces of safety to address suffering mute the voices of those who have suffered at the hands of abuse. Perhaps churches could include sermons to address the suffering that occurs in our world, such as sexual trauma and sex trafficking. Allowing survivors to acknowledge their uncensored pain without feeling the need to hold back on the rawness of their story, is a powerful form of unmuting. There is much discomfort in the uncertainty of suffering. Unmuting is allowing those questions to arise without feeling the need to answer with surface-level statements and to not only welcome pain, but to sit with it.

The Church may rely on the dominant language, perspective and expertise to analyse and contain the subordinate experience to shield their own sensitivities. Hearing the suffering of others may cause the dominant group to experience a sense of guilt as they contrast the suffering and pain of others with their Christian responsibility to live by the words of Matthew 25:42–6 and provide for those in need, to feed, clothe and take care of them. The muting serves as a shortcut, enabling them to evade responsibility by not allowing the person to speak. Trauma Theology seeks to unmute that pain and create a space where it is not only welcomed, but it is deemed holy and sacred (O'Donnell and Cross 2020:2).

## Healthcare

The issue of healthcare is a topic that incites frustration and anger in many survivors. Women have spoken of the times they felt unheard when visiting their healthcare provider. One woman expressed the feeling of being medically gaslighted. After describing the pain she was experiencing in her body, she was told that it was 'all in her head'. This is highly problematic for those who need trauma-informed healthcare post-trafficking. Furthermore, to be told by a person of authority that personal pain is not real negates the need for treatment. Additionally, it pushes the person towards accepting the authority figure's dominant language as truth, similar to the manipulative 'grooming' of the pimp or boyfriend to mistrust the sensations in her own body. This experience of muting gives the message that she cannot be trusted with her own body, and that her body once again is not her own. In her book, *Invisible Women*, Perez (2019:195) explores the issue of healthcare and claims that it is women specifically who have had their health needs ignored or disbelieved. Creating a space for broader understanding of non-medical terminology would validate acceptance of each patient as a whole human being.

## Muting methods

Acknowledging those who mute is important to understanding which aspects of cultures are prone to muting survivors' voices. According to scholars West and Turner (2000), four main methods are used in the muting process. These are: Ridicule, Ritual, Control and Harassment. Some or all of these are clearly expressed in the survivors' narratives.

### Ridicule

'Ridicule' denotes the act of diminishing the voices and opinions of the survivors while denying them the essential space to express their thoughts and ideas. Their experiences are often disbelieved and ridiculed. Quite simply, the act of saying 'no' in the face of sexual advances, for some, has been ignored. Sanyal (2019:1) shares, 'The best-known anti-rape slogan is "No means No." As redundant as that statement may seem, for much of history, "no" used to mean simply "I am female."' The mere fact of being female expresses that the taking of women's body is the right of a man. Women are without power; women are the property of men. While much work is being done to actively combat violence against women, more is still needed in addressing the power dynamic between the dominant and subordinate that perpetuates ritual abuse of women at some level in society.

### Ritual

The rituals of accepted behaviour towards survivors were addressed in my research in terms of how survivors were muted in church contexts. Rituals in this instance refer to sacraments, such as the act of taking communion. While this looks different in a variety of denominational settings, in mine and many Evangelical Anglican churches, the act of taking communion often involves kneeling before a male figure (usually a White male) and receiving the bread and the wine. Walton (2000:12) expresses the need for feminist liturgy. She goes on to say that traditional liturgical patterns have been shaped by 'patriarchal values' where men are typically given power and authority over everyone else, therefore excluding females and marginalised demographics.

For survivors, the act of kneeling before a man and hearing the words 'This is my body, which is given for you' (Luke 22:19 ESV) can be triggering. Walton's call for more inclusive liturgy is imperative if one is seeking to create an environment of safety and inclusion for survivors of trauma which subsequently allows for a more embodied experience of spirituality in a way that is safe for survivors.

## Control

West and Turner discuss how control can manifest through interruption in conversations between men and women, particularly in workplaces where men may frequently interrupt women who are sharing ideas. This subtle form of silencing reflects a power dynamic implying that women's voices are less valued. In the context of survivors, control may take the form of caregivers assuming the survivor's needs without giving them space to express their own. Through my experience in nonprofit organisations supporting survivors, I've observed the importance of shaping programmes based on survivors' input. Without their voices, those unfamiliar with survivors' challenges hold power, potentially hindering the healing process.

## Harassment

The *Cambridge Dictionary* (2023) defines harassment as 'behaviour towards a person that causes mental or emotional suffering which includes repeated unwanted contacts without a reasonable purpose, insults, threats, touching or offensive language'. This behaviour is common in those seeking to groom and traffic their victims. At first, communication may include subtle tactics that are manipulative, such as extreme expressions of affections known as 'love bombing' or affirming words. Eventually, when the survivor is worn down under the control of their trafficker, insults, threats and sexual assault begin.

# Unmuting through Trauma Theology

The concept of Trauma Theology intersected with MGT may be further developed through the tool of physical fitness to unmute a survivor's voice and body by freely allowing her to express both her story and trauma by her choice and at her pace.

Trauma theologians seek to understand people's experiences and reshape theologies in light of that experience, referring to it as 'Trauma

Theology' (O'Donnell and Cross 2020; Jones 2019; McBride 2021; Rambo 2010). Traditional theologies have been constructed by those who are less likely to understand the experiences of women or those who have undergone traumatic experiences. This is an expression of muting the voices and experiences of women and other marginalised demographics. Trauma Theology seeks to advocate for those who have experienced trauma and attempts to understand how one's image of God is affected through the framework of trauma.

When approaching trauma healing, an understanding of both the psychological and spiritual approaches to recovery are important. MGT can be used here to highlight how many survivors' experience of spirituality is ignored in the context of institutional religion. If survivors do not fit into the beliefs and doctrine of a prescribed church or denomination, they are left feeling as though their questions and doubt are heretical and therefore fail to see how the message of grace might be extended to them.

Growing up in the Church, the overriding narrative of what it means to be a Christian was simplified down to the belief I held about Jesus dying on the cross. It seemed that the teaching of one theory was more prominent without an offering of alternative interpretations. Scholars such as Ritskes (2018:311) subscribe to Penal Substitution Atonement Theory, which suggests Jesus Christ died on the cross as a penalty for humanity's sins to 'appease Divine justice'. Ritskes states that since humanity continues to break the holy law, it creates separateness from God. For reconciliation to happen, punishment must take place. According to scholars such as Jones, this theory is problematic for trauma survivors who may associate this imagery and language with their trauma. Instead, perhaps the question should be: what does it look like to bring a trauma-informed approach to the language of reconciliation and redemption in the context of the life, death and resurrection of Jesus?

Allowing survivors to contribute to theology in light of their trauma experiences is a powerful expression of unmuting. The acknowledgement of the pain and suffering and its release via slow and controlled movement of the body is an example of sacred integration of the body and spirit. It encourages survivors to recognise the holy presence in their body and to honour the experiences and suffering that it has experienced.

The choice to engage with fitness is in and of itself a way of taking ownership and agency of the body. It is a personal choice to contract the muscles, to sweat in a way that feels strong and wholesome. Physical fitness can restore the trauma-induced disconnection of body, mind and spirit and bring a sense of empowerment. For me, participating in weightlifting felt like a homecoming celebration for my body. I no longer connect physical pain in my body with the trauma that occurred, but celebrate the breaking down of muscle tissue, knowing the inevitability of the strength that would occur after the rebuilding phase takes place.

Vest (2000:125) states that the Church has struggled to shake off the 'gnostic contempt for the flesh', which refers to the separation of body and soul, thereby assuming the flesh as inherently bad. Martin (2001:8) refers to the 'flesh' as the 'innate drive of the human personality toward self-aggrandizement and self-preservation'. This is in reference to Paul's statements in Galatians about the flesh desiring what is contrary to the spirit (Gal. 5:17). The misinterpretation of this theory can lead to a negative outlook on the body and its needs, thus it is detrimental to a survivor's healing. Learning to own, appreciate and respect the body is crucial for a survivor's healing and to aid the process of unmuting.

The type of language used when addressing the body is important as the survivor can carry an inherent shame attached to their body. Survivors have believed that their body is a commodity for the sole purpose of someone else's pleasure. Using Scripture to reinforce negative thoughts towards the body can affirm what a survivor has already wrestled with for most of her life, leading to a further disconnect between spirit and body. Furthermore, to believe the body is bad can result in a disregard for its human needs. Many survivors do not see the need to nourish their body with rich, nutritious food and so open the way for disordered eating.

McBride (2021) references 'purity culture'. The negative messaging received about the body and sexuality can be damaging when it comes to 'associated bodily beliefs'. These beliefs manifest as: body shame, body dysmorphia, eating disorders, lack of arousal and out-of-control sexual desire. Many survivors attach shame to sexual desire and do not recognise that the sexual pleasure of women is a beautiful and healthy thing. Part of the healing process could include the reintegration of body and spirit though the acknowledgement of sexual desire and pleasure as part of human nature. To own one's sexuality is the ultimate act of agency over one's own body. Using Scripture to attach negative connotations to the body can be damaging; therefore, it is important to be aware of one's own personal theology before exploring this with a survivor (McBride 2021:7).

# Muting through Scripture

For church to be a safe and inclusive environment for survivors, elements such as language and biblical interpretation are key, as well as allowing survivors to share their stories of suffering and to be listened to and believed (Moder 2020:237). Regarding the image of God, it is important for survivors to explore a God who is loving and kind and, as Moder states, 'one that suffers with' for them to feel empowered and to heal from abuse. In the interviews for my dissertation, both participants struggled with the language that was used in their church spaces growing up. They speak about the image of God that was conveyed to them, as well as being immersed in purity culture-based teachings that focused more on restriction of sexuality and damaging messages regarding the female body. To stand and claim that this body was created in the image of God is in contrast to the patriarchal messaging that so many women have received within the Church. The collective reading of Scripture can be spiritual to some and damaging to others. To hear women throughout the Bible who have experienced sexual trauma deemed as 'sinful' can create a distrust and even a hatred of one's own sex. To fully gaze upon the naked flesh of a woman, to look at her breasts and her scars and claim that it was modelled upon and by the Divine is to reclaim the beauty and power of the female body.

Reflecting on my own personal church experience, I vividly recall the interpretations and communication surrounding the book of Esther. The events that occurred in her life were to be celebrated and modelled, but this led to verses being taken out of context and being told that perhaps my trauma happened 'For such a time as this' (Esth. 4:14 ESV). Taking this verse at face value negates the trauma that occurred in Esther's life and refuses to acknowledge that her story includes a narrative of sex trafficking. The Shiloh Project (2017) claims, 'There are troubling silences in the book of Esther that have been … ignored throughout the history of interpretation.' With verses that state, 'Let beautiful young virgins be sought out for the king' (Esth. 2:2–4 ESV), it is hard for survivors of sexual trauma and trafficking to enter church spaces where evil that took place in the history of the faith is not acknowledged. Just as Esther and Queen Vashti were muted throughout this book, so too are survivors' past, present and future if these scriptures are not explored through a trauma-informed lens.

As part of a fitness routine, survivors would explore and meditate on a passage of Scripture in the book of Esther. Wrestling with this text can be healing when trauma is acknowledged and handled with care. After studying the passage, survivors practised physical and spiritual exercises, by creating a way to meditate on the scripture, immerse themselves in the text, and allow their trauma to move through their bodies. Showing solidarity with other women who share similar experiences is a powerful act in reclaiming the body after sexual trauma. It offers a restorative and empowering experience. For these survivors, engaging with a text featuring a survivor of sex trafficking followed by physical exercise became a powerful way to express and release their suffering. They could move through the trauma at their own pace. Instead, they could pause, breathe, feel the pain and connect with it. According to Van der Kolk (2014), trauma recovery involves befriending sensations in the body. By this practice, women bravely sit with their bodies, hold space for the pain, and honour their trauma in an empowering way. This, in my belief, is a path to unmuting in order to heal.

## Unmuting through physical fitness

For some people, expressing trauma through words is a challenging or even impossible task and they prefer to release their trauma through movement. O'Donnell and Cross (2020:1), two experienced trauma theologians, coined this concept as 'Unlanguageability'. They refer to the 'unlanguageability' of trauma and how physical activity gives language to traumatic experiences that can be deeply challenging. Expression and release of emotion via use of the body could be helpful for survivors struggling to find words for their trauma.

Van der Kolk's (2014:3) discussion on the body and physical sensation connection states that trauma compromises the part of the brain that communicates the 'physical embodied feeling of being alive'. McBride (2021:6) supports this and suggests that when we are fully connected to the body, we understand what it means to be alive. If this connection is important, exploring ways to re-establish that connection is key for trauma survivors who have felt a profound disconnect from their body. For those who experience sexual trauma as a standalone event, the consequences can be hugely damaging to one's psyche. For survivors of sex trafficking, their bodies are used sometimes multiple times a day. The body and mind may dissociate from one another as a powerful survival technique to create resilience. When a survivor is safe from her exploitation, the journey to reconnect the body with the mind can be a long process and requires patience, a safe environment and techniques that meet the survivor where she is at.

The cultivation of a sense of safety within the body is key for survivors moving through their healing and allows for an openness to exploring spirituality and a connection with the Divine. To have agency over the body means to claim ownership over the things that happen to it. For someone who has had so much taken from them, it is a rebellious act against the abuser to claim that the body is good, it is powerful and it houses the spirit of the Divine. When looking at all that Jesus endured while on earth, survivors have the right to stand in solidarity with the abuse that he suffered. We read in the Gospel of Mark 'They struck him on the head with a reed stick, spit on him and dropped to their knees in mock worship' (Mark 15:19 NLT). I wonder if Jesus still acknowledged his body as a temple of the spirit, whether he gazed upon his wounds in his moment of abuse and claimed that his body was still good? Survivors are closer to the experiences of Jesus in a way that many will never understand.

When I began my fitness journey, I discovered a profound sense of strength and empowerment when I realised I was the only one who could give it to me. I noticed the difference in how I walked into a room and the willingness I had to take up space. Fitness nurtured a robust self-esteem and an inner confidence that grew more accessible as I learned to trust my voice and body.

# Conclusion

In the context of survivors of sexual trauma and trafficking, MGT can be applied to acknowledge experiences by recognising how survivors' voices and bodies have typically been muted, not only by those who have sought to exploit and do harm, but indeed by those who claim to protect survivors. Assuming the body to be a commodity is the first stage in the muting process, which occurs when traffickers and abusers seek to dominate and sell.

In reference to faith-based settings, muting can occur in the ways in which we interpret theology and Scripture. When exploring Trauma Theology, language around the body is important and ensures the connection between spirit and body. Furthermore, the language used when interpreting stories in the holy texts needs careful consideration in order to engage appropriately with survivors. Approaching theology through a trauma-informed lens is the difference between creating sacred space for a survivor to really address their own trauma and creating a shame-based faith that disconnects experience from Scripture. Recognising that Jesus experienced this world in the human body and endured the most horrific trauma suggests that the human body is something to be held with curiosity, love and compassion.

Trauma-informed fitness builds a bridge between spirituality and the body. McBride (2021) states, 'Embodiment is a way to heal the mind–body divide we experience within ourselves and more systemically, within Western cultures.' Growing up in the Evangelical Church, there was a distinct assumption of separation of body and spirit, which created a narrative that my body was bad. This is a disservice to humanity itself. Survivors seeking to release shame and to find freedom within their bodies may apply MGT to create dialogue regarding this topic and to explore how they can find strength and empowerment through movement of the body and how they can continue to grow into the people they were created to be.

Using fitness has allowed for the unmuted exploration of spirituality and physical freedom both in my own life and in the life of other survivors. The more I had a healthy love and appreciation for my body and soul, the more I began to recognise the voice and image of God within me, leading me to a distinct and unashamed unmuting of myself as a survivor.

# 5

# Muted Group Theory and Disability Theology: whose voices?

### DONNA JENNINGS

Around ten years ago, my (then) 3-year-old daughter, Tabitha, commented on her way out of her children's church group, 'Micah does not have the "God-stamp" in him. He doesn't know how to speak to people, he can't create beautiful things and he needs help to understand what's going on around him.' The 'God-stamp' was the subject of the Bible teaching theme for that month, explaining *imago Dei* in the human experience as being relational, creative and rational.

Micah, our (now 15-year-old) son, Tabitha's older brother, lives with autism, a profound intellectual disability and is non-verbal, that is, he inhabits this world in a way that is beyond the use or understanding of words. As is often the case, Micah also experiences complex needs that often emerge in the combined experience of his diagnosis. His presence in our world has radically transformed our perception of what it means to be human and be human together.

Some time later, Tabitha and Micah were starting school and I had the proud mummy social media posts ready. Tabitha's picture in her new uniform, was narrated by a written sign, 'My name is Tabitha. I am going into Primary 1. When I grow up, I want to be a baker.' 'Now, its Micah's turn – write a sign for him,' instructed Tabitha. I drew a deep breath, poised to explain that Micah's future did not include a university programme, a professional career or paid employment. Employing a discerning parenting trick, I reflected the question back to the child.

'So, what should Micah's sign say?' I asked, ready to explain the concept of disability, autism and the divergent life paths of our son and daughter.

'Write this…. Micah is going into Primary 3. When he grows up, he will be Tabitha's children's uncle.'

Tabitha had filtered the teaching she received in her children's church through her sibling relationship with Micah and narrated her own perspective, through the lens of relationship and inherent value. Tabitha's experience of teaching, delivered as a sealed package, from systematic theologies with little filtering, question or consideration to the real human lives within our real church communities, or local communities, has also been my experience.

I have studied Theology to master's degree level, with a focus on missiology and ecclesiology. Yet, the theological framework and substance that had formed my faith could no longer contain the deep questions about my son's humanity, about salvation, the Church, Christian witness that had broken into my own life and were stretching my theological horizons. My deeply committed faith, seeking understanding, searched volumes of biblical and systematic theology, only to find more questions than answers.

As I became increasingly active in leading several advocacy campaigns for Special Educational Needs and Disability (SEND) children, I sat at tables of policy and practice in the public spheres. Conversing about human rights ideology, using social activism language, speaking on media channels, I easily narrated my passion for human dignity, justice with *imago Dei* and 'kingdom of God'. While my deep faith intersected this work, I recognised that it would remain unfulfilled without full submission to the One who is the source and end of all justice and righteousness. Yet, these conversations felt so far from the imagination of the people of God, the Church, which should have been at the forefront of this societal change.

# Nothing about us without us

'Nothing about us without us is for us' is a mantra that features heavily within disability activism, and now emotively articulated by movements seeking social justice across several interest groups (Charlton 1998).[1] The

---

1 Originating in Polish politics, the phrase 'Nothing about us without us is for us' has subsequently been embraced by the United Nations International Day of Persons with Disability and the Convention of the Rights of Persons with Disability.

mantra expresses a cry for justice, to be heard, to be seen, to be perceived, to be required at the tables where social knowledge is formed and societal structures are built. 'Don't talk about us, listen to us, make space for us and talk with us. We have something to say, a valuable contribution that you need to hear.'

Disability Theology (DT) is a space where voices have been allowed to speak, and still seek to be heard by both theologians and practitioners. Similarly, Muted Group Theory (MGT) asks: 'Whose voices are dominant within the Christian community, whose are muted, and why?' DT also attempts to unmute and articulate the questions that arise from the disabled experience. DT is defined by Swinton (2010:140–1) as,

> the attempt by disabled and non-disabled Christians to understand and interpret the gospel of Jesus Christ, God, and humanity against the backdrop of the historical and contemporary experiences of people with disabilities … [resulting in] a variety of perspectives and methods designed to give voice to the rich and diverse theological meanings of the human experience of disability.

Therefore, MGT and DT potentially form a mutual partnership, which might bring 'Nothing about us without us' into the realm of Christian theology and practice. While MGT offers helpful insights into the voices and lived experiences that are dominating social knowledge and structures within the Christian sphere, a theological response might question the theories on which MGT is based.

In this chapter, I do not wish to relegate the voice of disability by asking a dominant question in Christian communities, 'What do we do with these disabled children?' Rather, I seek to begin a conversation within this volume, as to how DT offers a unique evaluation towards a fuller ecclesial understanding and response to the questions being raised by MGT for the wider theology and practice of Christianity. What can we learn about our Christian theology and practice from the voices and questions raised within DT? Critical dialogue between MGT and DT will be explored within two corresponding questions; First, whose voices dominate the narrative formation of theology and practice, and whose have been muted? Second, what constitutes 'voice', and so how do we do the unmuting to secure the intended listening and learning together?

With reference to disability, whose voices have been dominant or subordinate within theology and practice? Where and how does mutedness occur, and to what effect?

# Conversations from Scripture: whose voices?

While Christian theology and practice reserve the central, authoritative role of Scripture as sacred, foundational text, the authoritative role of Scripture is too often taken for granted within a modernist assumption. Theologies of biblical interpretation have increasingly acknowledged that no objective platform exists from which we read and interpret the text; the interpretation of Scripture is never neutral, but infused with the lived experience, or social locatedness (Barram 2007:42–58)[2] of those few who are tasked with hermeneutic agency. Adopting Swinton's previously referenced terminology, we ask to what extent have non-disabled voices and disabled voices and lived experiences participated in the interpretation of Scripture and formulation of Christian theology?

Yong refers to the 'ableist' and 'normate' lens applied to Scripture, which continues to be interpreted, through the experience, assumptions and questions of non-disabled persons, to the exclusion of disabled voices and experiences. Consequently, whereas Scripture itself does not convey a devalued perception of disabled humanity (or a superior, normative perception of non-disabled), the dominant voices within the Christian community interpret the biblical texts in a marginalising way.

Hermeneutic lenses of lived experience discriminately define what meaning is extracted, but also how meaning is extracted from any given text. Persons with disability appear in the narratives of Scripture

---

2  Social location is a term used in reference to missiological concern for 'cultural' context, and refers to the external, environmental factors that frame the human person's lens on Scripture and theology. See Barram (2007).

with their own story, their own agency and experiences of life. Yet the dominant priorities of the Christian reading community tend to detach these characters' personhood from their own, a hermeneutic act of 'othering' with marginalising consequence. Subsequently, these human characters are interpreted as little more than evidence for Christ's deity, as the passive, faceless recipient of miraculous healing; or a metaphor to denote a non-disabled reader's spiritual state before God. It is not surprising that persons with disability have struggled to find their place within the story of God (Rose 2019).

My son's own lived experience of profound intellectual disability and complex needs disrupted my detached, systematic reading of biblical texts into a narrative reading. Armed with new experiences and questions, I reread Scripture using a renewed lens that read Scripture's story *with* his disabled humanity, not *to* his disabled humanity; and uncovered new theological insights. My story became one with the mothers who brought children to Jesus, but who were refused (Mark 10:13–16); or the father who desperately sought Jesus' healing touch for his son's challenging and complex behaviours, but was met with the flawed faith of the arguing disciples (Mark 9:14–29).

MGT and DT both highlight a new hermeneutical conversation, which clears the interpretive space for voices previously marginalised to read Scripture in new ways.

## Conversations about God and humanity: whose voices?

Underlying the muting of the disabled hermeneutic voice is the community's perception of human personhood. What constitutes the type of humanity that could contribute to an understanding of the Divine and human interaction? MGT and DT urge the Christian community to explore deep questions of ontology, and human 'being'-ness. These questions must begin with our theological construction of who God is; for, as Swinton rightly perceives, 'the type of God we assume God to be, will ... determine how we understand what it means to be human, which in turn will determine how we respond to disability' (Swinton 2011:300).

The lived experience of being human is closely correlated to the Christian construction of the character and capacities of God, as 'we have a tendency to make God in our image' states Swinton (2011:296). Human beings experience the capacity to love, and correlate this experience to the divine love, that is, God's love is infinitely purer and greater; human beings experience the capacity of strength, competency and agency, and correlate this lived experience to the divine strength and power. So, the select human experience of the able-bodied, able-minded person creates the criteria, the language and conceptual framework from which a theology of the Divine is constructed.

Within this normative framework, dominant voices from non-disabled experience have constructed systematic theologies that locate the image of God within the human categories of being rational, having a desire for relationship, and enacting a creative agency; none of which easily correlates to the most profoundly disabled human experience, and not that of my son, which Tabitha was quick to discern.

Even within those Christian congregations who explore a better practice, the dominant voices articulate the power-laden question of 'how might we *include* disabled people'; a question that will only construct what Swinton calls 'thin model of inclusion' (Swinton 2012a:183). The key question Swinton insists must be articulated as, 'What does it mean to be human?' because a rereading of *imago Dei* is required to adequately address the former question, that moves beyond inclusion to belonging.

Rather than receiving the *imago Dei* as an endowed status, an identity that is integrally bound up with the mere existence of being human, the dominant voices have interpreted the *imago Dei* in such a way that it 'almost universally excludes the body from the image (whether explicitly or by omission) … continues to perpetuate an implicit devaluation of the concrete life of the body in relation to spirituality' (Middleton 2005:24).

In this way, the dominant understanding of our image-bearing humanity has become one of performative functionality, and this perspective has directed the way we perceive, value and relate to persons with disability. This is not surprising, given the Western, utilitarian world view that strives for self-autonomy, self-identity, self-sustainability and self-agency.

When discussing the image of God and its relation to the body, Klyne R. Snodgrass asserts,

> The focus is not on the body, but what the body should do. The real task of the body is to seek the kingdom and God's righteousness. This is merely another way to emphasise that humans were created for relation with God, bear his image, and are engaged in his work. (2018: 138–9)

The dominant perception of being human does not explicitly deny or diminish the human personhood of those who do not meet the performative criteria. Yet, the operant theology communicates a perpetual 'othering' of persons with disability through the implicit interactions of the non-disabled approach that responds largely by seeking to remove the disability, or as a project to serve in sympathy (Mills 2006:1–16).

Non-disabled voices read Gospel passages that narrate the removal of disability from the person and dominate the Christian interpretation that projects the ultimate goal is the removal of impairment. Nancy L. Eiesland's (1994) groundbreaking work, *The Disabled God*, critiques the Church's 'othering' perspective that emerges in a fixation on healing, 'touched by hands that have forgotten our humanity and attend only to curing us' … the Christian Church assumes that getting rid of … disabilities is the chief concern of people who are disabled and the ideal for all people.

Correlating to MGT, Reynolds (2008) identifies normative Christian language of 'caring for the needy' as formulated by this dominant narrative and perpetuating the 'othering' of the subordinate group as 'if they are helpless subjects with nothing to offer'. Likewise, Tam observes that church congregations tend to perceive persons with disability as projects, rather than persons, identifying as the 'giver' to those who 'receive' from their Christian benevolence (Tam 2002:21–34).

Within the Church, I hear a commonly repeated slogan that we 'serve the least, the last, the lost', a mantra that narrates a social barrier between 'them and us', wherein the Church identifies as the 'good people who do kind things to poor people'. A questionable perspective, in light of the reordered life of the kingdom of God, wherein those who are first, are actually last, and those who are last are, in reality, the first. Likewise, those who are the greatest in society's value system, become the least, and the least perceived as the greatest. If the voices of disabled men, women, boys and girls have been silenced in sympathy or service by the community of God, then how might the counter-cultural witness to his kingdom be expressed?

The medical (or individual) model of disability is critiqued for being purely deficit focused, where disability is perceived as an individual tragedy, and dominated unilaterally by the non-disabled expert's perspective (Rieser 2006:135). In contrast, the social model emerged in the 1970s as a corrective response to the dehumanising dichotomy created by the medical model (Union of the Physically Impaired Against Segregation 1976). Giving voice to the previously muted group revealed that the whole disabled experience extended beyond impairment, to include environmental factors and societal structures, such as restricted accessibility and demeaning social attitudes.

While the social model gradually influences community and society, regrettably it is the individual or medical model that prevails within the Christian community. Reynolds (2008) outlines the 'cult of normalcy' at large within church communities, wherein a binary 'Them and Us' are construed according to criteria of being able or disabled; and where disability is perceived as a disruptive deviance to the normative perception of being an able-bodied, -minded human person.

There is a significant concern, not only for individuals living with disability and their families, but for the whole Christian community and our witness to the world. While a growing current within the public sphere has identified the problem, and responded in various forms, the Christian Church largely remains oblivious to any problem. While the zeitgeist asks, 'What does it mean to be human, and to be human together across social divisions', our witness to the kingdom has failed.

As a rereading of the imago Dei, which is at the root of our perceptions of and interaction with persons with disability, Swinton suggests that instead of perceiving each person through the lens of a performative capacity, we receive each person, each body regardless of capacity or characteristic as a human person created, sustained and animated by the gifted nephesh of God (Swinton 2012b). We, therefore, attend to each one with the expectation that in our meeting, we might also attend to God.

Hans Reinders extends this thought by stating, it is in the face of the 'Other' that we might become aware of our own human and personal weaknesses and limitations. Attending to others, including the most profoundly disabled human being as a meeting place of God, opens up the revelation that might lead us to understand an 'otherly' character of God, and therefore of self.

As we seek a rereading of the *imago Dei* could it be that one aspect of the divine character and *modus operandum* that the dominant voices have overlooked is exposed by the unmuting of disabled voices? Specifically, that God created humanity in the image of a mutually dependent Triune community, and repeatedly embraces a kenotic vulnerability as the means by which he engages in and with his world; moreover, it is the means by which he redeems the world. Hauerwas avers,

> the God we Christians must learn to worship is not a god of self-sufficient power, a god who in self-possession needs no-one … Absoluteness of being or power is not a work of the God we have come to know through the work of the cross.
> (Hauerwas 2005:296)

There are individuals and families whose approach to Micah have been to acknowledge his limitations associated with his autism, intellectual disability and the level of support that he requires. They articulate their own lack of understanding, use their skills to support him and us, and yet engage with Micah, receive him and offer themselves to him as a person – Micah – not a set of disabilities that has to be addressed or ignored. Simply as Micah. His disability is a reality, yet it is not the focus within the mutual, reciprocal unforced relationship being built in every interaction.

## A cultural conversation: whose voices?

The second question of this exploration between MGT and DT offers a unique critique of MGT's theoretical assumptions and imperatives particularly in what constitutes 'voice', and how is unmuting performed to secure the intended epistemology?

The development of MGT surpassed social analysis, to insist that change is possible. Meares et al. (2004) perceives MGT as a tool that not only facilitates the identification *of* the marginalised, but it can provide hope and voice *to* the marginalised group in the intentional resistance of their muting.

West and Turner (2017:493) summarise four elements of such resistance. First, to name the silencing; second, to elevate subordinate group's voice; third, to create inclusive language; and fourth, to use media platforms towards cultural change.

MGT's theoretical assumptions for the resistance of muting are largely reflected within the Western post-structuralist quest for epistemic justice; and are implemented within human rights frameworks and social movements towards equality, diversity and inclusion. Buzzwords of deconstructionist activity that encapsulate aspects of MGT include the drive to *elevate* marginalised individuals' *own voice*; to secure and empower the *authentic representation* of *diverse lived experience* across the spectrum of media outlets. Thus, giving self-autonomy, self-expression to the self-defining individual towards the resistance of dominant voices by insisting on 'Nothing about us without us'.

DT challenges the criteria of humanity by the utilitarian valuing of what one can enact, achieve or produce. Within this cultural backdrop where changes in technology, medicine and social norms are radically reframing the accepted perception of personhood, it must be noted that despite outlining an increasing range of rights for humans, 'the human being the [human rights] convention is designed to protect remains undefined' (Reuter 2000:181–94).

DT critiques the idealised and imagined self-formulated human personhood that constitutes the voice to be elevated and unmuted. Thus, Swinton's previously referenced ontological insights, to create 'thick' models of epistemic justice, and ask the fundamental question, what does it mean to be human – or, given MGT's theoretical assumptions, we focus the question as, what kind of human is being defined?

# A complex conversation: whose voices?

MGT acknowledges that muting is a complex reality; wherein those who experience muting, may, in turn, enact a muting of others. This reality is observable within the muted group of disability. For example, within disability activism and media narratives, a preferable and *more able* experience of disability tends to dominate the discourse. The lived experience of individuals with a physical or sensory impairment, or a mild to moderate intellectual disability have become disability's voice and representation across media platforms. I wonder if the presented personhoods and their more moderate experience of disability is somehow more palatable, presentable or persuasive of their social activist argument.

In recent years I have worked alongside several statutory and third sector agencies to protect and develop the Special Educational Needs and Disability provisions at state level. A consistent message conveyed within disability activism is the need to draw a strong and tiered distinction between children with physical and sensory disabilities, and those with severe intellectual disabilities.

Disability activism has significantly increased on media channels in recent years. Yet, the argument centres on the disabled person's capacity to perform the human roles prescribed and celebrated by non-disabled people. The disability rights campaigns for Down Syndrome prenatal screening and termination argues, 'I am a valid person, with a valid humanity because I can do x, y, z – just like non-disabled people.' It is concerning that the voice, message and representation of the disabled lived experience mutes the voices and demeans the humanity of those who cannot perform x, y, z and does not fit into the premise and persuasion of the more dominant disabled voices. MGT notes the tendency for, and urges against, such dominant group members speaking for the whole marginalised community. Speaking 'for', it is argued, leads to the 'own voice' being lost as it is 'filtered' into the dominant narrative.

Thus, *own voice* and *authentic representation* is rigidly applied within arts, literature and media as the actual verbal or written voice of the disabled person. My daughter, at the age of 11 wrote a book about her brother. The BBC covered the story and it went viral, globally. We were inundated by requests for the book. However, seeking out a publishing house who would publish the book proved more complicated. Even publishers intentionally committed to unmuting disabled voices insisted rigidly on the verbal articulation or written authorship only by the person with disability. Tabitha's story, which narrated her mutual relationship with Micah, was deemed 'inappropriate and dehumanising'.

Therein lies the weakness of the theoretical assumptions that undergird MGT. Specifically, that own voices are largely verbal and inhabit media platforms through self-expression and self-agency. Thus, MGT's quest to unmute require the muted individual or community to self-assert, self-express, from a capacity to self-identify and self-define using a level of self-agency. Tasks that are moulded into the modern ideology of 'self' and exclude my son's personhood. Where, and how then, is Micah's non-verbal voice to be represented into the public discourse and media channels that are rapidly reshaping society's perspectives on disabled persons?

Consequently, the theoretical assumptions intended to unmute the wider marginalised disabled group, only result in the further muting of the most profoundly disabled experiences, which will subsequently lead to a tiered valuing of humanity, and more extreme social divisions based on flawed ontological assumptions.

## A language conversation: whose voices?

Finding an inclusive language has proved even more treacherous for those who live with profound disability. I imagine that through these ideas, I have already offended half my readers; and by the time you are reading this, there might be a new set of sensibilities and sensitivities around the language and concepts surrounding disability. I urge my audiences to hold grace, patience, so that we may reflect and rebuild together in a better way.

While the medical model defines the term disability purely as the impairment that creates a deficit on the individual, the social model intentionally broadens the scope of the term to refer to the wider landscape of environmental and social factors. The distinctive lens of language within each model creates a framework or an imagination for societal structures.

The social model intentionally strives for person-first language, which refers primarily to the person, and the specific experience of disability as an additional consideration. The goal is to alter social perception and interaction. Rather than the autistic/disabled boy, the preferred articulation might be 'the boy who lives with autism/profound disability'. More recently, an emerging 'social construct model' shifts the use of language around disability even further. This model questions how society has accepted not just the language of disability and impairment, but the concept of disability and impairment that is consolidated by the use of the terms within disability discourse. It seeks to eradicate any language that categorises impairment or disability at all.

An increasingly emergent terminology that seeks to correct the social constructs of disability refer to 'so-called disability'. This language gives voice to an articulation that 'we are not disabled, you have told us we are disabled because our experience of being human does not correlate with your own normative experience and perception of humanity'.

Similar to the 'social construct model', MGT theoretically argues that binary language sets have been created by societal structures. The term 'disability' in itself, is increasingly a contested term, defined in the world of intellectual disability by the alternative articulation of 'neurodiversity', and the term 'impairment' is replaced by 'characteristic' of the individual's personhood. While leading a Disability Missiology consultation in 2019, a group of academic delegates contested the use of the word 'disability'. Within the group discussion, Christian practitioners argued for their use of 'not disabled, differently abled'. One group of disability theologians insisted disability terminology was dehumanising and belittling. Their alternative language and terminology was: 'creative learner'. In my opinion, this imposed a detached and dishonouring narrative about my son, which denied the fullness of his lived experience and personhood.

Within the world of autism, families who experience a more complex diagnosis increasingly express a frustration with the removal of any 'offensive' language that adequately communicates our children's more profound needs. Any reference to the aspect of difficulty, challenge, incapacity, limitations, struggle is actively resisted, which further mutes this extremely marginalised group. I and other agencies active in advocacy continue to observe the impact of this ever-changing language representation and selected elevation of voices on public services and policies (Singer 2022).

# A flawed conversation: whose voices?

The assumptions inherent to MGT and similar human rights frameworks may widen the boundaries for certain experiences of disability, but they consolidate barriers of mutedness, oppression and dehumanisation of the more profound experience of disability. These barriers are rooted in the underlying hypothetical vision of the human being as the 'autonomous and independent subject'. This has been constructed according to the Western narrative and sense of 'self', which redefines the criteria for human personhood as being inherently self-autonomous, self-defining and self-expressive (Fineman 2008:1–24). These self-oriented criteria blur the definition of personhood within gender, disability and increasingly trans-humanist narratives of AI and robotics (Flood 2021).

What happens then, to those who lack the cognitive capacity to perform the tasks of self-identity, or self-definition? How does the elevation of marginalised voices occur, if the situation of mutedness pertains to the innate lack of self-autonomy and self-expression?

DT defines the human person as being created in the image of God through the life breath of God, worthy of dignity and honour; then we must present a wider 'voice' and a 'thicker' model of unmuting, which enacts 'Nothing about us without us' across the spectrum of disability. My son's profound intellectual disability renders his experience of the world as non-verbal. He does not interact with or process his understanding with language, and does not construct his existence beyond the immediate and experiential. He receives from the world through sensory, social interaction in proximity; and his contribution to the world, our shared world, inhabits the same form.

The 'voice', 'representation', or contribution of people who experience such a profound disability is therefore not 'own', or 'self', but 'together'. Within embodied encounters with others, each gives and receives a mutual sharing of life. A voice of this nature is not communicated in self-formed objective propositions, or in verbal articulation, but in the existential shared understanding that comes from being 'with'. This voice is not self-derived, self-imposed or self-expressed, but is received by those who accept the wordless 'voice' of the marginalised 'Other'.

People with profound disability have a contribution to make to us, to those who are able to posture themselves to receive the 'wordless voice', which speaks silently through presence. Those who draw near, enter their space, and perceive the person, create a space for mutual belonging. The preferences, personalities and peculiarities of both connect, in a shared moment in time and space. This is the reality of classroom assistants, social services and charity staff, who gaze upon his whole person, and who receive the other's gaze upon their own.

We are urged in the Church to pause and explore that as *imago Dei* calls to *imago Dei*, as 'deep to deep'. Receiving from 'the face of the other', an emphasis of Levinas, is a disruption to our pace and path of life. Brueggemann (2011:28) also narrates the life-changing contribution from those who are 'Other' to us, urging the Church's way of knowing to open up to 'the intense personal and interpersonal quality' of knowing with our typical Evangelical hold on 'reality understood as static or as rule or as proposition'.

However, Tam (2002) notes the lack of engaged exposure to persons with profound disability as a significant barrier for this interpersonal knowing. Exploring Fitch's notion of *faithful presence* within a lived experience of profound autism, Tam suggests holding up the sibling relationship as a model that is present with and attends to the contribution of each person as an image-bearer.

## A corporate community conversation: whose voices?

It is within this corporate congregation, the expression of the family of God, that this community conversation can be most fully formulated, understood and implemented. While a number of 'identity theologies' within the theological academy seek to explore Christian theology from a specific lived experience, they do so in academic discourse that is often siloed from other disciplines and voices. Swinton (2011:276) urges caution to fragmented 'identity theologies' that in isolated existence tend to 'create God according to our image'. For people with a disability who have felt excluded from the story of God, from the community of the Church, and whose image-bearing humanity has been indirectly diminished, Eiseland's *The Disabled God* intentionally disrupted that disconnection between disabled humanity and Christian theology.

While each lived experience can find a place in God's story, and in the process reveal a vital aspect of his being, the sacred story of God extends beyond any lived experience, and the person of God cannot be contained within any one human category or experience, embracing each lived experience and voice, as one lens of the whole. 1 Corinthians 13.12 says, 'For now we see only a reflection as in a mirror; then we shall see face to face. Now I know in part; then I shall know fully, even as I am fully known.' But it is together in the diverse, but united community of God that we can understand now in a fuller sense. Within this ecclesial vision, we enact the koinonia unity wherein the lived experience of Jew and Gentile, male and female, slave and free (Galatians 3.28) that might be extended to contemporary social divisions of Black and White, able and disabled, youth and elderly, working- and middle-class that contributes to a body hermeneutic to understanding who the God is that we worship.

Against a cultural movement that urges the 'self-conscientisation' (Freire 2000) of the oppressed, subordinate group, calling each one to rise up, elevate self, impose 'own voice', the Christian Church must adopt 'the mind of Christ' (Phil. 2:1–11). As Paul addressed social power divisions within the new ecclesial community, he generally addressed, not the subordinate group with a message of self-empowerment, but the dominant, privileged group, instructing them to self-empty, to consider others before themselves, to have the mind of Christ and emulate his act of kenosis, stepping down to own their broken humanity, in the incarnation, person and work of Christ.

In the community of the Church, strength and weakness are reordered, the first become last, and the last become first. Self-autonomy and self-identity are subversively overthrown in the self-emptying, self-giving act of the king, and the cruciform way required by those who seek his kingdom come, here on earth (Gorman 2006).

What if the Church became a place that opened a safe space for everyone to receive healing from the invisible lived experiences of fallen, broken human beings? Just as Jesus sent his disciples towards persons on the periphery, it is when we go there, place our hands on their body, share a gaze in a moment in time, form words that connect us, that we find we are both walking towards Jesus in a mutual journey of transformation, together.

# Christian witness of a new conversation: whose voices?

Amid a *zeitgeist* search to articulate 'what does it mean to be human, and be human together', the Church at every level must offer themselves as an epistemological witness to what God has done, in Christ (Conner 2015).[3] Newbigin, narrating the local congregation as 'the only hermeneutic of the gospel', refers to the presence of persons with disability in the community 'without that witness from its own membership, the Church's witness is distorted and deceptive and the Church's discipleship is irrelevant to the real world in which men and women suffer' (quoted in Conner 2015:24).

Lest we forget the helpful contribution of MGT that instigated this paper, and the insights revealed as to the Church's normative theology and practice that potentially dehumanises persons with disability, Swinton reminds us that disability is required for both cutting through failing cultural assumptions, but also in 'reveal[ing] how the church in its theology and practice has become acculturated in ways that prevent it from functioning faithfully' (Swinton 2011:293).

Tabitha articulates and models her sibling perception for the Church and disrupts prevalent theology. She cannot understand why others in God's family do not perceive and receive Micah as she does. What if Tabitha's children's church session had not been shaped by a 'here's the knowledge I prepared earlier', but opened up space for Tabitha's voice to ask, 'But what about Micah, does he not have the "God-stamp"?' Or if the children's church leader had engaged with Scripture in light of the individuals within the church community, raising questions about humanity and healing that emerge from the real people in this real time and place? What if Micah's peers and their families, whom we have

---

3 Conner (2015:15–29) states, 'in this missiological way of thinking, people with disabilities are ... necessary contributors to the calling of the church to bear witness to the ongoing redemptive work of God in this world – proclaiming the Kingdom of God is at hand'.

grown to know and love, who struggle alongside us, find the local church community not only to be a place where they are served or receive sympathy, as the strong serving the weak, but honoured, empowered, perceived and received, as persons who can belong?

If Western culture hypothesises an imagined, idealistic self-sustaining experience of humanity, we remember that this ideal imagination of the Church is no human accomplishment. The Church was instigated by Christ, and is constituted by the Holy Spirit (Gunton 1993; 1998). As such, the ecclesial community is an eschatological community, inhabiting both now and not yet, both holy and unfinished. Between what is and what will be, the ecclesial people enact practices, rituals, performative acts that, if practised with and alongside, rather than to and for, in the way of *nothing about us without us*, we more fully rehearse, transform and mould ourselves gradually into that perfect way of being human, and being human together.

# 6

# Unmuting migrants: Greenford Baptist Church

## DAVID WISE

Greenford is situated in the London borough of Ealing. I became the pastor of Greenford Baptist Church (GBC) in October 1987 and I was a full-time staff member until January 2015. In 1987, there were many first-generation migrants living in the community surrounding the church building. The biggest groups were from India and Pakistan, but there was also a significant number from the Caribbean. The ninety-three members of GBC in 1987, however, were almost entirely White British. In January 1988, the first people from India joined the church, and over the following three years, we welcomed two more from India, three from Hong Kong and half a dozen from the Caribbean. In 1991, the first people from West Africa joined the congregation. By the end of 2005, more than half of the 129 church members were not White British, and by the end of 2009, only one-third of the 181 members were White British, the majority coming from more than forty nations, and this became the settled proportion. This White proportion reflected the local community. We had a larger proportion of African heritage and a smaller proportion of Asian heritage than the surrounding community.

When I arrived at GBC, I was ignorant about racism and White privilege (the reality that people with white skin have social advantages). I was not aware of the extra challenges for people born outside of the UK to integrate into what was, in essence, still a White British church. I did not have any understanding of the cultural contexts from which people had come, so in the early years I did not intentionally engage with any of these issues as I was not aware of them.

This chapter is not about why people born outside of Europe chose to become a part of GBC, although some of the reasons may become obvious as you read. It is about how the voices of those who came from contexts outside of Europe became heard loud and clear within GBC, in the local community and beyond.

It was not my intention when I arrived at GBC to build a multi-ethnic church congregation. It was my intention to work to see a vibrant church community built, one in which all the new people who were joining became fully integrated and engaged. So initially moving towards hearing the voices of those from outside of Europe was a side-effect of inclusive community-building. It was only later as my own understanding developed that this process became far more intentional.

# Tapestry

I have recently completed doctoral research that examined the transitions that took place at GBC between 1987 and 2015. One of the findings was the significance of a metaphor that was used initially by me, then more widely within the church, to describe GBC. Using pictures or metaphors to describe the Church is common; popular ones are 'body' or 'bride of Christ'. GBC used 'tapestry' as a key metaphor for the congregation for over twenty-five years. It originates from Colossians 2:2, 'I want you to be woven into a tapestry of love' (*The Message* version). One of the most significant features of this metaphor is that in a tapestry, the picture is revealed only by the distinctiveness of the threads. These distinctives arise from the different ethnicities and cultures represented within the congregation. From Ephesians 2:8–10 and Romans 1:19–20, the phrases 'masterpiece' and 'everything God made' (the same Greek noun) make clear that it is the Church that makes known to the world something of what God is like. John 13:34–5 makes plain that it is through our relationships with one another that God is made known.

Using the tapestry metaphor, we see that it is through the juxtaposition, acceptance and development of difference that an image of God is revealed. In a tapestry, the predominant colour, usually the background colour, is the least significant. Colours that stand out because they only occur occasionally often indicate the most significant detail. This means that the least or the fewest represented cultures or ethnicities within the congregation can be the most significant. An implication of this for GBC was that it tried to ensure that the ethnic and cultural uniqueness of each ethnicity was expressed within GBC, so that all could be enriched. Always guiding was Revelation 7:9–12, an image of heaven, our destiny. It seems from this image that distinctiveness of ethnicity, both in physical appearance and language, is something that lasts into heaven. There is something about our joining together as one, but with our differing ethnicities, that is reflective of the nature of God. There is a real sense that living this out on earth is an anticipation of heaven.

As I write this chapter, it is clear to me that the use of this metaphor was a factor in the effective unmuting of people who became a part of GBC. We consciously chose to prioritise the voices of those who were least represented within GBC. As Kunle said,

The strength of each group comes out when we are all together … we are able to be a better people than if we just look at our individual cultural or ethnic group … to actually see people as equals, rather than one group being inferior to the other.
(Wise 2022:81)

Aspects of how this worked in practice will form the remainder of this chapter.

# Leadership Training Group

One of the most significant components that led to the unmuting of migrants' voices within GBC was the Leadership Training Group programme (LTG). The first group was formed in 1989 and groups became a regular feature of GBC life. The concept was simple. A small group, typically of four to seven participants, was formed, with the members being suggested by me and approved by the church leadership. Each group lasted for around sixteen months. During that time the group held a monthly meeting with me. Each time we met we explored one of the qualities listed by Paul for church leaders in 1 Timothy 3 and Titus 1, focusing on what this might look like in practice in the lives of the group members. In addition, there was honest sharing of what was going on in the group members' lives and prayer for one another. Group members were set ministry tasks by me, which, over time, involved them in almost every area of GBC's life. These tasks included leading worship/prayer and speaking in Sunday and other meetings, pastoral visiting, children's and youth work, evangelism and participating in leadership forums. In addition, when I was speaking or leading at a church or event outside of GBC, some of the LTG members always came with me and also contributed. At the end of each group, usually all of the group members took on leadership roles within GBC.

The first LTG had five members, four of whom were Black. As a part of my research, I interviewed Anthony, one of the Black members who was from the Caribbean. I asked in the interview if he remembered how, at that time, he thought I saw Black people. He responded,

> I would have thought your values meant you would have put Black people into a similar light as you saw yourself in that they can be educated and can be in leadership. They have potential … if you chose to choose them, certainly in the society as it was at that time, you must have had some value of them.
> (Wise 2022:130)

Anthony believed that I saw Black people in a similar way to how I saw White people. They were people who could be trained for, and could exercise leadership, even in a White Majority church. This perspective was particularly significant for him as I, the church minister, was the one who was setting up this LTG. His perception of my view was in stark contrast to his perception of his experience at school and college and of how wider society viewed people who were Black. In Anthony's own words, 'Black young men were to be feared or treated, regarded very suspiciously' (Wise 2022:130).

We needed to train future leaders in order for GBC to be able to continue to develop and grow. In discussion with the rest of the leaders, I invited to join an LTG those whom I thought had the most potential, irrespective of their ethnicity. As GBC's membership became more diverse, these groups reflected that. For example, the group that started in June 2006 was made up of one Iraqi, one from Sierra Leone, one from Jamaica, one British-born Caribbean, one British-born Nigerian and one White British. This investment in training leaders resulted in there being people from a mixture of ethnicities involved in every area of church leadership. Several of the LTG members went on to develop significant ministries within GBC and subsequently outside of GBC.

The impact on those who became a part of an LTG was profound. Alvita came from the Caribbean; when she arrived in West London it was her first time outside her country of origin. In her interview reflecting on her first visit to GBC in 2003, she said, 'Coming in was a bit daunting as I came by myself, the first time … I don't know anybody, but it was really good. I felt right at ease and comfortable with the people there' (Wise 2022:133). After some months she was invited to join an LTG. Reflecting on that experience she said, 'I left everything and came here. So, to come somewhere, be a stranger in a place and then to, in a sense, find myself fitting in and then being given opportunities I never, ever would have thought about; it was shocking (voice breaking)' (Wise 2022:133).

Alvita experienced welcome and acceptance at GBC. She experienced being invested in through a training programme and being given significant opportunities for ministry and leadership within GBC and later in the wider Church. This was so unexpected and life-changing that twelve years later, she was overcome with emotion as she recalled what had taken place.

# Unmuting the congregation: language

The routine use of languages other than English became an established part of GBC life. English remained the primary language used in Sunday meetings, midweek groups and for pastoral care, but there was freedom for people to use their own first language in prayer and worship, which meant people were able to express themselves in ways that would not have been possible if they had been restricted to English. In Sunday meetings, it was normal practice for several songs to be used that were in languages other than English. These songs were sung in the style that was used in the context from which they originated. For example, when a Hindi song was used, the singers and musicians, along with many of the congregation, would sit on the floor. The only instruments played were a tabla drum, bells and a drone sound. When a Yoruba song was sung, only drums accompanied it and there was a lot of dancing. When someone led in prayer, either from the front or from the congregation, they were free to use whatever language they were most comfortable with. During prayer ministry (when individuals came forward to be prayed for by members of the prayer ministry team), those praying were free to use their first language, whether or not the person they were praying for understood it. Similar practices took place in midweek and small group meetings.

Bunmi, another of the research participants, summed up her understanding of the approach at GBC, 'If you want to pray in your language then pray in your language. If you want to prophesy in your language then prophesy in it. It is not everything needs to be made more British to be acceptable' (Wise 2022:141). For another of the research participants, Ronke, the significance was profound,

To be able to be part of a church which not only embraces free worship, but also allows people to worship and pray in their first language and also puts a system in place to embrace different types of songs in different languages to allow me to come on stage to the podium and share testimony and break out in choruses in my language, but also at the same time translating so people understand and you can carry people along. That is huge, that is deep. So, it's very refreshing and has been very helpful.
(Wise 2022:142)

Tambara summed up the significance for her 'to have a church where your language is being spoken in the songs and the prayers, you feel welcome … [people] feel like they are human beings and not just second-hand citizens or whatever' (Wise 2022:142). This comment is striking, the unmuting by encouraging the use of first language led to people feeling that they were recognised as being fully in the image of God, fully accepted, fully human. Of course, this also significantly changed their self-image when *outside* of the GBC community as well.

# Unmuting the congregation: dance

At GBC dancing during the Sunday meetings became a normal component of worship. When we sang songs that had a Caribbean or African rhythm, members of the congregation would dance in their places. Often people would also use the space in front of the platform or behind the congregation to dance. It was common for the offering to be received accompanied by the entire congregation in turn dancing down the aisle to place their gifts in the offering plate or to touch the plate in recognition that all they had was given to God. Members of the congregation, especially those who had grown up in West Africa, saw this as an important part of their worship, presenting themselves and their gifts before God. The style of dancing was exuberant, drawing particularly on movements usual in West Africa and the Caribbean. For most GBC members who had grown up outside of Europe, dancing at home, as well as in church, is a normal part of expressing their devotion to God. Lavanya, 'Even at home when I get up in the morning ... I put on my Indian worship ... I'm dancing with it and I enjoy it, all the worship that God gives us' (Wise 2022:144).

Alvita became a worship leader at GBC; when she leads, she uses Caribbean rhythms, such as calypso and reggae. She commented that when she is at the front she sees 'people dancing, people raising their hands. It's just the whole-body movement that you don't get if they are maybe just doing a normal English song' (Wise 2022:145). From her cultural perspective, when people are physically moving, they are more engaged with God than when they are static.

For many migrants, dance was a normal part of their worship of God. Being able to dance as a part of their congregational experience was therefore welcome and helpful. Oluwasesan said,

I think a lot of Yorubas, Nigerians and maybe Africans generally like to express themselves and when we really express ourselves, we do it by dancing. We see a lot of that in the church [GBC] and I think it is the same for the people from the Caribbean as well.
(Wise 2022:145)

However, it seemed that there was a further spiritual significance to dance for the participants. Ronke explained,

> The Bible says … 'He delights in the praises of His people' and when you praise in my culture [Yoruba] and you praise a king, you sing and bestow accolades. You praise and worship that king. Kings don't dance, they sit down and their congregation will dance in honour and in worship. Now, we are talking of the King of all Kings. We are talking of the Ruler of the Universe. The Creator of Heaven and Earth and everything I have in my life I will use it to worship. My voice, my body, my song, my money, my family … So, for me, dance is integral. I can't keep still when I hear Christian music.
> (Wise 2022:146)

Tabia added,

> It shows that you are happy. It shows you are delighted, you are comfortable, so you are able to move your body freely because if you are not, if you are in a strange place and you feel frightened, you're not going to move your body … they feel connected. So, they express their worship through their movement, not only of their mouth, but all their body.
> (Wise 2022:146)

For Oluwasesan, Ronke and Tabia, dance is an integral part of their worship of God. It was a normal part of congregational worship in their home country. Dance expresses part of their adoration that for them cannot be communicated without bodily movement. Without dance, their worship is muted.

Perhaps there is a similarity here between the use of dance and the use of first language in Sunday worship. Both of these mediums allow cultural expression, but more significantly, the congregational embracing of these mediums communicates deep acceptance of people from those cultures. Being allowed to express worship via the medium of dance meant that people felt recognised and included, seen and heard. There is a connection here with Tambara's view, already quoted above, that when the first language of people in the congregation was being used, people 'feel like they are human beings not just second-hand citizens'. Dance as a bodily language seems, from this perspective, to function in the same way as first language. For some people at GBC to be unmuted, they needed to dance.

## Unmuting the congregation: congregational hermeneutics

From 1997 to 2000, I undertook a part-time MA in Biblical Interpretation, which particularly explored the way in which people from different cultures interpreted the Bible. I took the course out of a concern that my Eurocentric way of interpreting the Bible was marginalising the increasing proportion at GBC who came from elsewhere in the world. My learning from the MA transformed my understanding of hermeneutics and my preaching practice. From the congregation's perspective, the biggest change was that I began routinely asking the congregation questions during my teaching, and wandering around with a microphone so that answers could be heard. My questions aimed to help congregants use their imagination and engage with their emotions as they considered the biblical text. Towards the end of the teaching, I asked congregants to express how what they had learned would impact their own lives. This was designed to draw out different cultural applications of the text. This had the profound effect of unmuting non-European biblical interpretation. There is a good example of this early in this chapter where Ronke draws on her cultural understanding to interpret biblical teaching concerning dance. One of the research participants, Debbie, commented on the impact of my approach,

> The sort of interactivity of the church in terms of your style of asking questions and getting response, so that kind of dialogue going on … it encouraged the dynamic of the congregation having a voice and their thoughts and feelings being important and shareable.
> (Wise 2022:181)

Additionally, I invited visiting speakers from non-European contexts to preach on Sundays and I worked to encourage and develop some of the GBC members from overseas in their preaching at GBC, specifically encouraging them to draw on their own cultural heritage. This was a conscious decision to allow other, non-European ways of interpreting the Bible to be heard. This was part of an intentional strategy to enable the voices and perspectives of those born outside of Europe to be heard within GBC and, through the material being available on GBC's website, throughout the world.

## Unmuted in the community

In December 1997, there was a serious racially motivated assault on an Asian family who were a core part of GBC. In the early hours of the morning, three masked men forced their way into the family's home. The father suffered a dislocated shoulder, broken ribs and head injuries. The mother suffered bruises and cuts to the face, and the son required stitches as well as plastic surgery to the face. The family had been experiencing racial harassment from neighbours for several years. Shortly after the attack, the father was quoted as saying that there was a concerted attempt to force the family to move out of the area,

> When we would not move we were viciously attacked. We believe that there would have been far greater action if Black people had attacked a White family in this way. We thought the police were here to protect us, but they failed to do so.

Following what seemed to me to be a lack of appropriate action by the local police, I encouraged the family to make a formal complaint to the Police Complaints Authority (PCA). They were reluctant to do so as they did not believe that they would be listened to. I arranged a meeting between the chairman of the PCA and the father; this led to a formal complaint being lodged. Here is an extract from the complaint:

> The police never took any serious action over the harassment the XXX were suffering … Officers persistently failed to turn up to take

statements ... The police chose to believe the word of YYY [the individual who was the primary source of the racial harassment] ... By their favouritism the police contributed to an atmosphere in which it was easy for a group of thugs to invade the XXX home at night and viciously attack them. The police failed to follow up the attack actively or vigorously, apparently they did not even undertake house-to-house enquiries and witnesses who had seen the men thought to be involved were not immediately questioned. (Wise 2022:34–35)

Eventually, nearly all of the complaints were accepted as valid by the PCA. There was an apology from the police and changes were introduced into police procedures to try to prevent any re-occurrence of the police's failure.

In the meantime, GBC organised a public meeting to highlight the family's experience and put it into the context of other apparent examples of police and societal racism. I was invited to speak, alongside Neville Lawrence, the father of the murdered teenager Stephen Lawrence, and seven others. A BBC radio crew attended and recorded the event, journalists were present and there was subsequently extensive coverage in the Christian press and some in other media.

Following on from the public meeting, I was invited to give evidence to the second phase of the Stephen Lawrence Inquiry on 8 October 1998. I talked about the experiences of the family and another church member. I commented that 'these two cases illustrate the fact that the police here in West London seem to respond differently to Black and Asian people than to Whites'. Subsequently, I was interviewed by a BBC news team and by a *Guardian* journalist, which resulted in further publicity at the time and subsequently.

These shocking events had a profound effect on people, especially White British people, who were a part of GBC. During my research, I asked six of the research participants what they remembered about the impact of the events. Here are some of the responses. Betsy, who is White British, commented,

Well, you see I think that it was because we'd seen first-hand how terrible it was and talked to them and realised what they were going

through. But if we had just heard, oh so and so had been attacked, we'd say, 'Oh that's terrible isn't it,' and then go on and talk about something else. But when you sort of see first-hand and you are involved with the people it has a very different effect.
(Wise 2022:37)

Brian, also White British, noted,

Of course, it was around the time of the Stephen Lawrence stuff as well and because that was slightly remote from us, it didn't quite affect us in the same way, but then it did when it happened to them. You suddenly realised there is an issue within our society ... it made me think about my thinking with regard to other people from other ethnicities as well and so making sure I wasn't having prejudiced thoughts towards them because of somebody's ethnicity.
(Wise 2022:38)

Janice, White British, commented, 'When it happens to your own, then you start thinking and questioning yourself, your thinking and your beliefs and what you understand about race and people' (Wise 2022:38). By 'your own', Janice was referring to her perspective that when someone you know who is a part of your own church community is a victim of a racist attack, the reality of racism and its impact becomes real to you.

For Betsy, Brian and Janice, three White British members of GBC, what happened to the family brought home to them the reality of racism in a way that the high-profile murder of Stephen Lawrence elsewhere in London had not. Because this attack happened to some of 'our own', what was a reality on the outside of GBC became earthed inside. The fact that I, as the church pastor, with the support of the church leadership and membership, was to the forefront of not only campaigning for justice for the family, but also in exposing the systemic racism in our society and its institutions further made clear some of the challenges that faced us.

Within GBC, racism was exposed as an ugly, dangerous, daily reality that afflicted the lives of people who were a part of the church congregation. It was seen as sin and consequently something that needed to be confronted in our lives and in the life of the congregation. The attack on the family and the subsequent events, as the comments recorded above demonstrate, changed the self-understanding of people who were a part of GBC, especially the majority White British attendees. GBC's voice was unmuted, it spoke loud and clear to the local community, to the police and, through the media coverage, to the nation. The people who were attacked were seen by the whole of GBC as us, not them.

# Unmuting the congregation: food, flags and art

Eating together was an important part of GBC life, such as monthly church lunches. The format varied, but the most common was 'bring and share' where people were invited to bring some food that would be put out on tables for people to take. Generally, people brought food that reflected their own ethnic background. In the view of some of the research participants, eating one another's food meant accepting one another's culture. Oluwasesan commented,

> I like my food and I like tasting different things, different food from different places. It was another way of getting to know people and different cultures as well … And then I'm happy to explain what it is, when it is eaten, how it is eaten, how it is prepared. So, it's just erm, sharing my experience of Nigeria and just letting people know a bit more about the foods and the culture. I'm very happy when people try Nigerian food and then ask questions about what it is and how you actually prepare it … So, it's a way of saying, 'Yes, this is what we do in Nigeria.'
> (Wise 2022:155)

Graham observed that,

> I think we have embraced things like church lunches and international evenings which always express integration and something of an introduction to other cultures … I think the fact we have a long table with food from however many cultures on offer and people fill their plates with it, for those who are bringing and

preparing the food there is massive acceptance. A massive sense of belonging.
(Wise 2022:156)

Tabia commented,

It makes you feel very proud. You feel appreciated. They don't just like me; they like what I eat and they are eating it too, so they are connecting with me. They are connecting with me; they are acknowledging me. It's very important.
(Wise 2022:156)

For Oluwasesan, Graham and Tabia, eating food prepared by different members of GBC created opportunities for people to talk about their own culture and context. It led to a 'massive sense of belonging'. People were united in their diversity through eating together. For Tabia, when someone ate her food they connected with her and acknowledged her. So, sharing her food involved being accepted in her ethnicity by others; she was seen and heard. As Ronke expressed it, 'the impact of food is very, very significant' (Wise 2022:156).

On three sides of the rectangular worship space, there were (in January 2015) forty-seven full-sized national flags on display. Each of these flags represented a country that at least one member of the congregation had come from. Members of the congregation whose flags were not on display were given the opportunity to pay for their flag to be purchased and displayed. On the left-hand wall behind the platform, from where the meeting was usually led, was an art installation consisting of twenty-eight large hand-painted canvases. The canvases were painted during a workshop at GBC. Each had the name of God in the first language of the person/people who painted the canvas and each was surrounded by colourful decoration. From top to bottom, the canvases reflected the colours of the rainbow. On the right-hand wall behind the platform was a plain wooden cross, which, from time to time, was surrounded by a colourful seasonal display. Additionally, on the walls of the worship area, there was other art on display painted by people who attended the church, usually drawing on their own ethnic, cultural styles. For example, there were two paintings using traditional Chinese artistic forms and Chinese letters illustrating Bible stories that were painted and donated by a Chinese attendee.

There was no flag displayed on the wall that people usually faced during Sunday worship. This was a deliberate choice on my part. I had noticed that in the mono-ethnic churches I had visited it was common for the national flag of the dominant ethnicity to be on display at the front. At GBC I wanted the displayed flags to be a marker that people from all ethnicities were welcome, the flags in a sense marked out their space, a recognition that GBC was united in worshipping the same God. This was visually achieved through the names of God art installation and the bare wooden cross on the wall that the congregation usually faced during the service. Although at GBC God was addressed in different languages, everyone came to relationship with God through Jesus' death and resurrection (the bare wooden cross represented this). GBC was diverse in its ethnicity, but united in its acceptance and worship of God through Jesus Christ.

Bunmi was at the workshop that produced the large artwork. She said,

I remember we made some artwork with different languages demonstrating God's name. And it was so beautiful the work that everyone did because everyone worked independently, yet created a rectangle decorated beautifully with the name of God in their native tongue. Then we put it all together … all working together to create that artwork was really beautiful.
(Wise 2022:148)

Bunmi remembered that 'everyone worked independently' yet 'all [were] working together'. Each contributed something unique drawn from their own ethnic heritage, but built together, it made something 'really beautiful'. There is here an obvious link to the tapestry metaphor that underpinned GBC's understanding of congregational church life.

Tabia was one of those who paid for her national flag. She reflected,

We were the only Cameroonians before and we paid for the flag. So, when the other Cameroonians came and they found the flag it was

'ooh our flag is there,' and I'm always beating my chest – I paid for it (laughter). So, when they find their flag there they also have that feeling of 'they know my country here – I belong here'. I think that also makes them feel at home because they can see their flag here and they are represented here. So, my identity is here.
(Wise 2022:149)

For Tabia, having her national flag on display was a marker that at GBC her ethnic identity was welcome and accepted; she was not muted. It was her view that, at least for Cameroonians, seeing their own flag on display meant that they felt welcome, 'at home'.

Harnoop related an account of a visit to GBC by some Nepalese guests,

I brought some like people whom I know who are Christians and Nepalese … And the first impression they had was that it was a traditional kind of a British, you know, church and also, they were a bit taken aback because they didn't see much Nepalese except us, but then something caught their eye. It was the Nepalese flag and that really you know brought: 'I've never ever seen a church in the UK that has got a Nepalese flag, you know, hung on the wall.' So, I told them that, you know, not just the Nepalese flag, but all these flags they bow down to the cross at the front, so they were like: 'Wow, really?' … And every time I see that flag, I feel like I am a member of this church and part of Christ's family.
(Wise 2022:149)

In his account, Nepalese people who had never attended GBC before noticed the Nepalese flag on display and it was significant for them to see their flag displayed in what they felt was a traditional British church. For Harnoop, seeing his national flag on the wall meant that he felt 'like I am a member of this church and part of Christ's family'. For Harnoop, the displayed flag was a marker that he was an accepted part not just of GBC, but of 'Christ's family'. He was a fully accepted member, not a muted observer.

The intentional actions of embracing food, flags and art that were drawn from the ethnic contexts of ALL the people who were a part of

GBC unmuted everyone. There was no power disparity where any group dominated the spoken or visual discourse and thereby muted others.

# Conclusion

As explored elsewhere in this book, it is all too easy for entire groups of people to be muted, unable to make any significant contribution to their current context. This chapter has given real-life examples of what the theological ideas expressed throughout this book can look like when lived out in a local church congregation, enabling people to be enriched by encountering difference and diversity. In looking at Revelation chapters 5 to 10, Paul Woods noted the affirmation of cultural and linguistic identity with no groups being marginalised in heaven. A taste of this was experienced in the life of GBC. In looking at Revelation 21, the affirmation of human creativity was observed, with people using the gifts that God had given them. This was seen at GBC especially with artwork, food and dance. Finally, the command to be salt and light was viewed by Woods as 'an instruction to unmute and bring change'. This chapter has given examples, not least the complaint to the PCA and the submission to the Stephen Lawrence Inquiry, of how this took place at GBC.

A wide range of actions were taken that enabled people who had arrived from outside of Europe to be heard within the church community, in the surrounding community and beyond it. The unmuting of migrants at GBC helped to create a genuinely intercultural local church congregation where every person was seen and heard.

# 7

# Unmuting together: an Ethiopian in Norway

## LEMMA DESTA

I recently encountered Muted Group Theory (MGT). It is an intriguing and relevant method to assist in the transformation of social relations in Church and society. During the Covid-19 pandemic, the use of digitisation increased significantly. Struggling to sustain businesses, production, relations and engagements, everyone turned to web-based communication applications such as Zoom, Teams, etc. Consequently, *muting* and *unmuting* became frequent words during these digital meetings and conferences. Thus, we became cognisant of the power of having a voice in its practical, as well as in its political, sense. Voice is unique, deeply personal and precious. Having a voice to express oneself audibly is a right of a living human being with power and agency to define one's own destiny. It is also a means at our disposal to take part in the struggle for power, in the distribution of roles, and in securing rights and integrity as individuals and even communities. Having a voice is not limited exclusively to its audible form. People with listening or speaking disabilities also express themselves with other forms such as sign language. But the mundane act of utilising one's voice in safeguarding and sustaining one's own rights and integrity is not accessible for everyone everywhere. In our world of inequality, injustice and exploitation, human interactions are often experiences of being muted and muting others.

This chapter attempts to present an account of my personal experiences of being muted. It is an endeavour to try out MGT from the angle of the lived experiences of being muted in Church and society.

I will revisit my upbringing, the Church relations in my country of origin, ecumenical interactions and international migration. I will start with MGT itself, including its limitations as well as affinities to critical theories in various fields of study. None of the other subjects in this chapter have been consulted for their opinions, so in a sense there is some muting while I, as the writer of this chapter and, thereby, the speaker, am unmuted. Readers are therefore advised to read with the awareness of this limitation. The chapter strives to contribute to the academic work exposing injustices of mutedness by sensitising those in positions of power and privilege and enabling those who are denied a voice.

## Muted Group Theory: a theory or an analytical tool?

MGT emerged within the field of anthropology through the works of British anthropologists, Edwin and Shirley Ardener, who studied women's conversational behaviour in relation to men. MGT assumes that the dominant group determines the culture and content of the communication system in social relations. In such relations and interactions, the muted group exists in subordination to the dominant group. Linda Lee Smith Barkman (2018) attempted to transform MGT from theory to *analytical tool for hearing marginalised voices*. She identifies three basic tenets of MGT in how dominant and subdominant groups communicate. These are: dominance, acceptability and subordination. In other words, the dominant group creates and defines the terms, while those in the subordinate group are muted. The subordinate groups must use the *modus operandi* of the dominant group lest they endanger acceptance. The core idea of MGT relates to similar critical theories born of lived experience of injustice, inequality and discrimination – see Kimberlé Williams Crenshaw's theories of intersectionality (2020) and the theology of marginality by Jung Young Lee (1995), among other theories; theologies of liberation also belong to this category.

# From theory to experience

We live in a world of asymmetric distribution of power and resources that has consequences for the integrity, sustenance and enjoyment of life for many. Some dominate others in hosts of ways, including muting or denying them a voice and opportunities to be 'thinking beings'.[1] The injustice of muting takes place on many levels starting from the micro-level interaction at home, to relational dynamics in the local community, at schools, in the larger society, as well as in international relations. It occurs at workplaces, in the marketplace, at institutions, including our faith communities.

## Muting homes and agrarian society

I grew up within the power hierarchy of a traditional society in rural Southern Ethiopia. The etiquette dictates that the elderly by virtue of age, wisdom and experience occupy a place of prominence. In their presence, everyone must stay silent and attune to their advice, stories and even jokes. Cognisant of their pedagogical, administrative and arbitrator roles, the elderly exercise the power ascribed to them with uttermost seriousness. They never let you down in terms of sharing words of wisdom and guidance. The elderly, mostly men – and in rare, exceptional cases on occasions some elderly women – enjoyed the privilege of speaking and being heard. Although it had its own merit and justifiable cultural and practical benefits, that distribution of power clearly favoured the dominant group perhaps at the expense of others. Wisdom, age and experience, coupled with warnings about a curse or promises of blessings, sanctioned the communicative behaviour. That was the social order in our society.

Even at home, fathers enjoyed prominence over everyone. In that social order, some spoke, most had to listen and obey. To the latter group belonged younger people (as they are not yet regarded as mature) and women, as well as those from economically underprivileged backgrounds. Elders ought to talk, teach and tell stories, and arbitrate conflicts. The

---

1 This assumes 'thinking' is one of the widely accepted premises of human rights in line with the philosophies of René Descartes' famous line of thought, *Cognito, ergo sum*, 'I think, therefore I am.'

younger ones were to listen, learn and submit to the collective wisdom gained through the ages and guarded through those mechanisms and institutions. Even in the parent–children relationship, the culture muted children, thereby reserving the speaking and decision-making to parents, and disproportionately favouring the fathers (Poluha 2004).

# Muting schools

Modern schools were not available for my parents and the preceding generations. It was only after my parents' childhood that modern schools were erected in the local market towns, later expanding further out into distant villages. Education via schooling became the path for newer generations pursuing hope in securing a better future. When schooling became common, it was assumed that the school with its teachers possessed new knowledge to transmit to students who were sent there to acquire the asset of education. To this day, we have a teacher-centred educational system. The teacher teaches, the student learns. Such a *tabula-rasa* learning approach mutes the students or learners. Modern pedagogy, by contrast, and perhaps rightly, is learner focused. The student takes a prominent role in the learning process. I went through a school system that kept students as passive receivers or almost copy machines. Although asking questions for clarification and participation in answering questions posed by instructors were encouraged, the skewed relationship between teachers and learners did not enable students to raise critical questions.

During my schooling, the national *lingua franca* was the medium of instruction. Schooling in one's own mother tongue is a relatively new policy (Negash 1996). In our day, Amharic, the national *lingua franca*, was the medium of instruction. We had to simultaneously learn the content of education and the language of instruction. This was a double burden. In addition to the fact that the mother tongue was suppressed in favour of the national *lingua franca*, therefore, the content of modern education remained foreign in its content and medium, but not in application. The claim that education empowers must be understood with all its related aspects, such as content, method, medium, access, quality and assumptions of that education (Freire 1972). Modern education in a foreign content and language, with ineffective pedagogy, kept many people educated yet muted. Such is the situation for many countries with an imported education system under the hegemonic paradigm of development and dependency along the pattern of the industrialised world. Education did not unmute me.

# Muting government

I started out with my story at home and reviewed my schooling. I now turn to experiences within society. I have already noted that I was born and brought up in a rural agrarian society in Southern Ethiopia (Rahmato 1984; Wolde-Mariam 1986). A large portion of Ethiopia remains an agrarian society, but the pace of urbanisation and modernisation has increased over the last fifty years (Benti et al. 2022). Still, Ethiopia remains one of the least urbanised and industrialised countries in the world. Urbanisation and modernisation started to change our society. It brought modern education, health services, local administrative structures, roads, electricity, telephony and the internet. The modernisation has also changed the power structures in society. With the rise of modern forms of governance and bureaucracy, the old power structures of village, with parents and elders in the centre, began to fade away. New structures and power relations have replaced the old system. This was one of the drastic social changes we witnessed.

According to the new modern systems, age, wisdom and experience are all relevant, but they are not decisive. Education, political affiliation, professional skills and levels of income secure dominating positions in the community. Such hierarchical system power structures enable those in positions of power to dominate others. Although the elderly are still respected, elected or appointed local government officials now occupy the top positions within the power structures. Modern, educated, yet relatively younger persons now lead agencies, and run businesses and institutions, including churches. They are becoming the dominating group. Although the democratic forms of government assume the rights of everyone to be heard and represented, in many places democracy serves those who ascend the political, economic, educational and cultural power structures. They use their power to produce consent directly or indirectly. Elected, enabled, enriched, they define policies and priorities.

The political history of many countries shows that the ruling dominant group, military or civilian, make up a government both local and national. The recent history of our country is marred by violence as dominant groups deny others the opportunity to participate in the political processes and in the distribution of power and resources. Political mutedness is the worst of these denials of rights, and violence is taking place, especially in parts of the world where the political evolution has not transformed into a democracy (Global Findings 2023). In some cases, the situation worsens, moving from muting to persecution and forcing politically active citizens into exile. Repression and muting lead to violent reactions. Ethiopia has suffered several decades of armed confrontation between the state and armed groups on the claims and perceptions of domination and suppression (Redie 2013).

# Muting Church?

In recent years, unethical and exploitative churches and leaders have been exposed. There is a growing interest in scrutinising interpersonal relations in churches and society as well. One would hope that muting would not occur in the Church and in Christian ministry. Indeed, on the one hand, churches provide a breathing space for everyone, especially those it elevates to worth, contrary to the fact that they were counted unworthy both in spiritual and social terms. Christianity attracted the poor and marginalised in Ethiopia (Eshete 2009), as it did all over the world and throughout history (Anderson 2013). Churches have functioned both as places of liberation, emancipation and worth, as well as being places of submission and sanction, thereby sustaining social stratification. The workings of power structures in the life of the Church and in ministry take various forms. For example, in the Ethiopian context, there is a strong hierarchical power relationship between the ministers and the faithful in Ethiopian Orthodox Christianity, the largest faith community. From the outward appearance, one would assume the Ethiopian Protestants have a greater degree of relative egalitarianism with lay leadership, strong participation of women and youth, impacted by the theologies of the priesthood of all believers (Bakke 1987). This does not mean Protestants do not have power structures that keep the faithful subordinate to leaders.

Another area of the dynamics of power relations is between the missions and the national churches. I grew up in the Ethiopian Evangelical Church Mekane Yesus (EECMY). It came about as result of the missionary endeavours of Lutheran and Presbyterian mission organisations from Europe and America (Arén 1978; 1999). Missionaries came from affluent industrial societies with accumulated material, political and technological wealth. They occupied important positions of power and decision-making in the churches they helped to establish. I grew up in a church close to the missionary compound that also included a medical clinic. The clinic played a huge part in sparing many lives and eradicating tuberculosis in the area. It would be unfair to doubt the sacrifices of missions and missionaries in building churches and society in our part of the world. However, missions and the missionaries' mode of operation should not escape scrutiny. Missions must listen to the critiques of cultural imperialism, and allegations of co-opting with exploitative political powers. Without going into the details, as much as I benefited both spiritually and materially from the work of the missions, it also bothered me to observe the affluent missionaries and their enclaves surrounded by abject poverty and those in dire need.

The missionaries in our village lived a very different life compared with the rest of the local population. They had extravagant fancy houses and cars and their kids had books, toys and bicycles. They spoke English, thus connecting success to the powerful English language. English-speaking missionaries were given places of prominence as guests and as representatives of the powerful world. Perhaps knowingly or perhaps operating from a specific world view, missionary–native dynamics muted the local community in favour of the missions and the missionaries.

Our native Ethiopian mission and ecumenical relations with the industrialised world did not bring equality nor people-to-people bonds between the mission-sending and mission-receiving societies. We were, and perhaps sadly still are, on the receiving end, while our counterparts in the Western world are on the sending end. The old missionary paradigm created dependency as it promoted a conception of mission and church growth spreading from the hegemonic Western cultures of the world to the Majority World, often perceived as uncivilised. Such paradigms failed to enable strong churches in the native mission areas.

The state of Christianity in many of the traditional mission-receiving countries in the Global South might not be as glossy as we have often heard. A simple illustration is the number of abandoned mission stations as the Western mission organisations withdrew from those places. The old hegemonic missionary paradigm left local leadership marginalised, in matters of contextual as well as global missional and theological needs. Today, churches in the Global South are struggling to build necessary cultural, technical, administrative, linguistic skills, competencies and resources. The EECMY strives to fill the gap in producing resources for local and national theological needs, as well as taking part in global mission and ecumenism. Despite the claims of the centre of gravity of Christianity shifting southwards in the last century (Walls 1996), the political, cultural, theological domination still marginalises the voices of the Global South.

The missionaries with their financial resources enjoy the privilege to speak, to write, plan and execute projects and maintain expertise, including in the affairs of others. When missions and missionaries dominate the field of experts, native and indigenous voices are muted. The hegemony still influences the priorities and the framing of theology and mission. Further ongoing research is required on how churches in the Global South are being organised and financed and in identifying which issues are their priorities within their contexts and into their cultural spaces.

## Muting in the context of international migration

Mutedness and vulnerability is prevalent in international migration and mobility (Kretsedemas et al. 2013; Lee 1995). International migration and mobility occur for a variety of reasons. Some had to flee as refugees escaping conflict or persecution. Others pursue a professional career in the industrialised high-income countries or even venture to start or expand businesses. Some move into other countries due to family ties. The opportunity to travel to other countries, especially to high-income countries from low-income countries, is filled with hurdles. The picture is different for citizens of high-income countries mainly in the West. We live in a world organised according to income. Birthplace determines prospects. Those born in impoverished countries will most often struggle for survival. Those born in a middle- or high-income country have a great variety of possibilities in their life choices. Getting a scholarship to study abroad was a dream for many of my peers. A little over twenty years ago, I had such an opportunity via the Norwegian scheme for those in the Global South to pursue higher education in Norway. Sadly, the scheme was scrapped and the opportunity is non-existent now. Looking back, it would probably have been impossible to get a Schengen visa as young student under the age of 30 from an African country. For my part then, the visa process was smooth, despite my anxiety in meeting someone from the embassy during the application process. On my arrival in Norway, I was nervous facing the border control for fear of denial of entry, even though I had everything in order.

Contrary to the ideals of freedom of movement, international travel is an arena where lived inequality, prejudice and racism persistently lurk in the name of security, law and order. It is filled with hassle for citizens originating from low-income countries, especially in the wake of 9/11. Arriving, adjusting and residing in a foreign land was also an overwhelming experience. The first years come with a mix of distress and displeasing encounters, not only due to the emotional experiences of uprootedness and homesickness, but also because of the difficulties in adjusting. As a newcomer, I had to start from scratch to acquire the Norwegian language and to gain cultural proficiency. The time between arrival and acquiring the language skills was daunting. Although I had much in my heart to share and engage in social conversations, I remained muted, lacking the language skills, except the use of English, which was my third language. International travel involving crossing diverse linguistic and cultural boundaries impedes social interactions. It unintentionally mutes the outsiders (the foreigners, the immigrants, the guests or the visitors).

Those who have travelled to distant places with less linguistic and cultural affinity share the emotional toil of being muted in migration. Only as we get acquainted with the people and their language and culture does the burden lighten. In many places, access to acquiring linguistic and thus cultural skills costs money. New language learners, in fear of making mistakes, might tend to avoid practising, and thus lack the confidence to engage with native speakers. Language is knowledge and knowledge is power. Power dynamics are displayed through the use of language (Fairclough 1992). In the migrant communities, many highly qualified persons take jobs way below their qualifications due to their lack of language proficiency. Language proficiency requirements are also used to discriminate in the labour market. Language and culture proficiency is not based upon the mastery of grammatic and conversational skills, it also involves building an experience in understanding the codes, the nuances and the formal–informal ways of using language. This is part of the instrumentalisation of language in power politics.

Even after mastering the technical aspect of language proficiency, people might still lack shared cultural experiences and racial markers, meaning that they would remain outsiders in conversations. In my case, it took a couple of years before I half-heartedly attended Norwegian language classes. Once the formal courses were over, I struggled for years to feel confident in using the language in public. Still, even now in social interactions involving shared cultural experience from the past, such as sporting events and memorable national incidents, I am muted as I was not part of those historical cultural events. Linguistic and cultural nuances subtly underlie the used language and create a sense of belonging and valuable shared life experiences. I find myself unable to relate and contribute and thus feel muted and I learn to live with it. One would assume the universality of the Church would be less restricted in terms of belonging and contributing.

## Muted missionaries?

A difficult form of muting took place in my encounter with Norwegian Church life. I worked with Lutheran missions from the Nordic region back home in Ethiopia. During my theological studies, I had Norwegian and Nordic theologians as instructors. The seminary compound was also a meeting point for missionaries and visiting travellers from the Nordic region. Therefore, I had relations with the Nordic region and its Lutheranism through those encounters before my arrival in Norway. With our common liturgical and denominational tradition, I had hoped to find easy passage into parish life for my own needs and contributions in ministry. As mentioned earlier, in the first years, the prospects of participation in liturgy were confined to a minimum due to the constraints in language proficiency. Worship via translation did not adequately respond to my dire needs for spiritual care as a newly arrived immigrant with a different culture and upbringing. In my naivety, I had hoped for a warm reception and the opportunities to contribute in Church ministry, given that I was coming here with ministry experience from Ethiopia. I had such expectations because that was the tradition back home in Ethiopia. Upon the arrival of a guest missionary or visitor to any of our congregations, there would be an impromptu invitation to bring greetings, to take part in welcome feasts afterwards, thereby continuing the practices of the apostolic community in the New Testament (Acts 13:15f).

It was during my studies at university where I found spiritual pasture for my soul through the Christian Union students' fellowship dedicated for international students (Christian Union 2023). For international students, English was the common language for fellowship, as we shared our lives and the Word of God. In addition, I arrived in Oslo at a time when a small group of Ethiopian and Eritrean Lutherans had initiated a joint Bible study. The group later joined a few similar groups to start an English-speaking service, and this later became an international congregation. However, many were not used to using English as the language of worship and fellowship, and they met with others from the same country or language group for prayer, Scripture reading and fellowship. Many of those small beginnings resulted in new churches becoming established, led by migrants and comprising migrants. These emerging trends are transforming the Church landscape in most countries in Europe and America (Jackson and Passarelli 2021).

There is a growing effort to raise awareness about the hindrances that mute fellow believers from all over the world experience as they arrive in other countries as migrants and refugees. The process of immigration and settlement involves waiting, acquiring language and culture skills, and getting acquainted with the existing Church and mission structures. Yet getting those practical problems solved does not automatically unmute migrants. Raised awareness about the need for migrant inclusion and diversity helps to open up the churches for general attendance and participation. But access to ranks of participation remains restricted and complicated in any ministry, but specifically in ordained ministry and employment and occupying positions in the churches. Lack of language and culture proficiency is the most common excuse proffered. Basic language skills ought to provide a starting point. However, no amount of language proficiency is considered enough when the visual appearance is that of a subordinate. Those who have undergone the educational and vetting processes towards ordained ministry share gruelling experiences of the bullying, intimidation, prejudice and racism they have experienced while qualifying for ordination. Norwegian pulpits are still sparsely open for migrant pastors or preachers. Many migrants with a calling for ministry are still muted.

The muting of migrants happens not only in Church ministry in Norway, but also in mission organisations that work in the countries of origin of the migrants. With my background from the country that is still a mission field for Norwegian missions, I occasionally get invited to mission gatherings to talk about the mission needs of Ethiopia, underscoring the life-saving importance of Norwegian missionary assistance. My participation in these events comes with a dilemma. The decision is made, the message is clear, my face and presence may fascinate mission friends. I am welcome to add my confirmation to the already reported image of achievements of the missions. My agency, my quest, my concerns, my questions and my wishes do not matter. I am ascribed the role to help the mission gather more funds; thus, I am muted. Even if I may turn down such invitations, it is not going to change the practice. When these agencies draft strategic plans for their work within the foreign mission fields, the voices and the expertise of migrants are not considered. Problem analysis, policy and programme responses, priorities and even theological materials prepared for use in the churches in the mission field overlook any possible contribution from the subordinate migrant status.

## Muted in global mission and ecumenical relations

Muting is an issue to grapple with in world mission and ecumenical relations. In 2010, the centenary of Edinburgh World Mission Conference was commemorated in many places, including Norway. I took part in a conference organised by the Norwegian mission and ecumenical organisations. A host of commemorative publications were produced (see the Oxford Centre for Mission Studies website[2]). In this regard, having examined the process and conduct of the 1910 conference critically, I discovered that interracial relations was a suppressed topic. The Edinburgh 1910 World Mission Conference assembly did not consider the Black African Church important, even relevant for world mission, because the prevalent idea was that Africans were not yet mature and they were to catch you up on the human development ladder. The centenary commemorative process also failed to acknowledge the racism, the Darwinism and colonialism that defined the World Mission Conference of 1910. The fact that Africa was underestimated in 1910 was not unexpected, but the failure to acknowledge the problem even 100 years later during the centenary was distressing and a realisation that macro-level muting was taking place in global mission and ecumenism. I lamented this glaring shortcoming of the 2010 centenary commemoration, writing,

> from a critical African point of view the Edinburgh conference could easily be suspected to be the missionary counterpart to the 1884 Berlin conference of the scramble for Africa. But the fact that there were no Black Africans represented and there was no discussion about it remains a big shortcoming of the Edinburgh 1910 missionary conference. Not only what happened then is discomforting, but also the fact that this was not exhaustively addressed in the course of Edinburgh 2010 anniversary. This could be too sensitive an issue to address even today.
> (Fagerli et al. 2012:136)

Over the years, I have had access to European and global ecumenical structures based in Europe. I examined at length the World Council of Churches (2012) new mission document, *Together Towards Life: Mission and Evangelism in Changing Landscapes*, as approved at its assembly. I had the privilege of meeting one of its editors during a mission seminar

---

2   https://www.ocms.ac.uk (accessed 7 August 2024).

in Oslo. I raised critical questions challenging the perspectives in the mission document. Unfortunately, the questions were blatantly dismissed. In a hope to contribute to the mission conference that was scheduled to take place in Arusha in 2018, I started to engage with the African delegates of the World Council of Churches (WCC). I raised concerns that such a world mission conference taking place in the African context must take up African priorities. I passionately appealed to the planners to address issues such as: mission and colonialism, Africa's place in World Christianity, the state of Christianity in Africa, world mission and African migrants, the quest of Africa and people of African descent. These concerns were muted at the 2018 Arush World Mission Conference.

Having published via the WCC during the days of the refugee crisis in 2015/2016 in the wake of the Syrian war, I wrote another article questioning the WCC conceptions of justice and peace in its policy document (Desta 2014). Although it was not published, I appealed to the central committee that was meeting in Norway, expressing my hopes that the gathering would dare to raise big issues such as peace between Russia and the West, the exploitation of poor countries by the rich, issues pertaining to world peace, refugees, ethics in the marketplace and religious freedom. In the years preceding the WCC general assembly in 2021, I tried to convince the WCC and its assembly to address slavery, colonialism and its repercussions. The quest was silenced due to reasons including reluctance by the African leaders. It was painful to be muted by both African and global ecumenism.

## Are Evangelicals any better?

Living and working in Norway has given me great opportunities to access European and global ecumenical networks. Through the advocacy work for migrant inclusion and multiculturalism in Europe, I detected the disconnect between the ecumenical movements represented by the likes of the World Council of Churches, the Conference of European Churches, and the Evangelical movements represented by the Evangelical Alliance and the Lausanne Movement. Having been interested in the Evangelical movements during my term as moderator for Churches Commission for Migrants in Europe (2017–20), I reached out to those who were planning the Lausanne Europe gathering in 2021. Together with Usha Reifsnider, we conducted a networking seminar on decolonising mission (Desta and Reifsnider 2021).

Decolonisation is a sensitive and awkward subject. It touches on aspects of history, culture, identity, justice and power primarily for the victims, but for also those in positions of power and privilege. Both in the larger society and in the churches, there is still much resistance to openly addressing these issues with courage and caution. The Lausanne Europe digital conference did not attract a large attendance, but it generated conversation about the subject. The leadership of Lausanne Europe picked up the call of the seminar in its later planning. In 2023, European Evangelicals gathered in Budapest, Hungary, for a regional conversation to prepare for the Lausanne 4 congress. The event brought together a representative body of Evangelical leaders including migrants, women and youth (Memory and Reifsnider 2023).[3] The intercultural, interracial and interethnic listening, and trust-building efforts were to be intentionally tried out in a few places, with Norway as an example. The expectations were high for Evangelical gatherings, networks, associations and movements. The result is an expectation that new directions of inclusivity and justice will be charted regarding intergenerational, intercultural, interracial and interethnic interaction, stewardship and participation in world mission and evangelism.

# Conclusion

Muting starts early in life as world views take shape. We need to be mindful of the voices of children and minors and those underprivileged and under-represented. From the earliest levels of education, an environment that encourages and stimulates multiple ways of learning should be prioritised. The overall atmosphere should stimulate the ability to think, to speak, to unmute oneself and encourage others to speak out. Unjust restrictions hampering critical thinking and true learning should be carefully addressed.

---

3  https://lausanne.org/gathering/lausanne-4-regional-gathering-europe (accessed 7 August 2024).

Since few voices speak louder, and dominate media and academia, it is easy to assume the ideals of human rights and dignity as universally respected. Billions of people are still denied basic and birthrights of freedom of expression, voice and association. International migration enables the rich and powerful to exercise more power while it mutes and restricts access to many others. Discrimination, prejudices and racism in human mobility architecture are jeopardising the voices, integrity and dignity of migrants and refugees. There is a dire need to deliver on political visions of an inclusive and sustainable development that does no harm to anyone, nor leaves others behind.

Mission and ecumenism cannot continue sustainably by banking on the systems of mutedness in society, let alone succumb to muting themselves. Our human history is filled with the injustice of muting and denial of voice for many people. From participation in political, economic and civil life to Christian ministry, the denial of opportunities, the injustices and domination have robbed the dignity and potential of many people. In so doing, the Church has become poor in expression, in passion and impact. No single cultural expression or dominant centre can represent the wealth, width and intentions 'of him who fills everything in every way' (Eph. 1:23).

In the past, the narrow form of Christianity that dominated architecture, music, theology, models of Church organisation and government, was translated and spread all over the world. The goals of translating and spreading Christianity gave Western education the dominant voice all over the world. Yet, in many places, radical Church growth took place when the gospel was translated, contextualised and indigenised. Muting others, denying them a voice, and preventing them from participating, influencing and partaking in their own collective development is unjust and untenable.

Everyone has agency that should be acknowledged, with the commitment to upholding the values of equality, liberty and freedom applicable to all. Simultaneously, maintaining the uniqueness, integrity and dignity of each human person is the task remaining, to ensure that the whole of humanity has the ability to strive. Such a radical vision sounds alarming and may initially trigger fear in those who are used to privilege and hegemony. Enabling and unmuting everyone does not mean dethroning those in positions of power overnight, nor sanctioning disorder and noise. Our human interactions need order without polarisation.

Respect for rights and dignity cannot be achieved without orderly, mutual and multifaceted engagement. But if the cry for justice and recognition remains unattended, everyone turns to their own means and to the methods aided by technologies. In our age of digital technologies, with democratisation and decentralisation, the monopoly of access to knowledge, information and network limits and makes redundant the benefits derived from personal, physical interaction and still favours the 'haves' over the 'have nots'. With web-based, simplified access to social media, including self-broadcasting, mutedness is counteracted with noise. Those who can speak up and speak out hold court. Conversation, orderly exchange, mutual reasoning, remorse, repentance, renewal and reconciliation are replaced with radicalised and polarising noise.

The cry for justice voiced by those who have been muted should not offend us; rather, it should call us to humility, admission of wrongdoing, the courage to change. It is only when we attend to each other, bear with one another, acknowledge each other, that we all benefit, upholding the dignity of all. God's people cannot deny the fact that colour, race, ethnicity, gender are determinant factors with the potential to magnify the beauty, or become misused for discrimination and favouritism. God's people are not without ethnicity and culture, but beyond the limitations, bondage and barriers of cultural and other identity-markers, they are called to embrace the integrity of each and the diversity of the whole. The call of Bishop V. S. Azariah of India at the 1910 World Mission Conference in Edinburgh echoes much that is relevant today.

The exceeding riches of the glory of Christ can be fully realised neither by the Englishman, the American, and the Continental alone, nor by the Japanese, the Chinese, and the Indians by themselves, but by all working together, worshipping together, and learning together the Perfect Image of our Lord and Christ. It is only 'with all Saints' that we can 'comprehend the love of Christ which passes knowledge, that we might be filled with all the fullness of God.' This will be possible only from spiritual friendships between the two races. We ought to be willing to learn from one another and to help

113

one another. Through all the ages to come the Indian Church will rise up in gratitude to attest the heroism and self-denying labors of the missionary body. You have given your goods to feed the poor. You have given your bodies to be burned. We also ask for love. Give us FRIENDS!

(World Missionary Conference 1910)

# 8

# Unmuting racial ambiguity: a theological perspective

## DR GIGI KHANYEZI

I leisurely wove my way in and out of grocery aisles and browsed the shelves as I went. It was the grocery store in East Oakland just around the corner from where we lived, and I knew it like the back of my hand. My heart swelled with joy being out and about in my neighbourhood. This community was my place of belonging; quite literally the place that birthed the woman I've become. Although predominantly Black and Brown, we sat just next to the intersection of 'predominantly white-bodied' with 'predominantly melanated'. Just like my physical appearance, my neighbourhood was the in-between.

Just as I felt my heart fill my chest with the joy of being out in the neighbourhood, a feeling I cherished, a strong hand squeezed my shoulder. To understand the shockwaves that surged through my system, you'd have to know the particular unspoken code in my community. You don't put hands on someone uninvited unless you are either ready to throw fists or you have the kind of relationship history where such touch is welcomed. The heart swelling with joy quickly leapt into my throat in a fraction of a second. I whirled around to see a middle-aged white-bodied man looking down at me, 'I've been watching you and I just *have* to ask… What *are* you?'

The ridiculousness of such a question was apparent even to me, an 8-year-old Brown girl living in a predominantly Black neighbourhood situated on the edge of the in-between. And yet it was a question I was all too familiar with. Apparently, to this man of European descent, his right to know preceded my bodily autonomy *and* the neighbourhood

115

code, which even my childhood mind knew he was oblivious to. The entitlement of need-to-place-you-in-the-hierarchy took precedence over any sense of dignity that a human descending from the Global Majority deserved.

I was asked this exact question so frequently that I already had a formulated response, *at 8 years old*. That response quickly pushed past the heart that had lodged in my throat to reach his entitled ears, 'I'm a human, what are *you*?' With that, I bounded away not waiting for a response and *certainly* not giving time for another iron-fisted grasp of my shoulder. It is amazing how quickly the warm sense of security that comes with belonging can be snatched away in an overt or covert act of 'othering'. Even that 8-year-old child could feel the dehumanising nature of a question that needed to justify her existence. So many of us Black and Brown children learn how to take such dehumanisation in stride with a little outward sass, while quietly masking the grief that weighs like stones in the soul.

We exist in a social context so embedded with racial hierarchy that our identity has become defined by it in ways we are largely unaware of. The construct of race has always been about power and wealth, and in whose hands they both belong. The enforcing of that system has always been about violence, so our bodies and psyches have interpreted racial dynamics as a literal fight for our lives. Hence, if our unconscious minds understand that racial identity is tied to life-and-death danger, we must, therefore, be very clear about where every human lands on the hierarchy. Essentially, our lives depend on it.

This life-and-death danger would have been acute to many of our ancestors: enslaved folk of African descent understood clearly that behaving as anything other than enslaved was a life-and-death decision. Our indigenous siblings understood that any form of behaviour indicating their own human dignity could mean the loss of life. Furthermore, we know that many of our European-descended ancestors who came to colonise North America had been in the lowest echelons of peasant society in Europe, having been thrown off lands and relegated to poverty and indentured servitude (Dunbar-Ortiz 2014:36). Hence, much of the driving force that compelled the settler colonialism of North America was the promise of land and attaining status above peasantry, because many came from a social location of powerlessness, poverty and sometimes loss of life. Gaining status was a life-or-death endeavour, which meant that the threat of losing that status was always a life-and-death danger as well.

Unless conscious healing work has been done, our bodies hold that trauma through many generations. We may not know why we vehemently cling to racial categorisations, both our own and others', but our bodies have the cellular memory telling us that racial identity is a life-and-death matter. It is from this decontextualised trauma that questions such as, 'I just have to ask, what *are* you?' emerge. If our subconscious believes our lives and safety depend on clearly defined places in the racial hierarchy, those categories *must* be crystal clear. Ambiguity, then, is not merely an annoyance, *it is a threat*.

This chapter is *not* about offering a solution to the overarching problem of racial hierarchy and racial categorisation. Rather, it is describing one particular aspect of harm that has resulted; a voice that is rarely heard. This chapter explores the silencing of those of us who exist in the in-between. We do not fit neatly in any racial category; we exist in the borderlands. In a society that functions quite literally in the binary of Black and White, our very bodies place us in the grey that isn't allowed to exist. We will explore the role of empire in the construct of race through the lenses of a Palestinian theologian, Dr Mitri Raheb; an African-American woman journalist, Isabel Wilkerson; and the sacred text of Genesis 1. We will go on to explore both the grief and the gift of lives lived in racially ambiguous bodies, the ways that empire silences us, and, finally, Jesus of Nazareth as the unmuter of silenced voices.

## Life in a racially ambiguous body

As I've grown into an adult, my response has shifted. First, I correct the question, before making a statement of self-identity, 'If you're asking what my ethnicity is or what people I come from, I am half-Brazilian and half-Amish.' Then I watch their eyes search me over trying to put the pieces together of my physical appearance. They *must* place me in a recognisable category; remember, their safety depends on it.

I spent the first thirty years of my life learning to navigate a racially polarised world in a Brown, marginalised, othered body seeing through the lenses that East Oakland imparted to me. Learning how to manoeuvre on the front lines of racial justice and healing work in a Brown, marginalised, othered body. Even despite more than fifteen years following the history of South Africa's transition from apartheid into democracy, nothing could have prepared me for what I encountered when I relocated there. During the 'forced removals' of South Africa (primarily in the 1950s and 1960s, but continuing to 1983), Black South Africans were forcibly removed from the cities and suburbs into distant residential areas created by the Apartheid Government on the worst land well outside the cities. Although the removals in the early years included Indians and what is known as 'Coloureds', a staggering 3.5 million Black South Africans were forcibly relocated in one of the largest mass removals of people in modern history. Those residential areas outside the cities where Black South Africans were forcibly relocated are called townships. They are, by definition, 100% Black and are a direct result of the brutality of the Apartheid regime.

When I relocated to South Africa, I planted roots to live and serve in Soweto, the single largest township in the nation, estimated at 5 million beautifully melanated African folk. Being the only one who looked like me did not feel unusual to me, as that is often the demographic context in which I find myself. Yet, it meant something very different for my new community having me in it. During Apartheid, it was against the law for anyone not racialised as Black to step foot inside Soweto, even just to visit for an afternoon. That is part of how the Apartheid regime controlled the narrative. The rest of the country could not see that townships of African folk were not savage communists if they never got to go there themselves.

What I did not expect was how I would be racialised in this context. I found that in the cities and suburbs, I was viewed as 'coloured'. That was no surprise. But in the township context, the very place I had relocated to, to plant roots indefinitely, I was viewed as 100% *White*. The first phrase I learned in Zulu was, '*Eish, ubani lomlungu?!*' because I heard it everywhere I went. I learned it meant, 'Geez, who is this White person?!' In the first couple of years, I would respond with, '*Angingumlungu ...*' meaning, 'I'm not a White person,' followed by an explanation of my ethnic makeup; how I have never been viewed as White in my home country; how I've never had domestic workers, which they assumed I'd

118

grown up with. That did not bode well for me, nor for the trust I was trying to build within my community.

It wasn't until I accepted my perceived 'Whiteness', understanding that everything I said and did was seen as coming from a white-bodied person. It profoundly shifted my orientation to the world, to people, to activism, to ministry … to everything. Not one part of my life was untouched by this change in racial status. It was a crucible for this Brown girl raised in East Oakland that is impossible to adequately express with words.

Understanding race and muted voices begins with understanding empire. In the context of the United States, we hear 'empire' and we think of age-old societies such as the Constantinian Empire or the Ottoman Empire or maybe the British Empire. We do not typically imagine the United States as an empire, and yet it very much is. From 'leftist' author Howard Zinn, who wrote of the 'global American empire', to politician Pat Buchanan on the far right, warning that the United States is 'traveling the same path that was trod by the British Empire', some are beginning to wake up to this reality (Immerwahr 2019:13). Empire has always been about power, control and domination.

While our society may frame things as racial 'conflict', the reality is not conflict, but colonisation. We are a nation built on dominating, subjugating and dehumanising certain groups to keep a small population in power, wealth and control. We began as an occupation of indigenous land. We now have literal 'colonies' in our own country and around the world lurking behind the smokescreen of democracy. Welcome to a hidden empire.

## The lens of Palestinians: Dr Mitri Raheb

Palestinians are a people well acquainted with occupation; they have been living under it for 2,500 continuous years (Raheb 2014:4). Dr Mitri Raheb, a Palestinian theologian and pastor of the historic Christmas Church in Bethlehem, offers a pivotal framework in understanding the intersection of empire and faith in his book, *Faith in the Face of Empire: The Bible through Palestinian Eyes*. Raheb states that empire provides the 'hardware' that holds its power in place through military arms. Yet, according to Raheb, empires cannot survive by their military, political and economic power alone. Rather, the justification for violating basic human rights must be endorsed by something much bigger. It must be inseparable from divine purpose 'set within an ideological and theological framework' (Raheb 2014:64). It is this justification that Raheb calls the 'software' of empire: the promoting of dangerous biblical interpretations and doctrines that condone and even inspire such domination and brutality.

Over the nearly three-thousand-year history of occupation of Palestine, these settler-colonial theologies are largely responsible for the devastation of Palestinians' daily existence. Just as the construct of race lives in our bodies as a matter of life-and-death threat, so also the commitment to re-interpreting the ways in which we read Scripture is a matter of literal life and death for Palestinians and other colonised peoples.

The narrative claiming that God has given a people the right to violently possess lands and peoples is not unique to the Palestinian occupation. We see similar dynamics in other contexts around the world and throughout history: South African Apartheid was authored and justified by theologies in the Dutch Reformed Church. Colonising immigrants sought to perpetrate genocide against Native American peoples in North America, as well as Australians against the native Aboriginals, all fuelled by similar theological narratives. The trouble is, in the United States' context we do not place ourselves in the same category. Thus is the paradox of a hidden empire; perhaps even more sinister and brutal.

## The lens of Isabel Wilkerson: caste

The hiddenness of our empire is what makes Isabel Wilkerson's *Caste: The Origins of Our Discontents* (2020), one of the most seminal texts of our times. She holds the history of the United States alongside two other civilisations: India, with their caste system, and Hitler's Germany. The remarkable similarities between our history and that of two societies that we readily condemn, is jarring to say the least. It is meant to shake us awake!

Wilkerson notes that in 1944, the Swedish social economist Gunnar Myrdal and a talented team of researchers from across the country created a 2,800-page work entitled, *An American Dilemma*. To this day, it is still considered perhaps the most comprehensive study of race in

America. This investigation into race led him to conclude that the most accurate term to describe the mechanisms of American society was not *race*, but *caste* (Wilkerson 2020:24).

After years of thorough study, Wilkerson goes on to say, 'In the American caste system, the signal of rank is what we call race, the division of humans on the basis of appearance. In America, race is the primary tool and the visible decoy, the front man, for caste' (Wilkerson 2020:18).

She clarifies that race is phenotype – what we can see of physical features that have been given arbitrary meaning for who a person is. Caste, on the other hand, is the infrastructure that holds each group in its place on the hierarchy (Wilkerson 2020:18). 'Caste is fixed and rigid. Race is fluid and superficial, subject to periodic redefinition to meet the needs of the dominant caste in what is now the United States' (2020:19). In other words, what was defined as 'White' 100 years ago, is not the same as what is defined as 'White' today. Today, 'White' includes Italians, Polish and Irish, for example, all of whom were categorised as non-White previously in this same country. When greater numbers were needed to bolster 'whiteness', the boundaries of European distinctiveness became more fluid.

Regardless of who is included in any particular racial category at a given time in history, the reality of a dominant caste has remained constant, being granted the rights and privileges that secure life at the top. At the other end of the spectrum, subservient castes likewise have been fixed from the beginning. Who is included in which one may shift depending on what is needed to hold the hierarchy in place at any given time (Wilkerson 2020:19).

Both Dr Raheb and Wilkerson see theological belief systems as a central component to the apparatus that makes up empire. What Dr Raheb describes as the 'software' of empire, Wilkerson describes as 'Pillar #1' in the eight pillars that are present in every caste system. In order to hold empire in place, interpretations of God and the sacred text connected to God must inspire and condone the subjugation and domination of other peoples. This is why our task to bring about a society that more reflects the God who created us necessitates a commitment to *decolonising our theological beliefs*. This chapter is an invitation for you to dive in right here, right now. Let's decolonise our reading of Genesis 1.

# The lens of the sacred text: Genesis 1

The Hebrew people had been conquered and exiled into Babylon, a foreign land populated by people who subjugated them harshly. Not only did they experience forced removal (remember South Africa?) into a land not their own, a culture and language not their own, but they also found themselves held captive by a people whose theological world view said humanity existed to worship gods who were cruel, vengeful and merciless (Harper 2016:26). The fall of Babylon marked the liberation of the Hebrews and the long-awaited return to their homeland after generations in captivity.

Most scholars agree that Genesis 1 was written by Hebrew priests emerging from exile in Babylon to their recently oppressed people whose trauma from oppression was still raw. As the priests were writing this text, the people were rebuilding the Temple. Indeed, rebuilding their lives (Harper 2016:29).

When we read Genesis through eyes that centre the voices on the margins – the colonised – the book becomes more than a narrative demanding scholarly analysis; it becomes *a text of hope*. Hope in a God whose very nature is the liberation of all who are oppressed, regardless of how hopeless our reality remains (De La Torre 2011:10). It is a direct affront to the theological and ontological world view in which they had been immersed and held captive.

As we read Genesis 1 centring the marginalised voices, we will take note of two important words in the Hebrew text of verse 26, *tselem* ('image') and *radah* ('dominion'), and ground the study in a particular Hebrew phrase, *tov me'od*, found in verse 31: in the climax of creation, the Creator said on the sixth day, 'Let us make humankind in our image … So God created humankind in his image, in the image of God he created them' (Walton 2019:6).

This text uses the Hebrew word, *tselem*, translated as 'image' three times in two sentences. It is emphatic! What the contemporary reader likely does not recognise is that the use of this word in a creation account would have been radical in the ancient Near East. An 'image' was not about physical likeness, but rather a representation of identity relating to the office/role and the value connected to the image (Walton 2019:8). In this context, to declare all of humanity – and not solely royalty – made in the image of its Creator would have been regarded as blasphemy. In the words of Lisa Sharon Harper, the writers of Genesis 1 'democratize dignity by redistributing it to all humanity' (Harper 2016:25) for a people in the aftermath of living as dehumanised captives for seventy years.

In the very same sentence in which God named humanity as made in God's image, God quickly followed it with the command for that humanity to 'exercise dominion' over creation. The Hebrew word translated as 'dominion' is *radah*. The writers could have used any one of eight other Hebrew words to communicate a rulership of creation, like that of a king ruling his empire. Yet the writers chose *radah*, a word that is clearly *not* a call to exercise imperial power (Harper 2016:27–8). *Radah* is not only not imperial power and control, but rather, as Lisa Sharon Harper asserts, is best described as a stewardship style of dominion (Harper 2016:28). It is the type of leading in which the led things *flourish*. Furthermore, the command to *radah* is not for a small privileged few; it is for *every single human.*

This declaration by recently liberated priests undermines the very foundation of the belief system we call race. The myth of race was designed to give one group of people the power to take away the human right to both the dignity of *tselem* and the agency of *radah*. God's declaration in Genesis 1 must be our North Star! It is our way back home. That is why it is a text of *hope*, even as we suffer under occupation and colonisation.

Six times – one on each day of creation – the same phrase occurs, 'God saw that it was good.' On the day that God completes creating, God uses a unique phrase for the first time, saying, 'Indeed, it was *very good.*' The Hebrew phrase translated 'very good' is *tov me'od*, a very indicator of what God intended when God designed all of creation. Contemporary readers today hear 'very good' and typically understand it to be a declaration of the goodness of the things created. The ancient Near East listeners, however, would have known that *tov* is not about the things themselves, rather it is about the ties *between* the things. In other words, the very-goodness of creation was not about the goodness of the created things, it was about *the relationships between the created things*. The writers then add *me'od* as an emphatic adjective.

The relationships between created things were not just good, but were abundantly, overflowingly good (Maschler 2009:171–5)!

*Tov me'od* speaks emphatically of *the interconnectedness and interrelatedness of all creation* being in a state of harmony. The construct of race has sought to destroy that harmony; it has fragmented the connectedness and replaced relational congruence with brutality, subjugation and flagrant, chronic abuses of power. The construct of race has categorically undermined and sought to dismantle three key principles of God's intent for creation: the image-bearing nature of all humanity (*tselem*), the call for all humans to exercise dominion and agency (*radah*), and the interconnectedness of all of creation that cultivates harmony. Furthermore, this decolonising of our reading of Genesis 1 is an invitation to co-create a society that embodies those three principles.

## The grief and the gift
## of the racially ambiguous

Science has now demonstrated the need for 'belonging' to be a fundamental human need. Feeling excluded activates many of the same neural networks in the brain that physical pain does. According to Geoffrey Cohen (2022:ix), 'Psychologists call it "social pain," saying people are as motivated to alleviate it as they are to slake thirst and find shelter' (Cohen 2022).

When it comes any fluidity to racial identity, those of us who are viewed as racially ambiguous sometimes have privilege above that of our Christian brothers and sisters – our 'siblings' in the faith – who are in a fixed location in the bottom caste. This reality means we have a responsibility to stand in solidarity with those siblings and fight for the abolition of the system that allows us privilege. In addition to the ways in which we could potentially benefit from our ambiguity, when it comes to the fundamental human need for belonging, those of us who live in bodies viewed as the in-between often suffer immense, ongoing grief. We see folk in their own ethnic enclaves in tight-knit community with a clear display of belonging and inclusion among them. We are often looking in from the outside. It is very lonely on the outside. We are often regarded as too much of one thing to be one of 'us' over here, and not enough of another thing to be one of 'us' over there.

The grief of the racially ambiguous is the rejection from belonging. It is a soul wound that words cannot adequately articulate.

When a person loses something or someone in their life that is valuable to them, but their loss is not valued or recognised by others, it is called *disenfranchised grief.* Those of us who live in bodies that are racially ambiguous often exist in a state of chronic disenfranchised grief. Not only are we scorned by the dominant caste (white-bodied Christian brothers and sisters), we are often rejected by communities of colour as well. Our bodies and experiences challenge the reality that defines entire peoples. Those whose places are fixed in the hierarchy resent and attack us, whose places are not clearly identifiable at a glance. It is a vehement and violent resentment because, remember, our unconscious programming registers racial uncertainty as a threat to our safety.

Add to that the long history of select folk claiming to be about the work of justice until sacrifice or suffering becomes a necessity. Then some folk have chosen their extra rung of available privilege even if it means stepping on someone else's neck. This history adds yet another layer to the violent resentment and alienating of those of us who appear racially ambiguous. Again, the grief of the racially ambiguous is the rejection from belonging. The construct of race is a declaration of war on one another and a declaration of war against our Creator. This is a different kind of war, though; one that is fought on the battleground of the human body. I suggest in addition to the *grief* of the racially ambiguous, there is also the *gift* of the racially ambiguous. The gift, however, admittedly does not feel like a gift to most of us who are actually living in the borderlands of ambiguity. And it is a gift that very often does not directly benefit us. I believe it is a gift in the struggle to dismantle the hierarchy.

The gift is this: our very bodies expose the lie that is race. The bodies of the racially ambiguous expose race for the myth and illusion that it is. I was Brown enough to be harassed by the Ku Klux Klan (KKK) for four years in a suburb outside of Oakland, but 'White' enough to be targeted and attacked as a white-bodied person in Soweto. I could be Brown and marginalised in one context and White and privileged ten miles away while living in South Africa; such a reality exposes the absurdity of this manufactured system of beliefs we call race. The fact that there are bodies which do not fit into the boxes designated as a fixed racial identity, casts doubt on the validity of the entire system. Our very existence challenges the foundation of an erroneous belief system that has formed our society and informed our identity. If we, the resistance, could recognise this for the gift that it is and leverage it in the struggle to dismantle race, we may find resistance not only more unified, but also more effective.

# Jesus as the unmuter of silenced voices

Jesus' life was a demonstration of navigating at least two empires: the empire of the coloniser, Rome, and the empire of the religious establishment of which he, himself, was a part. Both empires demonised certain groups of people, and both subjugated certain groups of people. He stood for none of it, and he resisted all of it.

In Jesus' first public declaration of who he was, the long-awaited Messiah, it wasn't enough to declare himself the fulfilment of the Scriptures (Luke 4:16–22). He had to do so by quoting a passage, Isaiah 61, which declared the Good News to be for the poor, for the captives, for the uniquely abled (aka 'disabled'), and for the oppressed. He did so with a passage that culminated in a declaration of the practice of Jubilee, a tradition that prevented intergenerational (unjust) wealth and liberated people from intergenerational poverty.

As long as his people believed the declaration was to their own benefit, they celebrated him on that day. The moment he continued with two stories in which he made heroes of Gentiles, his very own people sought to kill him. Jesus of Nazareth stood in such solidarity that he, himself, became rejected just as vehemently as those he had given voice to … those whom empire villainised. Jesus, our Messiah, had been muted. But he didn't stay that way.

Jesus modelled the middle caste. He lived the suffering of his own colonised people *and* he fought for the liberation of those relegated to a place below him on the social hierarchy. *Our Brown Saviour was the unmuter of silenced voices.*

A Palestinian himself, Jesus of Nazareth sought to purposefully eradicate both the 'hardware' and the 'software' that held empire in place. He sought to dismantle the castes that held groups of people in a fixed and subjugated location in hierarchy. The entirety of Jesus' life and ministry displayed a theme of giving voice to those whose voices were muted and empowering those whose value was defamed. In his own melanated body, our God incarnate modelled efforts to repair the *tselem* image-bearing dignity of all, the *radah* capacity to lead and influence, and the *tov me'od* interconnectedness that brings relational harmony and justice. Jesus constantly made heroes of those that empire villainised as a way to challenge and reorder the social system.

Jesus' life is an invitation and a call to follow his lead. May we recognise the little 8-year-old bounding through the grocery aisles inside all of us longing to be seen and embraced for who we are. May we see that child in ourselves and may we see that child in those around us. Refusing to mute the voices of others and refusing to be muted ourselves comes with holding the daily intention to stay rooted in our image-bearing worth and our call to dominion. When we stay rooted, we are no longer a servant to the desperate pursuit of safety that makes us reject and mute others. When we stay rooted, naming racial identity is no longer a life-and-death endeavour. We become freer to embrace the humanity in ourselves and the humanity in others. We become freer to cultivate the *tov me'od* connectedness that co-creates harmony and re-imagines a society grounded in equity.

# 9

# Unmuting the Roma

## MELODY WACHSMUTH AND RAFAEL NĂSTASE

There is an uncomfortable irony for a non-Roma scholar to begin a chapter on unmuting the Roma; for centuries, the Roma have been conceptualised, historicised and imagined by the non-Roma. Before the reader has time to note and rightfully critique this irony, I wish to immediately draw attention to it in order to contend with it. Indeed, as many Roma scholars and others have problematised the discourses that have historically framed images and perspectives of the Roma, this has increasingly become an important nexus of discussion in academia, arts and culture, civil society and politics. Further, in the last decade, as interest in the Roma in relation to Christian mission has soared, are these kinds of discussions happening in the Christian world, and if not, how should they be brought to bear on perspectives and discussions in the Church and in regard to the Church's mission? I will try to offer the general and wider terrain to which these questions are rooted, first in academic discussions and then I will bring those conversations into the relationship of Roma and non-Roma in the context of Church and mission. Rafael Năstase, a Romani scholar himself, will then locate some of these issues into his particular context – Romania – paying special attention to the period of Roma slavery in Romanian history and the current impact of Evangelical and Pentecostal churches in Romania among the Roma.

Through the lens of Muted Group Theory (MGT), Roma groups have been living as long-term subordinate groups to the majority cultures for centuries. Particularly in Central and Eastern Europe (CEE), addressing their social marginalisation is often spoken about in terms of 'success' or 'integration' or, in the words many people in CEE have spoken to me, 'being normal'. At a grass roots level, this often implicitly means cultural, social and lingual assimilation into the majority culture. 'Normal' is the dominant society and 'abnormal' are the Roma who, in people's minds, 'refuse' to live like us. In other words, often Roma groups' ways of being (communication, culture, language) are deemed irrelevant (at best) and not-normal or sub-normal, or even sub-human (at worse).

This is also connected to 'Romaphobia' or anti-Gypsyism, which is, in the words of scholar Aidan McGarry (2013), 'the last acceptable form of racism' in Europe. Jan Selling (2018:44–61) defines it as, 'excluding and discriminating discursive practices which are centred around the constructed image of a "conceptual Gypsy"'. It is a specific form of racism that not only involves concepts of biological race, but also distinguishes between cultural differences (Mirga-Kruszelnicka 2018:8–28). When we think about 'unmuting', we cannot address it until we begin to understand the pervasive and endemic issue of anti-Gypsyism, which is deeply interwoven into not just the systems and structures of society, but also various societies' identity – as people in relationship to this 'Other'. There is European history, and Roma history in Europe. There is Christianity in Europe, and there is Roma Christianity or Christianity among the Roma. In other words, somehow the Roma are 'different' than other minority groups who are included in European identity, history or Christianity.

This 'conceptual Gypsy' is related to the issue of identity – who are the Roma? For centuries, conceptualisations of the Roma were written about and portrayed primarily by non-Roma – and this contributed to an essentialisation of identity (Mirga-Kruszelnicka 2018:10; Hancock 2007:39). Many people have never listened to how a person, whom they see as simply 'Roma' or 'Gypsy', might identify, nor been interested in the reasons behind this identification. For example, one of my interlocutors in my anthropological research was a woman in a village in Serbia who identifies more with Romanians since they speak an old Romanian dialect, but they are forced to adopt a 'Roma' identity that the government puts on them, even though, in her words, 'We don't speak Romani.' She said: 'I don't know how, who decided to call this a Roma village. It's really lame. This is supposed to be called a Romanian village.'[1] In reality, the Roma are a heterogenous minority living within a wide range of different societies and cultures, and can have shared or diverse cultural practices and language (Kovats 2002). And yet, on the one hand, while acknowledging the importance of self-identification and defusing the monolithic myth of the 'true Roma', on the other hand, there is also the risk of an over-dilution, which dissolves a sense of collective belonging (Mirga-Kruszelnicka 2018:22).

## Shifting conversations

Although Romani activists working for political and social change have been around for some time, in the twenty-first century, there has been an increase of 'unmuting' as more Roma voices are increasingly involved in academic, political, education and cultural initiatives and civil society initiatives.[2] In addition, transnational conversations on human rights and the pressure of the EU on member states and those wishing to be member states have contributed to new directions and engagement (Selling 2018:51). For example, there is now a strong acknowledgement by political, civil and religious bodies regarding how Romani minorities were persecuted and killed during the Holocaust. As another example, a Digital Archive of the Roma (Romarchive) has been developed in which Roma 'reclaim' their identity, history, art and culture in their own voices and on their own terms (Roma Archive n.d.). Since the Decade for Roma Inclusion (2005–2015), activists borrowed the slogan, 'Nothing about us without us', in order to critique and reorient policy, civic organisations and activism (Ryder et al. 2014:518–39).

In the academy, there has been lively and sometimes polarising conversation around knowledge production – how Roma have historically been portrayed by *gadje* (non-Roma) researchers and academics which, at times, contributed to the racist discourses in society. In fact, although scientific racism was discarded by academia in general after the Second World War, Thomas Acton (1998) describes a 'twenty-year lag' before this

---

1  Interview in Serbia, 2017.
2  For example, the first World Romani Congress took place in London in 1971. This was a landmark event attended by representatives from fourteen different countries, and they adopted a flag and an anthem.

rejection took effect in Romani studies. Non-Roma scholars have created constructs and images of the Roma without reference to their voices or their own ways of conceptualising themselves and the world (Selling 2018; Silverman 2018:76–97).[3] As the academy in general has become increasingly influenced by critical studies, postcolonial perspectives and second wave feminism, this has also caused a reflexive turn among academics working in Romani studies and 'raised new questions about epistemology and the political responsibility of scholarship' (Selling 2018:51). As Angéla Kóczé put it in 2015, 'Right now Romani intellectuals are in a historical moment when they use their epistemic privilege to "speak back" to the dominant cluster of scholars who created discourses and knowledge systems about the Roma that objectify them' (2015:86).

This shift could be seen concretely in the formation – by two prominent Romani scholars – of the Romani Studies Program at the Central European University in 2017 and the launch of the programme's journal, *Critical Romani Studies* (Beck and Ivasiuc 2020:4). Consequently, some non-Roma scholars moved towards collaboration with Roma colleagues and communities (Beck and Ivasiuc 2020:xiii) and even saw how activism has a role alongside scholarly research, as an 'engaged anthropology or sociology'. In other words, using the research for the purpose of improving people's lives, rather than merely keeping it in the academy to solely build one's career.

Of course, as mentioned earlier, these conversations tend to be rigorously debated. For example, respected scholars of Romani studies question whether assigning scholarly validity on the basis of ethnicity will result in a 'closed-society research paradigm' (Stewart 2017). Some of the outcomes of various attempts to unmute the Roma – usually as top-down initiatives – are also hotly contested and polarising. For example, the initiative that created the Roma Institute for Arts and Culture (ERIAC) is intended to highlight a positive image of the Roma by the Roma. Critics argue that this frames exclusion only as a 'culturalist' issue, ignoring wider political and structural racism factors. Further, they argue it is Roma elites who use the space to 'produce forms of cultural

---

3   Of course, this is related to the wider conversations from second wave feminism, anthropologists, critical studies regarding power dynamics, positionality, and subjectivity in research.

"authenticity," deemed a valid tool for combating socioeconomic and political exclusion' (Beck and Ivasiuc 2020:4). Another critique is what some scholars have termed the 'Gypsy industry' of the proliferation of non-governmental organisations that run as a kind of 'ethnobusiness', making money and careers for a handful of elites with little impact on actual communities (Van Baar 2020:37).

This criticism on initiatives that seemingly offer (or claim) voice, power and social capital for the Roma minority is important to consider, as sometimes they can result in a different kind of muting – culture, voice, history, which, although now has the power to speak into society, either remains in its own little box as something exotic or 'Other', or which communicates its own culture to the majority society in a way allowed or carved out by the dominant paradigms.

# Roma Christians as European Christians

All of these conversations are pertinent when thinking about the Church's role in unmuting the Roma. Approaches from non-Roma Christians and Churches need to be problematised to see if they are still lodged in the 'civilising' discourses of eighteenth- and nineteenth-century mission. In fact, since the Catholic, Orthodox and later Protestant Churches all took a strong mediating role in enforcing and perpetuating standards for Christian morality and civility, they have thus often been complicit in furthering the stereotypes of the Gypsy as 'Other', collaborating with governments to assimilate or suppress Roma (Thurfjell 2013: 33, 34). When the Church became concerned for their 'heathen souls', as with many other initiatives, it often became a civilising mission, sometimes even attempting to stamp out their language as well as culture. For example, Verena Meier highlights Protestant missions to the Sinti and Roma in Friedrichslohra, Germany, in the early nineteenth century in which they were attempting to infuse Christian morality and work ethic so they could be 'useful members' to society. One short-lived strategy for this was to remove children from the parents to educate them and force the parents into workhouses (Meier 2018:86–126). This was eventually declared a failed mission as a result of many difficulties and, according to the Naumberg Missionary Assistance Association's writings, 'partly due to a deep-rooted disposition among this people to lead a roaming and wanton life …'. Also, the report noted that parents did not want their children taken: 'They regarded the placement, diet and upbringing of their children in this institution as an intrusion on their right to rear the children according to their nature, namely in jugglery, begging, stealing, and a vagrant life' (Meier 2018:99, 100).[4]

One can also note in this civilising dynamic the self-narration of Gypsy Rodney Smith, a famous Romani evangelist from England. In his first sermon, he tells the people he is 'only a gipsy [sic] boy,' and excuses himself to people in relation to his first experience of eating publicly in a 'civilised manner' by saying,

> Please forgive me. I do not know any better. I am only a gipsy boy. I have never been taught what these things [cutlery] are. I know I shall make lots of blunders, but if you correct me whenever I make a mistake, I will be very grateful. I will never be angry, and never cross.

In the twentieth century, various Church traditions began to recognise their complicity in Roma suffering and marginalisation, such as the Catholic Church, the Church of Norway in 2002, Luther World Federation in 2013, Churches Commission for Migrants in Europe, and the World Council of Churches (WCC).[5] More recently, large Evangelical gatherings such as the European Evangelical Alliance and Lausanne Europe have made attempts to include Roma voices. As with the similar movement in academic, political and civil society spheres, these are all positive developments.

However, in current mission and Christian work among the Roma, there is often a lack of a critical awareness of this past history, nor a

---

4  Disturbingly, Meier notes how these reports were sent, upon request, to the Racial Hygiene Research Unit in 1939, and became part of the developed classification of racial theories, which was used to deport Sinti and Roma.

5  For example, the Catholic Church has had several historic moments recognising and apologising to Roma communities. In 1965, Pope John Paul VI had a historic meeting with 'Gypsies and Nomads': 'You are not on the margins of the Church, but, under certain aspects, you are at the centre, you are at the heart. You are at the heart of the Church.' In 1970, the Pontifical Council for the Pastoral Care of Migrants and Itinerant People – Guidelines for the Pastoral Care of Gypsies was begun. In 2000, Pope John II includes Gypsies in his list of groups to whom to apologise. In 2019. Pope Francis in Romania apologises to the Roma.

reflexive sensibility regarding the current mission paradigm from which one is operating. From a theological standpoint, it can be easy to note our 'family status' as we are all one in Christ. On the one hand, to adapt what Paul says in Galatians 3:28, in Christ there is neither Roma nor non-Roma. On the other, in Philippians 2:1–11, the portrayal of Jesus setting aside his privilege for the sake of his mission should serve as a warning and model for us with regard to power dynamics. In fact, the true power dynamics will manifest in various ministry initiatives. As noted above, anti-Gypsyism is the 'last acceptable form of racism'. Sometimes I wonder if mission to the Roma is the last acceptable 'colonial' enterprise. Is the implicit impulse as mission as transformation to 'become like us' or to 'become normal?' Or is mission still viewing the Roma as 'problems to be solved?'

I propose that one aspect of a new mission colonialism is a drowning in resources from another culture – which squashes creativity and imposes non-local theologies – instead of collaborating with and encouraging Roma Christians to develop their own. Further, to be willing and open to have one's own thinking and theology challenged by what they are developing. These kinds of impulses can become evident in different Christian initiatives, conferences or ministry endeavours. It is a significant mark of progress when Roma are being invited to mainstream Evangelical conferences. But are they being invited to 'create knowledge and culture' at the conference or just merely to be participants? Are they only sequestered according to the stereotypical gifts associated with Roma, such as music? Are they sequestered in their own 'Roma Christianity' or are they seen and listened to as one of the significant influencers on what Christianity is becoming in Europe? The *Eastern Theological Commentary* (Constantineanu and Renner 2023), although a substantial achievement and first of its kind, demonstrates this huge lacuna in theological knowledge production and the gap between Roma and non-Roma. Although it was lauded to be the first contextual biblical theology for Central and Eastern Europe, there was no entry written by a person of Romani ethnicity, and the Roma were only even mentioned in a couple of articles. Considering the hundreds of thousands of Roma Christians in Central and Eastern Europe, this silence is like a deafening trumpet on the Christian landscape in Europe.

# Final reflexive musings

As non-Roma academics reassess their positionality and role in research in Roma communities, so do I, as a White American female Christian researcher in Europe. I am aware that the knowledge and research I produce are shaped by my epistemology, my understandings and definitions of such key things as poverty, mission, practical theology and cross-cultural dynamics. My goals and ideas have shifted over the years. My first impulse when I arrived in 2011 was to tell the story of the Roma 'revival' in terms of conversions, healings, the things that God was doing. The story grew more complicated and nuanced, however, as I saw the struggling pastors and churches, and engaged with my own experience as an elder in a Roma majority church for ten years, beginning to understand the impact of trauma on Roma communities, and to see complicated dynamics between Roma groups as well as the deep, persistent prejudice in the wider Church.

In reaction to this prejudice, I began to try to write numerous positive stories to be 'positive press' about the Roma, for example, what God was doing in Roma communities, how Roma responded during the 2015 refugee crisis in Eastern Europe and in the war in Ukraine. I have no doubt this has brought help to various Roma; on the other hand, I must recognise that it is still a kind of muting of the Roma. As I try to broadcast the Roma voice and advocate for them, what I pick and choose is highly subjective and based on what I think should be shared and is still according to my perceptions of reality and life. Although I conduct interviews and ask people for their thoughts and perceptions, it is me who is ultimately telling the story for an article or book. The only thing that can challenge this, is for more Roma Christians to be part of these 'knowledge production' spaces, whether in writing, speaking, theological education, online spaces, and for others to be listening and learning – not as a 'special project' or separate stream of Christianity, but as active agents who have some things to say to the global Church. In this, I currently see myself moving toward a more collaborative role. Certainly, this includes collaboration in writing and research, and thus I now hand the shared writing space over to my colleague, Rafael.

# Romani muted in the Romanian context, a historical perspective

For myself as Roma researcher, I observe the discrepancy between statistics presented by the Council of Europe, which finds Romania the country with the largest number of Roma in Europe (Council of Europe 2014),[6] and the Romanian census from 1990 to today. To understand this dynamic, it is essential to have a historical bird's-eye view over the Roma situation in Romania.

It is important to have a special look at the historical dynamics in Romania within the Romanian Principalities: Moldova, Valahia and Transylvania, where the Roma have lived for a thousand years and thus where various empires have had a special influence on their habits, language, culture, religion and behaviour.

From 1038 until the abolition of Romani slavery in 1859, Romanian territories were in a vassalage relationship with the Hapsburg and Ottoman Empires. Roma people were 'countryless' people without centralised leadership and they travelled around Europe. This historical context was favourable to Roma slavery, which existed in certain principalities from the thirteenth century to the middle of the nineteenth century. From 1385 to 1434, historical archives presented by Adrian Furtună in chronological order reflect various selling contracts and donations of entire Roma villages and houses as monastery possessions (Furtună 2020). From Furtună's analysis, we can conclude that in Romanian Principalities, there were two methods of subjugation: one was related to Romanian paysans who had no land possessions, working for Romanian or Hungarian aristocrats, but they had the freedom to own a house and to travel. Another category was 'Gypsies slaves'. Historical sources demonstrate that the legal slavery system facilitated the existence of *jobbagy* (term of Hungarian origin) in Transylvania and *Sherbs* (term of Latin origin – *servus*) in Moldova and Wallachia. These *robi* (Romanian term) were Romanian peasant servants without properties, working on Romanian aristocrats' lands. The legal difference between Romanian

---

6   In Romania, according to the Council of Europe, there are 1.8 million Roma.

servants and Romani slaves is in status, demonstrated in the total lack of social, economic and family rights of the Gypsies.

In the wider European continent, between 1497 and 1774, 146 decrees were issued against the Gypsies by churches or Imperialist authorities. One of these, which seems representative of the Imperial European context in the Austro-Hungarian Empire, and especially for the Romanian space, in the historical relationship between the Roma and the church, was *De Regulatione Zingarorum* (1758) (Kenrick 2007:103). This regulation represents the attempt to settle the Roma by Maria Theresa and Joseph II, by transforming the 275,000 Gypsies from the Habsburg Empire into the 'new Hungarians'.[7] On this occasion, compulsory school and church attendance was instituted. Another aspect imposed by the regulations was listening to the priest's advice. This sounds positive, but other instituted laws were also difficult for the Romani: they were forbidden to speak in their own language and wear their own national costumes. This was an intentional muting of the Romani national identity and dignity. This could explain why today Romani-Gabors from Transylvania have a closed national attitude characterised by endogamy and a very distinctive dress code (Olivera 2012). This could be interpreted as a self-protective attitude and for perpetuum reason of their ethnic identity. In this historical context, we may conclude that despite its positive points, *De Regulatione Zingarorum* proved to be a factor muting the manifestation of ethnic identity and freedom to use their language.

Between 1848 and 1856, the statutory situation of the Gypsies was changed in the Romanian Principalities. Venera Achim (2005) identifies in the archives of the time that there were more than 260,000 freed Gypsies, representing 7.6% of the population of the Romanian Principalities. According to various laws and regulations, only between the 1848 Revolution and 1859 were there voices that became 'voice givers' for Romani in the Romanian Principalities. The appearance of fascism in Romania extinguished voices working for Roma emancipation.

Throughout the last 165 years, since the abolition of Gypsy slavery, the precarious conditions of the ethnic Roma can be observed. The

---

7 For five hundred years, Transylvania was under the Austro-Hungarian Empire. Because Hungarians were a minority in the Empire, they tried to 'transform' the Gypsies, changing them into 'new Hungarians'. In 1918, it was annexed by Romania.

two World Wars, the pogrom (extermination camp), the lack of ethnic recognition during communism, discrimination, poverty, nomadism and the high level of crime all accentuated the lack of community transformation. Even though in the interwar period, there were signs of an ethnic emancipation, Romani efforts for self-emancipation proved that Romani were used in mass political manipulation, as officials tried to buy their votes. It could be seen in historical newspapers from archives that Roma leaders were present in various political elections from 1918 to 1940. Shortly after the important historical moment of the formation of Greater Romania, there was a movement towards a great Romanian patriotism or even nationalism, which culminated with the Holocaust where Roma were sent over the Dnister River to extermination camps/villages. A recent documentary inspired from national archives revealed how 25,000 Roma[8] were asked to fight in the Second World War, but their families were sent to an extermination or labour camp in Transnistria (National Center for Roma Culture 2023).

After the Transnistrian episode, the Roma survivors' return to Romania in the summer of 1944, and in the 23 August 1944 change of regime, the 'Gypsy problem' ceased to exist in the eyes of the Romanian authorities. The reinstatement of the survivors was made without much noise. In the eyes of the new authorities, the Roma became what they had been in the period before the Antonescu regime: a marginal social category rather than an ethnic minority.

Romanian communist government officials recognised the Hungarian and German minorities, but as László Fosztó (2007:83) observes, there was no cultural recognition or artistic manifestation of the Roma ethnic group even though it was the largest ethnic group in Romania.

# Current perspectives of Romani emancipation in Romania: a glimpse of Romani evidence

During communism, there was no historical mention in schools or mass media about the Roma Holocaust. Communism erased the ethnic

---

8   Approximately 500,000 Roma from the territory of Europe died during the Holocaust.

consciousness of the memory of both slavery and the Holocaust. After 1990, the European Union and other European forums provided support to identify problems and solutions that could at least mitigate the problems of Roma during communism, trying also to resolve social and economic problems. These inclusion policies were costly and did not have the intended effect. Iulius Rostas (2020) refers to these European funding projects for Roma inclusion and cohesion programmes, observing that ethnic variety, linguistic divisions, lack of unity and a clear identity meant that many of these institutional attempts failed.

From a religious perspective, due to the double meaning of the word *robi*, there is now a dispute between Roma activists, including the self-titled king of Roma people (King Cioaba) and the Romanian Orthodox Church (ROC) (which also had a large number of Roma slaves), arguing for historical reconciliation or asking for public forgiveness. The argument of ROC is that there was slavery for both Romanian paysans and Roma, so there is no need for forgiveness.

However, there are legal, historical and narrative arguments that Roma were slaves with different economic, social and family statutes compared with Romanian paysans. In defence of this argument, I would offer Prime Minister Mihail Kogălniceanu's [9] memories, which refer to the *Gypsies* as:

> human beings with chains on their hands and feet, with iron hoops around their foreheads or metal collars around their necks. Bloody whippings and other punishments such as starvation, hanging over a smoking fire, imprisonment and throwing, being stripped, into the snow or frozen water of some river, this was the treatment meted out to the wretched gypsy. The sacred character of marriage and family ties was also mocked: the wife was separated from the man, the daughter was torn from the mother, the children were taken from the breasts of those who brought them into the world and then sold like cattle to different buyers in the four corners of Romania.
>
> (Kogălniceanu 1908:14)

---

9  Mihail Kogălniceanu was Prime Minister, Minister of Foreigners of Affairs, and Minister of Internal Affairs from 1863 to 1879.

# Contemporary efforts to unmute Romani voices

Because of these historical factors, some of the Roma lost (or maybe even gave up) their Roma identity: language, traditions, even denying their relatives' origins. This is probably the reason for the huge discrepancy between the latest census results in 2021[10] and EU statistics. We may interpret this reaction as 'self-muted attitude'. The dominant culture does not feel so guilty since they never recognised the fact that the Roma were repressed. We as the Roma self-mute, which helps the ROC to not recognise or take responsibility for the history.

Looking at many Roma families from Romania, including my family, I was raised with a natural pride of being Gypsy. However, this happens primarily with individuals or families, not in whole communities. Unfortunately, many Roma with higher education, who are involved in sports, showbusiness, business or schools refuse to recognise their Roma roots. They argue that they separate themselves from the Roma identity because Roma identity is associated with negative stereotypes such as poverty, crime, low education, etc. In their minds, the only way to emancipate their identity is to leave their Roma identity. This only perpetuates the muting cycle since if being 'successful' in society requires a self-muting, thus society does not connect 'success' with the Roma nor do other Roma have enough role models in various occupations.

Breakthroughs for the Roma came after 1989, as the memory of Roma slavery within the Romanian Orthodox Church came alive among educated Roma people. They started promoting historical milestones of the Roma, and in 1992 the Romani language was promoted in the Foreign Language department in the University of Bucharest.

In the midst of these historical discrepancies, Evangelical Churches have had a great impact in unmuting the Roma, particularly as they were not part of this history. As Fraser and Miroslav Atanasov (2010) observe, in the UK and Bulgaria, the attempt to 'change' the Roma community

---

10 See the Population and Housing Census (2011).

was not for control or manipulative reasons, but for love, care and especially spiritual reasons. In contrast, slavery or historically harsh situations as far we understand from Bulgarian writers (Marushakova, Popov, Atanasov, Slavkova), British writers (Fraser, Acton) or more recently Romanian (Mihail Ciopasiu), contributed to the extent to which the Roma are muted today.

# Conclusions

According to Anne-Marie Kool, there are *signs of rebirth among Roma,* intentional or not, unnoticed by the EU's official radar. Having an Evangelical perspective, the author justifies the lack of progress of European forums because they operate with other methods – secular – on the world that is incapable of *understanding the incarnation in Christ* (Kool 2016:520–43). In this way, Christ became the role model for the Roma. The questionable origins of Jesus and his illegitimate birth, and his traveller and refugee life experience are characteristics with which Roma could identify themselves. The fact that the God of Israel is manifesting his power among the least of the world (1 Cor. 1:26–8), and that Christians are seen by Peter as 'strangers and travellers' in the world, while expecting a new country at the end of their wandering (1 Pet. 2:11), offers another perspective of Christianity, not like a religion that betrayed them.

Evangelical Churches in Romania after 1990 were listening and used an active conversion 'to speak up for those who cannot speak for themselves'. In Roma Evangelical communities, active listening and engagement are foundational in fostering transformation. Listening becomes a catalyst for bridging the gap between understanding and action, empowering genuine conversion as individuals act.

Another aspect observed in my field research was individual *metanoia* (Dirksen 1932)[11] in collective transformation. Individual transformation, especially within the context of collective *metanoia*, emphasises the

---

11 Among the definitions found in biblical theology, we believe that the most appropriate for the context of Evangelical Roma in the communities surveyed is that of Aloys H. Dirksen who defines the terms μετανοέω and μετάνοια as 'a conversion from sin that requires regret and confession of it' (Dirksen 1932:31).

interdependence of personal change and collective progress. *Metanoia* initiates a radical shift in perspective, setting off a wave effect that inspires broader societal transformations. The continuous process of conversion rooted in Galatians 3:28 (NIV), stating, 'There is neither Jew nor Gentile, neither slave nor free, nor is there male and female, for you are all one in Christ Jesus.'

Dignity and identity are rediscovered in conversion and transformation. Romani people resonate, in a special way with the idea that they are the 'handiwork, created in Christ Jesus to do good works' (Eph. 2:10 NIV). Embracing cultural heritage and fostering pride in one's identity are pivotal steps towards empowerment, transcending basic social change. Embracing cultural heritage and taking pride in one's identity empowers individuals to counter internalised oppression, challenge historical systemic oppression and advocate for their rights. This might explain why 27% of Roma people declared themselves Evangelicals. I observed that the consequence of discovering their dignity is a healing from internalised oppression – a self-muting for protection, a mechanism of self-defence.

In this way, *metanoia* acts as a healing force, allowing individuals to reject damaging narratives and to embrace new self-images, particularly countering the internalised prejudices imposed upon them. In this way, *metanoia*, coupled with faith, empowers individuals to bandage historical systemic oppression (Năstase 2023:160). Through renewed mindsets and spiritual strength, individuals can confront racism and challenge discriminatory practices. Community development and transformation finds its roots in *metanoia* within Roma communities, producing significant markers of transformation. Acts of kindness, empathy and solidarity serve as tangible evidence of conversion, nurturing empathy and compassion within communities.

Holistic transformation is another fruit of *metanoia* that emerges as a transformative force within the contexts of Black Theology and Liberation Theology. It not only restores individual dignity, but also empowers individuals and communities to resist oppression actively. This transformation extends beyond personal spheres, leading to solidarity, social justice advocacy, economic and educational empowerment, empathy and cultural pride. Through this process, Roma individuals embark on a journey towards genuine empowerment and social change, enriching individual lives and strengthening the entire community. Ultimately, this journey nurtures a future where dignity is the inherent right of every member, transcending backgrounds and heritage, and the muted will have a chance to speak and to be heard.

# 10

# Unmuting local theologising: an Asian perspective

## CLAIRE T. C. CHONG

'You have let go of the commands of God and are holding on to human traditions.' *And he [Jesus] continued*, 'You have a fine way of setting aside the commands of God in order to observe your own traditions! For Moses said, "Honor your father and mother," and, "Anyone who curses their father or mother is to be put to death." But you say that if anyone declares that what might have been used to help their father or mother is Corban (that is, devoted to God) – then you no longer let them do anything for their father or mother. Thus you nullify the word of God by your tradition that you have handed down. And you do many things like that.'
(Mark 7:8–13)

Do we, in our present day, 'do many things like that' – instruct lay believers that they do not need to give what is due to their parents and fulfil familial and social obligations, and instead, focus on them performing religiously pious acts to demonstrate their allegiance to God? Lay believers are not in a position to say or act otherwise when missionaries and missionised leaders invoke God's Word in laying down the dos and don'ts of discipleship, albeit with the best intentions. Generations of Christians in Asia have in this way been theologically, socially and culturally muted. Building on Usha Reifsnider's introduction of Muted Group Theory (MGT) in the context of cross-cultural missions, this chapter invites you – the readers – to reflect with us whether we have unwittingly muted others. If so, how we can be more sensitive to the power dynamics of missions? Thus we will be able to craft more culturally respectful theologies and practices, so that 'As a prisoner for the Lord, then, I urge you to live a life worthy of the calling you have received. Be completely humble and gentle; be patient, bearing with one another in love' (Eph. 4:1–2).

# A historical problem

Students of mission history will be aware of the notorious Chinese Rites Controversy (c.1640s–1742) – the polemical debates between the Jesuits on one hand and the Dominicans and the Franciscans on the other hand, who vehemently opposed the Jesuits' *Il Modo Soave* mission approach of cultural accommodation and their acquiescence to the ancestral practices (Mungello 1994). However, lesser known are the muted voices of the Christian Confucian intellectuals who defended their time-honoured traditions to the West and their vision of a culturally Chinese Christ-centred faith.

This contentious issue allegedly arose in an unassuming conversation in 1635 between a Franciscan missionary to China, Father Antonio de Santa Maria (who arrived in China three decades after the founding Jesuit, Father Matteo Ricci) and his Chinese-language tutor. Father Antonio

> stumbled upon a word, which is pronounced '*ji*' 祭; he did not know its meaning, nor could he understand the explanation given by a Christian named Tadeo, who was his tutor. Finally, unable to make him understand, Tadeo said: 'Father, this character means "to sacrifice," and explains what you say during mass.'
> (Hsia 2018:29)

This led to an extensive inquiry and ecclesiastical and political dispute, which culminated in the *Ex Illa Die* (1715) and the final anti-rites papal bull, *Ex Quo Singulari* (1742), forbidding the practice of the Chinese ancestor rites by Chinese Catholics.

In the run-up to the papal decree, especially during the period between the 1680s and 1720s, numerous collective appeals and literary works written by Chinese Christians, including those from the Confucian literati and imperial court and even the Qing Emperor Kangxi were submitted to the Vatican to explain the Chinese side of the argument (Hsia 2018; Standaert 2018; J. S. Lin 1994). Wang (2022), who studied the works of Yan Mo, one of the prolific defenders of the Chinese rites, explicated the polysemous nuances of the Chinese meaning of *ji* and contended that the rites performed towards the ancestors and the great sage Confucius, in contrast to the cultic practices of tutelary spirits, were not idolatrous. However, it is apparent that the Chinese voices fell onto deaf ears; it was as if the theological reflection of the Chinese on the relationship between their inherited culture and their newfound faith did not count at all. 'What mattered in the end, however, was the decision-making process in Rome, not expert native voices, whose echoes still sound today in the luminous reading rooms of the libraries and archives in Europe' (Hsia 2018:48). The eventual banning of ancestor rites, among other factors, resulted in the proscription of Christianity and persecution of Christians in China.[1]

The Protestant missionaries who entered China in the 1800s were similarly ill disposed towards these Chinese practices, which was profoundly problematic for the spread of the gospel. At the 1890 General Conference of the Protestant Missionaries of China, the ancestor issue was extensively debated. After a heated debate, the 400-strong contingent of Euro-American missionaries voted against the ancestor tradition and forbade Christian Chinese to participate in the cultic rite, despite pleas for tolerance and suggestions on adaptations from voices in the margins, including William A. P. Martin and Timothy Richard.[2] Since then, this rejectionist stance towards the ancestor custom has been staunchly adhered to among Protestants.

In the postcolonial period, there was a resurgence of indigenous religions throughout Asia, and in China, church leaders struggled to find appropriate responses to the governmental rejuvenation of Chinese (religious) culture. In 1983, 'The Consultation on the Christian Response

---

1 In Korea, the persecution of Christians resulted in the creation of many martyrs.

2 The inside view of the heated debates can be read from the *Official Records of General Conference of the Protestant Missionaries of China* (1890); protagonist W. A. P. Martin's argument for tolerance and accommodation can be further studied from his biography and publications: Martin (1903; 1904; 1912:267–72, 276–7; 1896); the argument of antagonist Hudson Taylor against the ancestor case can be read in his biography published by Broomhall (1981a:283–8; 1981b:139–43). For further discussion, see Addison (1925); C. P. Lin (1985).

to Ancestor Practices' was convened, which led to the publication of the book *Christian Alternatives to Ancestor Practices*, edited by Ro (1985). Responses were mixed: some were convicted that ancestor worship had to be wholly rejected, others advocated contextualisation and local theologising. The outcome of the consultation is ambiguous. However, from the general responses of Christians today, it feels as if, by and large, these traditional practices are still categorised as religious worship and deemed pejoratively.[3] Except for a contextual model of a Hakka community in Taiwan, several other attempts of redeeming ancestor practices have not been well received by mainstream denominational churches.[4]

Finding a Christ-centred, biblically sound, people-loving response to the ancestor issue is indeed contentious and complex, and in this discussion, I shall use MGT as a conceptual framework and its categories of thought to analyse the issue at hand.

# Muted Group Theory and the call to unmute

MGT, which originated within the field of anthropology,[5] is largely used to study the interactive dynamics between dominant and subordinate groups and the structures and processes of communication between them. 'Mutedness' is a social phenomenon in which the voices of subordinate groups are not taken seriously; mutedness is not so much about the explicit suppression of subordinate voices as the implicit disadvantage of people of lower hierarchical social status. In any society,

---

3   E.g. Tong (1993); Bae (2008).

4   The contextual innovation by the Japanese Indigenous Church Movement has been denounced (Mullins 1998:129–55). The indigenous church-planting movement Free in Jesus Christ Church Association (FJCCA) in Thailand (Bailey and Martin 2020), which has non-conventional Christian practices including responses towards the ancestral custom, has sparked much debate among the missionised churches (personal communication with Bailey). Even in Singapore in 2023, a senior clergyman and scholar gave a sermon about loving our religious neighbours and illustrated his point by sharing a testimony about a Christian daughter helping her ailing mother clean the ancestral altar, which triggered a flurry of unkind responses on social media.

5   MGT was conceptualised by Edwin and Shirley Ardener (1972; 1975). Key contributors to the development of this discourse include Kramarae (1981) and Meares (2002). Although MGT was theorised within gendered issues, its application extends to engaged interactions between any dominant and subordinate parties that exhibit imbalanced linguistic and social dynamics.

or sub-sector of society, it is the dominant group that establishes institutional structures and determines the direction and development of discourses, and naturally, they would set up and perpetuate systems that benefit their interest.

As a result of imbedded biases, the subordinate group members would always be at a disadvantage and unable to realise their fullest potential. Even in communicative processes, members of the subordinate groups have to employ the conceptual categories, linguistic idioms and social conventions defined by the dominant group. Not being able to use their 'heart language', subordinate group members are not able to express and articulate their ideologies as eloquently, adequately and persuasively, and because of the inherent disadvantage, their voices become muted and their ideas marginalised. What makes MGT particularly significant is that it recognises that the imbalance of power is tacit and taken for granted. In many situations both muted and dominant group members may not even recognise that they are muted or muting the other. MGT is thus helpful as a conceptual framework for critical reflection and exposing inherent biases.

MGT has been applied to analyse communicative dynamics in a number of contexts, including those pertaining to gender and ethnic discrimination, people with disability, non-conventional sexual orientations, low socioeconomic status and work with various disenfranchised groups. It is important to note that MGT is not just a critique of powerplay; rather, it serves to understand the structures and processes of disparate dynamics and provide practical ways to rectify systemic imbalances and create healthier and more efficacious interrelations (Houston and Kramarae 1991). Orbe's (1998b) comprehensive study demonstrates how different subordinate groups from various cultures employ diverse strategies to resist muting and renegotiate their relations with dominant groups. MGT offers much promise in situations where both dominant and subordinate groups are mutually engaged in a constructive endeavour, but who are not able to achieve desired outcomes because of unconscious systemic biases. Referring to the processes of unmuting, Meares remarks, 'making change is the most difficult. The mechanisms of muting are easier to understand than the mechanisms for eliminating it' (2017:6–7). It is apparent that transforming power dynamics is not merely a matter of having good intentions and simply creating space for open dialogue. Unmuting requires in-depth understanding of the communicative processes, awareness of the preconceived assumptions and conceptual categories employed by both parties, profound self-knowledge and other-knowledge, and a willingness to make radical changes in order to nurture mutuality.

Most recently, Reifsnider (2022) has applied MGT to cross-cultural conversions among diaspora Hindus in Britain, analysing the dynamics of established Christianity and new converts. MGT is poignantly relevant to mission praxis, especially because historically, Christian mission is inextricably associated with imperialism and colonialism. MGT is helpful for analysing the interactive dynamics between foreign and local mission partners, missionised church and the larger non-Christian community, as well as the communicative dynamics in evangelistic and discipleship processes. By critically reflecting on power issues and systemic biases through the lens of MGT, some of the problems encountered in missions, such as shallow discipleship, stunted church growth and unempowered indigenous leadership, may be addressed.

## Analysis of the ancestor controversy through Muted Group Theory

In this chapter, I employ MGT as a conceptual framework to analyse the Christian treatment of ancestor practices. One of the central observations of MGT is that subordinate voices are often interpreted and evaluated through the conceptual categories and social conventions of dominant groups. This is evident in the conversation between the Chinese tutor Tadeo and the Spaniard Franciscan Father Antonio, who had difficulties understanding the Chinese term and practice of *ji*. After much explanation, Tadeo resorted to employing a term used in mass referring to sacrifice, which triggered the controversy. As explicated by Catholic Chinese scholars, *ji* is a multi-nuanced term; it describes a mother bird presenting worms to her nestlings, food gifting to parents, food ceremonies to Confucius, votive offerings to tutelary spirits, and worshipful offerings to the God of Heaven – the significance of *ji* in each instance can only be understood in the context of its usage (Wang 2022). By conflating *ji* as the Western Christian idea of sacrifice unto God/a god, the multi-layered nuances of *ji* are muted.

The linguistic issue raised in MGT is comparable to Zeng's (2011) concept of 'reverse analogical interpretation' – the academic phenomenon of explaining Chinese philosophy in Western categories.[6] In Zeng's critique of the Western exposition of the ancient Chinese notion of *qi* in Western categories and through Western logic, the profundity, dynamicity and 'internal "spirit"' inherent in the indigenous philosophical concept is lost (2011:112). Reconstructing and reframing Chinese theories using Western terminologies produce partial and distorted understandings of Chinese ideologies.

Yet, Gadamer (1975), the well-known scholar of hermeneutics, contends that the understanding of new and foreign ideas has to be built upon fore-understandings or fore-structures. Thus, deciphering the meaning of *ji* has to necessarily begin with the Western fore-understanding of sacrifice. The problem of misunderstanding occurs when we stop short at this and assume that *ji* is the dynamic equivalent of sacrifice. Understanding the meanings of words, and lived experiences, world views and philosophical ideas, is not a matter of one-to-one correspondence and translation using the language of the dominant group; it involves a complex and iterative process to achieve empathetic understanding. Any lesser method would result in the muting of subordinate voices and meanings.

To deepen our understanding of the phenomenon of muting within a mission context, it is helpful to also comprehend the concept of biblicality.[7] Biblicality is a cousin of coloniality and is distinct from Bebbington's use of the term biblicism as a characterisation of evangelicalism.

Bebbington's (2021:36–40) Evangelical Quadrilateral describes four salient features of evangelicalism, of which biblicism – referring to the

---

6  Analogical interpretation (ge yi 格义) was an ancient Chinese methodological approach of learning in which foreign ideologies such as Buddhist doctrines were understood through conceptual categories from Confucian and Taoist philosophy. Reverse analogical interpretation is using English terminologies to understand Chinese concepts.

7  The notion of biblicality was introduced at a seminar by Patrick Krayer at the Evangelical Missiological Society Annual Conference, 2022. His paper on biblicality and coloniality is forthcoming in *Missiology* (2024). Krayer is my colleague at Fuller Theological Seminary and he has kindly given me permission to engage with his concept of biblicality.

centrality of the Bible in Christian praxis – is one. Anthropological studies of Evangelical biblicism show that different Christian groups express biblicism in varying ways.[8] For some, biblicism can manifest as a rigid, perhaps unhealthy, legalistic and even idolatrous adherence to the Bible, opposed to the spirit of *sola Scriptura*.[9] This wielding of Scripture is sometimes used by religious exponents to mute nonconformist voices (as observed in Acts 15 described below).

Such biblicists assume absolute objectivity in their understanding of Scripture and are not aware of what Krayer calls biblicality, which is a parallel concept to coloniality. While coloniality refers to the dominance of Western ideologies and epistemic approaches over local knowledge and methods (Quijano 2007),[10] biblicality refers to the privileging of certain culturally bounded – often Western – biblical interpretations.[11] The tacit assumption underlying coloniality and biblicality is that Western/modern vision, mentalities, and methods, life and society, which also undergird much of the theological project, are definitive and universal. Krayer argues that interpretation of Scripture is intimately shaped by the world people inhabit – their culture, world view and philosophical assumptions; the theological project is contextually constrained. Without this awareness, biblicists extend their religious positions on other cultures; any variation from their dominant narrative

---

8 Malley (2004) and Larsen (2021).

9 Cummings (2012), Steffaniak (2020), Smith (2011). Popular Christian author Dallas Willard (2015) cautioned, 'To be a biblical Christian is not to have high views about the Bible' (2012:16), and by 'high view', Willard refers to the way some Christians pride themselves on their knowledge of Scripture and views and twist the Word of God to their own destruction (106).

10 The concept of coloniality was first espoused by Quijano. While colonialism refers to a historical past, coloniality is an ongoing reality. Even after colonised societies had gained independence from Western colonisers and expansionists, the Western ideologies and methodologies that continue to dominate are perpetuated in the thinking of the subaltern. Decoloniality seeks to deconstruct (not destroy and supplant) the ideological frameworks that undergird the thinking and working processes so as to carve out space for engagement with local wisdom and practices.

11 The idea of biblicality was also alluded to by earlier missiologists. In a comparative study of Charles Kraft and Paul Hiebert's missiologies, Chang et al. (2009) noted that Kraft's missiology was not as well accepted as Hiebert's in the earlier days, because Kraft was more critical of the cultural baggage of missionaries and Christian institutions. However, because of the lack of self-critique, although Hiebert's missiology is widely accepted, the impact of his model of contextualisation has not been as successful as desired (Shaw 2010; Shaw et al. 2016). Similarly, Duerksen and Dyrness (2019) also contend that a more critical assessment is needed to evaluate the current methods of Enlightenment-based theologising.

is considered heterodox.[12] The Western definition of sacrifice *vis-à-vis* the Chinese notion of *ji* is a case in point. Theologically muting subordinate groups by (unconsciously) imposing biblical interpretations constructed in other socio-cultural contexts has injurious effects on other peoples' culture; in some mission contexts, biblicality has resulted in 'an iconoclastic holocaust of the culture which already existed' (Collinson 1988:94 cited in Cummings 2012:178).[13] There is 'violence of silence'.

Unmuting helps us to identify our blind spots, become aware of our socio-historically bounded assumptions, so that we can begin a process of rehabilitating our mission approaches. Scripture, which is the Christian's source of inspiration and wisdom, is able to provide some insights as to how we can unmute others.

# An example of unmuting in Scripture

Acts 15 gives an account of a landmark debate on whether non-Jewish Jesus-followers should follow the religious practices of Jewish Jesus-followers.[14] As the gospel spread across Asia Minor, diversity of faith expressions flourished; the Greek disciples of Jesus in Antioch were so distinct from the Jewish Jesus-followers that they were identified by the term 'Christian' (Acts 11:26). However, some Jewish Jesus-followers or Judaisers contended that to be saved by Jesus and be a part of the family of God, Gentile disciples had to comply with Jewish worship forms, social norms, and Mosaic tradition, in particular, circumcision. Membership to the community of Jesus-followers was determined by the dominant group of Jewish Jesus-followers. In all fairness, the Judaisers were trying to be as biblical as possible for circumcision was a direct commandment of God and it applied to foreigners – non-Abrahamic

---

12 It should be noted that biblicality is not a problem of Western Christians alone, but also of missionised Asian Christians, who are great defenders of Western theology. After all the hard work that we have put into learning systematic theology, we have become attached to it; we self-identify with it and perpetuate it. Suppression of theological innovation puts the Holy Spirit in a box and does not give him room to move in new ways.

13 Original quote by Collinson (1988) and cited by Cummings (2012:178).

14 Detailed treatment of this watershed event in which the full panoply of leadership – the apostles and the elders – endorsed Paul's mission method are found in Dunn (2016) and Peterson (2009).

offspring – who were part of Jewish households (Gen. 17:10–14). Their insistence on Gentile circumcision was in keeping with this law of God. Their soteriology and ecclesiology were founded upon the socio-historically constructed doctrine of circumcision.

Having lived and ministered among the Gentiles, Barnabas and Paul, who were firsthand witnesses of God working among the Gentiles through signs and wonders, were not able to convince the Judaisers otherwise – they were part of the subordinate group. To resolve the dispute, the debate was brought to the Jerusalem Council where an open dialogue ensued in which dissonating voices and contesting convictions were all laid at the discussion table. Reflection on the proceedings of the Council can shed some insights into what unmuting might involve. Here, I discuss three observations.

First, there should be an earnest desire to listen and understand the non-dominant position. Barnabas and Paul and their missionary band listened to the struggles of the Gentile Christians over circumcision and the socio-cultural and political repercussions of it. James and the Jerusalem Council empathised with the Gentile Christians and acknowledged that circumcision 'disturbed [them], troubling [their] minds' (Acts 15:24) and 'ma[d]e it difficult for the Gentiles who are turning to God' (Acts 15:19 NLT). Like the Jesuits of sixteenth- and seventeenth-century China, the missionaries to the Gentiles took the trouble to deeply understand the vision of life and the societal norms of the people, even when they were contrary to their own convictions. They were not quick in labelling the Other as 'wrong'.

Second, Paul, Barnabas and the Jerusalem Council saw and perceived the new work that God was doing among the Gentiles (Isa. 43:19). God was forming a people for himself in a way that was different from that of the Jews, and this was clearly evident in the way in which the Holy Spirit was moving in signs and wonders among the uncircumcised Greeks.

Third, what the Jewish Jesus-followers saw opened their ears to hear Scripture in a new light and this renewed their theological understanding.[15] Reflecting on Barnabas and Paul's testimony in the

---

15 Bauckham (1996) describes the intricacy of the proceedings and the significance of the Old Testament Scriptures cited at the Council.

light of his own experience with the Gentile household of Cornelius, Peter came to the realisation that following the Mosaic laws was not the prerequisite for salvation, which is through the grace of the Lord Jesus. Rereading an Old Testament prophecy in an illuminating new way, James redefined what 'chosen people of God' meant: from one that was exclusively referring to Israel to one that includes 'the rest of mankind' and even 'all the Gentiles' (Acts 15:17). Similarly, Paul transformed the old interpretation of the doctrine of circumcision; emphasising the spirit of the law rather than the letter, he criticised the legalistic demands of physical circumcision and preached on the circumcision of the heart by the Spirit (Rom. 2:25–9). These doctrines – salvation by grace, universal family of God, and heart circumcision – may not strike us as particularly special, but at that time, these reinterpretations would have been regarded as radical. In fact, the decision that was made at the Jerusalem Council was not immediately rectified and by reading the epistles, it becomes apparent that the first-century church continued to struggle with these decisions.

This reflection has pertinent implications on the way we carry missions today. This is, however, not within the scope of this chapter, which seeks to focus on the phenomenon of muting within the mission context and the process of unmuting. In the foregoing biblical reflection, central to the unmuting process is a profound *metanoia* – a changing of mindset and paradigm. Instead of imposing predetermined theological conceptions, the apostolic workers listened intently and sought empathetic understanding, and by being perceptive and discerning of God at work, they allowed the Holy Spirit to illumine their minds to their socio-historically bound understandings, and in so doing, transformed their interpretive frameworks and long-established theological interpretations. This hermeneutical process that we see here is one that is co-dependent on text and context, one that is deeply rooted in the Word and yet sensitive to the work of the Holy Spirit in the present and God's continued authorship in writing history. In this sense, Acts 15 may also be considered as a narrative of how the Church 'unmuted' God, submitting to the authority of the Bible in a way that took seriously a range of cultural issues.

# A Cambodian example of cultural and theological unmuting

In Cambodia, there is a ritual act of obeisance, which involves kneeling and bowing three times, head to the ground. This act is called *tvaibongkum* and is ceremonially performed before parents – living or dead, elders, the king, monks and the Buddha statues. When Cambodians meet monks on the street where it is not appropriate to prostrate, they would greet the monks by saying '*kona tvaibongkum loak m'zhah*' ('I *tvaibongkum* Venerable').

Many Cambodian Christians are hesitant about performing this ceremonious ritual and greeting monks in these words because the Khmer word *tvaibongkum* has been inopportunely translated as worship and is used in Christian Scriptures and songs to express adoration and exaltation of God. Thus, among Cambodian Christians, bowing to or using the word *tvaibongkum* towards another person other than God implicitly amounts to idolatry. This creates profound conflict and cultural dissonance among Cambodian Christians.

However, anthropologically studying the lived experience of ritual bowing, it becomes apparent that the way in which the word *tvaibongkum* is used in Cambodia is quite different from worship in the Western Christian sense. In the Cambodian lifeworld, *tvaibongkum* is ordinarily understood as an expression of reverential greeting. In a YouTube video produced by a Cambodian monk to teach second-generation Cambodian Americans about Khmer culture, the Khmer phrase, '*kona som tvaibongkum loak m'zhah*' is annotated in English as, 'I express my greetings, Venerable' (Jupiter 2017). In the Headley's Khmer–English Dictionary (online), *tvaibongkum* is defined as 'to greet (respectfully); say hello' or 'to greet, pay respects/homage to, venerate, make an obeisance, salute'. In Cambodian society, not to bow to monks or ceremonially respect parents is not considered as religious impiety, but insolence. Some pastors from mainline denominational churches recognise the cultural nuances of *tvaibongkum* and its distinction from the Christian definition of worship, but they are cautious in the spoken use or demonstration of ritual bowing in non-Christian contexts.

What is of particular interest to this study is that this multi-nuanced act of ritual bowing is also observed in the Old Testament. The Hebrew word for ritual bowing is *shachah* and there appears to be at least two usages of this word. First, as an act of worship, people of God *shachah* God and God commanded his people not to *shachah* idols (compare with Gen. 22:5, and Exod. 20:5). However, *shachah* is also used as a cultural form of reverential greeting, brother *shachah* before brother (Gen. 43:28), subjects *shachah* before king (1 Sam. 2:36), tribal leader *shachah* before other tribal leaders (Gen. 23:7), children before parents (1 Kgs 2:19), and even before a parent-in-law who is a pagan priest (Exod. 18:7). While a more thorough theological consideration is needed to establish a theology of worship in Asian contexts, this biblical reflection stimulates pertinent paradigm shifts in the hermeneutical framework and provides assurance that God-fearing Cambodian Christians need to culturally unmute themselves.

Extending from the reflection of Acts 15, the process of unmuting involves an in-depth understanding of the practices of subordinate groups. The inquiry of cultural phenomena at surface level is grossly insufficient; it has to occur at the undergirding structures of lived experiences. It is only at these deep-lying levels that semantic or gestural resemblances can be distinguished – these are words or gestures that appear similar, but have different nuances of meanings. The Cambodia practice of *tvaibongkum* is comparable with the Hebrew practice of *shachah* and the Chinese practice of *ji*. It is apparent that in these lifeworlds, the meanings of a word or act are non-binary, but graduated, that is, it takes on different nuances in different hierarchical social contexts. Meanings can therefore only be grasped contextually. For cross-cultural workers, this implies that we should be more cautious of trying to translate words or ideas because it may be unlikely that we can find simple one-to-one corresponding equivalents.

As in the biblical reflection of Acts 15, the anthropological insight from the study of *tvaibongkum* opened the eyes to 'new' readings of Scripture and renewed understanding of *shachah*. This missiological phenomenon is comparable with what Duerksen and Dyrness call 'reverse hermeneutics' (2019:28). Resonating with Krayer's concept of biblicality, Duerksen and Dyrness contend that Christian ideologies and practices reflect the prevailing contexts from which they emerge.

[W]e believe that the church of Christ has always reflected its social and cultural setting; it has read Scripture in terms of its cultural assumptions about community and human goods. This had led to a wide variety of possible social forms that, we believe, should be seen not as a cause of painful division as has too often been the case but as a potential basis for mutual learning.
(2019:ix)

This means that our social and cultural embeddings significantly shape our reading of Scripture – what we find interesting, meaningful and valuable. As in the case of *tvaibongkum*, Western readers may skim over Moses' bowing before Jethro, his father-in-law who is the Midianite priest, but for the Khmer, this stands out because it is an existential reality for them. Duerksen and Dyrness further argue that the reading of Scripture, the methods of theologising, and the construction of Church and practices throughout Church history have revolved around reverse hermeneutics (2019:27–58). So, rather than denying and obscuring the subjectivities in the hermeneutical project, Duerksen and Dyrness advocate a reverse hermeneutic in which Bible readers 'use the values and insights of culture to illuminate aspects of Scripture' (2019:28).

And, when people of different cultures read Scripture together, what Wrogemann terms 'intercultural hermeneutic' occurs (2016), in which readers mutually unmute hidden dimensions of biblical interpretation, and in so doing, enlarge and enrich the global Church's understandings of God and his ways. In cross-cultural mission contexts, doing intercultural hermeneutic also produces what Hiebert envisions as a 'double conversion' – a transformation of the Other as well as the missionary (2008:321).[16] 'As we read the Scriptures with our Christian sisters and brothers in other cultures, we see its truth through new eyes' and uncover 'our own cultural biases that distort our understandings of the gospel' (Hiebert and Meneses 1995:375). Unmuting the cultural Other is not taking a step back and leaving the Other to study and interpret Scripture on their own. Rather, it is a collaborative endeavour in which

---

16 This is similar in ethos to the 'double movement' expounded by Pope John Paul II in the *Salvorum Apostoli* (Collins 2007:139–40).

people of different cultural and theological perspectives can come to the table and co-construct meaning in the creative tension of our differences. Instead of insisting on one's own biblical interpretation over another and creating dissension, the vision of intercultural theologising may help us – disciples of Christ – to be an answer to our Lord's prayer that 'all [of us] may be one . . . brought to complete unity' (John 17:20–3).

# 11

# Unmuting cultural practices in conversion

## USHA REIFSNIDER

Raksha and I are in her rented upper floor rooms of a semi-detached house in north London. We are both in the kitchen when our eyes are drawn to the street below. We lean over the sink to get a better view. Cars are arriving. First, we see women pour out into the street, dressed in beautiful *saris*; then little girls in bright *sharwal kamees* or *lengha*; men in fine suits or traditional *sherwani* or *kurta* paired with designer jeans. We peer out of the window further then look at each other. Raksha is wearing mismatched fluffy pyjamas and I am in my husband's old oversized grey T-shirt that bears the words, 'Every Tribe, Every Tongue, Every Nation.' Diwali morning and we are alone. Here we are, far from our family, unfamiliar with our mother tongue and somewhat deracinated.

Back to the bustle outside, people greet one another. Some are carrying packages of *gungra* and different types of *mithai*, the traditional sweets for Diwali. An older woman adjusts the sari of a younger one. The teenage girls huddle together and look at each other's saris, adjust a pleat here, stretching their hands through the flowing piece of fabric over the shoulder. Teenage boys step back and allow the elders to pass by into the house first. 'Selfies' are clicked. Cheeks are pinched. Kisses are shared as babies are passed from hip to hip. As some disappear into the house, others arrive, and the scene continues. We look again and point out various colours and styles of clothing. Slowly the crowd, oblivious of our voyeurism, vanishes into the house. We take a couple of *gungra* from the fridge and heat them up in the microwave. As British Gujarati Christian converts, this was as close as we might ever get to celebrating Diwali.

This story comes from the moment I realised how much of my life before conversion had been repressed. I had never taken time to dare to think what it was to turn my back on my whole family and culture in order to follow Jesus according to what I believed were the expectations of life of the convert from Hinduism to Christianity. At this moment, I recognised I had spent over forty-five years of my life with a narrowed Christian experience that had been defined for me through someone else's even more limited understanding of my life than my own. Until one October morning in 2016, I had never considered the idea of the impact of decades of being isolated from my family, community, language, food, dress and so many cultural aspects.

Muting in this chapter, and to a greater or lesser extent in this volume, refers to a set of limitations imposed sometimes inadvertently by the culture within the Western Evangelical context. The leaders within possess position and authority to represent from a tradition of cultural hierarchy. The voice of perceived authority is upheld, reinforced and perpetuated as those who are represented are considered unable to express for themselves in a way deemed acceptable to those who carry the highest influence.

The Old and New Testaments both provide examples of the benefits of audible expression that has been muted. 'Whoever derides their neighbour has no sense, but the one who understands holds their tongue' (Prov. 11:12). The sense of holding a neighbour's narrative as valuable at the expense of speaking oneself brings to mind the sense of shared living within close community where the marginalised are welcome to speak out loud.

In the New Testament, the works of Jesus are spoken of by those who witness his life and ministry. 'People were overwhelmed by amazement. "He has done everything well," they said. "He even makes the deaf hear and the mute speak"' (Mark 7:37). There is a spiritual dimension to the physical miracles of healing vision and healing, which are an analogous part of the revelation of the gospel to humankind. Thus, the realisation of the work of Jesus restores our capacity to speak to and be heard by God as our Father and releases the limitations imposed upon us through our sinful nature.

The apostle Paul also reminds us of a further condition of being part of the body of Christ that comes from hearing Christ, and accepting his ways, which enables us to have a new attitude in our minds. As a result, we are encouraged, 'Therefore each of you must put off falsehood and speak truthfully to your neighbour, for we are all members of one body' (Eph. 4:25). Looking at the analogy of the body, we must engage with the idea that a physical body is always changing, being renewed and growing. Similarly, the body of Christ is not a fixed entity. New believers from different cultures bring new ideas and experiences that become part of the body of Christ. Those within may experience changes of ideas and interaction with differences as an ongoing benefit of being a part of the body of Christ.

The Ardeners who developed Muted Group Theory (MGT) for explaining misogyny and sexism in the 1970s use the terms dominant and subordinate groups. The dominant group is not necessarily the majority group, but their authority holds more weight due to the standards they themselves set for the subordinate groups. In that sense, this chapter must delve into the roles of victim and perpetrator, but at the same time, it purposefully investigates and interrogates intentions and outcomes. West and Turner offer four responses to contravene the process of muting. Applied in the Evangelical context, the first of these is to identify or name the action that mutes as being derived from the positional perspective of Western cultural Christianity. Second, to reclaim or restore the redeemed customs of the cultural background of the convert. Third, to promote the value of pre-conversion cultural heritage and practices. Fourth and finally, to honourably observe and (in the case of conversion) celebrate with the convert, on their terms, without a hidden agenda. It is to simply acknowledge that the problem creates a victim and perpetrator division within which there would always remain an impasse.

Part of the difficulty in this chapter comes from the use of specific terminology. There must therefore be an unmuting of the terms 'dominant', 'subordinate', 'power'. After all, I am speaking as a fellow Christian, but critiquing the prevailing patterns of Church leadership authorities that may be considered a precarious act of a rebellious nature. However, muting is not merely vocal.

In the conversion experience, muting is a cutting off, extraction or diminishment from the pre-conversion self and everyone and everything in it with extreme consequences. The excerpt that opens this chapter reveals that the muting process is not necessarily limited to the physical space of inside a church, or through being in the presence of Western

Evangelical Christians. The muting process is conditioned within the converts as a part of the reinforcement of turning away from a sinful life of pre-Christian identity to be a new creation in Christ. For example, the life of the convert most often becomes regulated by weekly attendance at Sunday church services. The format of the programme falls within a pattern of prayers, sung worship and a sermon or talk, along with an encouragement to interact with other congregants after the formal part of the service for light refreshments. During the week, there may be Bible studies held at the church or in the homes of lay leaders.

The focus on attendance at Christian gatherings serves to shape or enculturate the new convert into Christian life, habits and relationships. An oft-repeated message in Evangelical Christian settings is, 'Christianity is not a religion, but a relationship with Jesus.' However, the relationship with Jesus is curated through the habitual patterns of interaction with those present at church. The process of cultural adaptation has an expectancy of assimilation to the new belief system with the hope of merging the convert fully into the Evangelical church 'family'.

The sharing of appropriate behaviour and thinking is to encourage the convert to conform. This is done through the weekly sermons and Bible studies with a focus on turning the converts away from their former religious beliefs and habits and replacing them in their entirety with the ones taught by seasoned Western Evangelical Christians. This incorporation of converts seeks to modify their cultural patterns, with the dominant culture within the church having the stronger influence. Inadvertently, standardisation and integration into the Christian community subject the convert to marginalisation and separation from their culture and community of origin, but at the same time from the new Christian community, resulting in them being culturally peripheral or extracted from both groups.

The impact of cultural extraction upon the convert has been discussed from the perspective of the leaders within the Church speaking on behalf of the convert and also the convert who speaks from their assimilated position in the Western Church on behalf of groups of converts from multiple non-Western religious faiths. This chapter aims to interact with their real-life experiences through glimpses into the lived experiences of the convert.

During my research on converts from Hinduism, my first port of call was to a number of Evangelical churches located in close proximity to South Asian communities. The pastors and lay leaders I met generally referred to their multi-ethnic congregations as 'multicultural', as there was a combination of people with a variety of skin tones and different English accents. Their church 'culture' as a combination of Western ideas, customs and social behaviour was welcoming to all, but distinctly monocultural in terms of hospitality, the relationships beyond church services, and emotional and spiritual support, which did not meet the needs of the non-Western Christian.

Enclosed in this setting, the complicated lived experiences of converts among family and community did not include the engagement and support of the Christian 'family' in terms of how family support systems function among those from non-Western backgrounds. Some church leaders knew of the difficulties of converts from Islam, but the converts and leaders acknowledged they were unable to engage in appropriate discussion and support.

Within the church setting, accessing the conversion stories that were shared during baptism were most common, but there was little information on the lived experiences and challenges of conversion that were not directly related to church life. The majority of the leaders were not sure of the family name or any details beyond the regular attendance at various activities.

I recognised my error in understanding the position and responsibility of the church leadership in cross-cultural interaction. It was not a lack of interest, but perhaps a combination of first, a lack of engagement with non-Westerners outside of the goal of evangelism; second, a lack of training and teaching of how proselytism and conversion are viewed through the tenets of other faiths; and third and finally, the engagement of the leadership with conversion stories simply to use for affirming Christian pre-eminence.

Many conversion stories contain pain and suffering that the Westernised leaders may not understand, but have a strong desire to fix or own vicariously, rather than learning to walk alongside the convert beyond the confines of the church building. In this sense, the leader, teacher and more experienced Christian is simultaneously muting the convert, and acknowledging that their understanding is incomplete. I became aware that I had looked for expertise on my conversion in the wrong places and needed to be with converts who would trust me with their stories. Arguably, the responsibility of communication is on both; however, the willingness and desire to hear from those whose lives are affected is on those who lead. Leaders have the more powerful and accepted voice among the more homogeneous group whom they represent.

The individual conversion stories from those of other faith backgrounds are often exciting presentations in the Evangelical Church tradition of the sharing of the 'testimony' that is based on the extreme opposites on the pre-conversion and post-conversion experiences. Converts are expected to demonise or at the very least distance themselves not only from the old belief system, but also any aspects that might compete with the new religious identity. This expectation is valuable in providing a contrast to validate not just the gospel, but the intrinsic higher value of Western forms of Evangelical Christianity.

Moves toward understanding the cultural contextual approaches to evangelism and discipleship were recognised and created by Western Evangelical Christians and also those converts who had gained something of an acceptance with the majority group. Approaches to evangelistic techniques are genuine attempts to 'give voice' to converts' cultures of origin for bridge-building, but most often with the purpose of evangelism.

There is a tendency for Western Evangelical Christians to create programmes using contextual approaches with some input from converts who appear to have successfully integrated into the Western Church space. Many of the converts find themselves glad to be able to contribute, but remain reserved in offering criticism. After all, the version of Christianity that we are all steeped in is from a perspective that positions the voice, intellect and indeed spiritual authority of the Western world above all other. Inadvertently, the postcolonial perspective continues to maintain, affirm and propagate an interpretation of Evangelical Christianity.

Many of the non-Western converts who are critical of contextualisation are those who are still sacrificing family relationships, friends, communities, jobs and inheritance and wear their sufferings as a badge of honour, having made peace with the extraction process as part of their sacrificial lifestyle. Often their experiences of suffering earn them a great deal of respect among the majority Western population, but not necessarily influence in the overall gradual adjustments of Church cultural practices. Converts seem to be perceived and treated as those to whom mission is 'done' and yet in some ways simultaneously honoured, pitied and kept at a distance. Within a monocultural fixed Church there are sometimes cultural practices that may be outdated. Contextualisation is an attempt to adjust and make relevant those outmoded practices. However, the shifts are posited and represented, based on what the Western culturally positioned experts deem as appropriate.

## Giving 'voice'

By examining the very basic definitions of what it means to be an Evangelical Christian, as based on the crucifixion, the Bible, and conversion and as demonstrated by active expression (Bebbington 1989), Western cultural expression can be seen as ultimately unnecessary to those from the Majority World, but partially necessary in their interactions with the Western Church, wherever the Western Church model may have been replicated. More and more Western Evangelicals are becoming aware that their culture has shaped Christianity for the rest of the world. In an attempt to address Western culture as the only vehicle or normative for Evangelical Christianity, there are various attempts to implement the idea of contextual Christian practices. The deliberate effort for leaders with a strong Western perspective to understand and appreciate the cultural practices of Majority World Christians has been presented through the translation of discipleship materials, hymns and songs into multiple languages. Furthermore, the inclusion of nationals in linguistic and cultural translation reveals a broadening of the Western Evangelical's ability and desire to include the pre-conversion culture.

Another attempt to create new practices is often through Western Evangelicals who have personal experience through visits to the Majority World and are therefore considered by the Church leadership to have a level of expertise of a non-Western culture. This is often through overseas mission experience of varied lengths of time. Overseas missionaries have a tendency to disciple new converts through and partially to their own Western culture whether deliberately or not. Often, they label their techniques as purely biblical. This suggests that all that is taught is entirely biblical and the cultural perspective of the teacher is completely without bias. Whatever is taught is biblical and whatever is not taught is at best irrelevant, but perhaps at worst 'heathen' or 'pagan' and must therefore be eliminated in its entirety.

Regardless of the amount of time missionaries have spent in a nation, it is impossible to comprehend the entire culture or the life experiences of a convert from a non-Western background. The Westerners gain a familiarity with that culture and build strong relationships with the converts who have absorbed the Western culture and have become accustomed to and perhaps unwittingly, accepted their own cultural knowledge as less relevant to Christianity than that of the Westerners.

At this point it is worth noting that convert voices are inclined to appear less significant and are filtered through what is inadvertently deemed relevant by the missionary. Even though this may not be necessarily deliberate, the natural inclination is towards the familiar. The dominant voice also takes higher agency and therefore picks and chooses what appeals as relevant, thus perpetuating a view in terms of what may be interesting and exotic enough to provide the necessary cultural overlaps. This gives the subordinate the limited ability to articulate (or at least be visible) by being 'muted but engaged' (Mears, Torres et al. 2004:4–27). Arguably thus, there are two other possibilities. These are first, to accept the limitations of engagement and inclusion that the prevailing culture offers or second, to remain muted and be (sometimes silently) angrily disengaged.

Western Evangelicals may attempt to unmute and be aware of some of the difficulties of separation of converts from their culture of origin and try to provide a contextual approach to engage with foreign cultural activities. Contextual celebrations of festivals such as Diwali provide a show of inclusion of the convert culture, but at the same time are used for the purpose of perpetuating the core of Evangelical beliefs of biblicism, crucicentrism, activism and conversion from the dominant standpoint. The following is an illustration of a contextualised Diwali celebration.

In describing this event, I must reiterate my position that on this occasion I was there as a researcher primarily, but also as a convert. Additionally, I had prior knowledge of all the groups involved and significant interaction with the Evangelical Church culture in the form of my postgraduate degree in Theology and my experience in Christian leadership, as well as cultural and linguistic advantages.

At this event, the Western Evangelical Christians operated with the correct understanding that British Gujarati Hinduism was expressed in English, especially by those who were beyond 1.5 generation diaspora.[1] The event was located in the British Evangelical Church framework, but at the same time, it revealed an intentional scattering of religio-cultural expression. The approach of drawing upon the Diwali season and the use of the term 'celebration' was a way to access British Gujarati people whom the church sought to influence towards conversion to Christianity.

Three of the groups involved in planning the event were churches interested in the conversion and discipleship of Hindus to Evangelical Christianity. Two groups were South Asian Christian groups who had an interest in converts' religio-cultural practices and the interaction between their communities, and the conversion of Hindus in Britain and India. The last group was from a Bible college that specialised in training Evangelical Christians for Evangelical Churches and foreign mission vocations.

There were walk-through displays of Bible scenes using Indian artefacts, but nothing that could be connected to Hindu religious practices. A few Indian snacks and sweets and some soft drinks were provided as refreshments. Approximately eighty people were present, but there was a conspicuous absence of children and families. The presentations were mostly in English without the use of translators except during the Bible readings. An icon of Jesus was displayed by projector. The music leader instructed everyone to focus on this picture of a Western White Caucasian man. His distinctive White Caucasian features were in modern art form and coloured in blue, yellow, green and orange blocks. The sacred worship

---

1  The terminology for defining different generations of diaspora refers to first generation as those individuals who leave their country of origin from adolescence to adulthood. Children from the primary school age to pre-adolescence are considered the 1.5 generation. Non-verbal infants and children born in the host country are referred to as the second generation. See Rumbaut (2004).

using song was rendered embarrassingly devoid of any spiritual, cultural or linguistic value by the fact that a White British woman was attempting to sing in Hindi. Her pronunciation of Hindi was exceptionally poor. Her heavy English accent rendered the lyrics of the songs untranslatable and incomprehensible. The event bore all the characteristics of a church service aimed at children, especially as we were sitting on the floor. All of those present seemed to know each other. I met three Hindu people who were invited by friends or family who were converts. They were respectful in that they had been invited to a church as guests.

The event was purposed by Evangelical leaders as a culturally appealing opportunity to make a connection between Evangelical Christianity and what they perceived as appropriate engagement with Hindu religio-cultural practices. However, those for whom the event was organised engaged in a way that they believed was expected of them by polite attendance and appropriate, but awkward engagement.

The contextual approach was an acknowledgement of the limitation of the British Evangelical Christians' comprehension. Beyond inviting friends, the event lacked real participation by those for whom the event was intended. Rather than a celebration, the event felt like a poorly disguised attempt to convert Hindus to Christianity. The converts who attended were ingratiating, thus muted, but engaged. This is evident in that most of the converts were not accompanied by family or friends. Those in attendance came out of a sense of duty to those who organised the event. The majority of the converts who had been invited did not attend and thus remained disengaged. The Western Evangelicals had a specific group agenda based primarily on their wish to influence Hindus towards conversion, which is not necessarily wrong, but is at best misleading. Furthermore, it creates both a deceptive motive and a poor replica in the way in which converts are expected to celebrate.

The invitation that was created to publicise the event reveals the influences of the dominant group's agency and power. First, the colour black is not generally used in any South Asian religio-cultural celebration. Second, the inclusion of clear biblical references to Jesus as the returning bridegroom has no relevance to Diwali. Third, the term 'celebration' evokes expectations of happiness, merriment and joyful interaction with others. Fourth, the offer to explore and reflect is contrary to the idea of Diwali celebration. Fifth and finally, I felt insulted, cheated and diminished, not just as a convert, but as a person with a place, a history and a life that was being articulated for me by someone else, using what they concluded would be to my benefit.

The term 'Rice Christian' came to mind. This refers to converts to Christianity who, rather than responding to personal conviction, convert for food, education or other benefits. However, on this occasion of a Diwali celebration, the lure for the converts appeared to be the prospect of social respect and value among the Western Christians. This was by appropriating the converts' pre-conversion life experiences, regarding them as deeply significant and meaningful in building family and community relationships within the Western Christian arena. In my desperation to find a place of celebration, affirmation and belonging, I personally perceived the lack of respect that Western Evangelical Christianity had for me as a human being and the depth of suffering that families of converts experience.

This shows evidence of my own interaction with Western Evangelical leadership as a convert. I felt compelled to engage with the expectation of those with higher influence within a hierarchical group by complying to their expectations of my faith and cultural expression. The 'presentation' was actually an act of activism (as part of the Bebbington Quadrilateral) in an attempt to evangelise the friends and family members of the converts. It arguably cuts off avenues of inquiry by a subordinate group of British Gujarati Hindus by the dominant group by attempting to provide answers to questions that have not been asked.

On this occasion, and many like it, the idea of 'giving voice' is then revealed as little more than the prevailing group controlling the convert group's expressions of faith and consideration of the claims of Christianity by actively reinforcing their silence.

# Reclaiming, elevating and celebrating subordinate culture

The following demonstrates an alternative to external contextual perspectives. It illustrates a rare example of celebrating the culture of the converts with greater involvement from the converts. I use the term 'rare' as the majority of converts have become accustomed to the polarising of pre- and post-conversion performances. They mostly engage with Western Evangelical Christianity and are sometimes reluctant to challenge the cultural hierarchy within their context or feel guilty for doing so.

A year after the pandemic, a north London church continued to broadcast their services online. On occasion, I joined the church service remotely from my room in Oxford. On this particular Sunday, the small hall seemed unusually crowded. I tried to spot my friend Raksha, but I noticed there were many faces of people I would not usually associate with the convert community whom I had met during my research. The women were in colourful *saris* looking for friends and saving seats, and there were giggling girls of all ages, some in pretty party dresses or sparkly *sharwal kamees* and such lovely *lengha*! Young men were dressed in jeans or khaki trousers and a baseball hat paired with a *kurta* or a sports T-shirt. As the crowd settled down and the announcements were made, I realised it was Diwali. The unstable internet connection blurred the faces of individuals, so it was hard to differentiate Raksha, Rani, Mohan, Vina, my custom-made convert family, from their friends and family members. A young woman I recognised from my field visits stood up and shared the story of Diwali.

> Ram travelled through many dangerous dark places to rescue his wife Sita who had been kidnapped by an evil king. After defeating the king, the people set *diva* outside their homes to light the way back for the heroic couple. Light overcomes the darkness and shows us the way.

Someone had made a beautiful *rangoli*, a colourful piece of art used to decorate the floor at the entrance of a building during celebrations. Templates were used and were heavily dusted with vibrantly coloured powder. Every shift of the templates created more designs in a multitude of colours. Layer after layer of templates and colours created unique designs that, despite their breathtaking beauty, were eventually smudged by trampling feet and washed away in the next rainfall.

As the presentations ended, the chairs were moved back and some people disappeared to prepare the shared meal. Everyone else prepared for *garba,* the traditional dance of Diwali. The electric keyboard struck a chord and Sunita Darji took the handheld microphone and began the call and repeat style of *Prabhu Isu bhajan.*

In their north London church, the converts decided to celebrate Diwali, but chose to refer to it by the English translation as 'The Festival of Light'. With their pre- and post-Christian cultural and linguistic knowledge, they were familiar with the fact that the dominant group's language in the church favoured the use of the term 'light'. The overlaps with biblical terminology with the correlation of Jesus as the 'Light of the world' thus provided a strong connection with the language of biblicism and crucicentrism. They also invited their friends and family regardless of their cultural self-identity as Hindu, thus satisfying the two other aspects of activism and conversion in the Bebbington Quadrilateral.

Simultaneously, the converts incorporated the aspects of the Diwali celebration that were meaningful to their culture, such as the use of vibrant colours, multigenerational participants, mingling and interacting with friends and family through shared food, activities that involved the children replicating practices of singing and dancing that were shared among all.

# Subtle overlapping issues of influence

The function of influential positioning within the Western Evangelical Church may not necessarily be intentional in its representation of cultural expression. However, it is not necessarily intentional in honest and equal engagement with converts' cultural background and lived experiences. The Evangelical agenda in engaging with Hindus at the church during Diwali was for the purpose of conversion. The role of the converts at the Western Evangelical Church celebration of Diwali did not treat them as equals, but as those for whom ministry was being done, not those whom they do ministry alongside.

The first attempt at the Diwali celebration in the church was regulated by the prevailing Western Church leadership structure. It upheld and reinforced the terms of the gathering and perspective and used its expertise to define Diwali for and on behalf of the converts. In turn, those present accepted what was offered as secondary or less significant out of a sense of loyalty to the church structure and appreciation for the attempt out of politeness. This also revealed the lack of recognition of the value of their own historical cultural experiences and thus revealed a lack of self-respect or a self-muting. The converts' diminished position was thus reinforced as the points of reference were created and flowed from the more dominant, influential group toward the convert group.

It would be naïve to presume that the second celebration was totally directed by the converts. In fact, the same person created the publicity for both celebrations. However, the time between the two events had brought an adjustment in the approach by the member of the influential leadership group. Her interaction increased through living among the converts group and taking the posture of observer and learner of the converts' culture and this had altered her understanding of the value of her prevailing cultural position.

Creating on behalf of subordinate culture from a position of dominance puts the responsibility of success and failure in one arena, thus polarising the practice of authority. The exchange of culture through interaction provides a flexible interchange, within which cultural contributions can occur in fresh ways.

The influential position of the dominant group culture, and the subordinate convert group's conscious and subconscious acceptance of their positions and representation may be perceived as either completely valid or sufficient to register in a way that may be positionally perceived as unnecessarily insensitive. Unmuting may require extra steps between the thought being conceived, verbally expressed and action being taken. I find this useful in terms of how words like 'celebrate' or 'family' need an active involvement, a performance so that the conception of the thought connects with different experiences depending upon cultural context. This would require a certain flexibility in how the dominant groups in their intellectual and cultural space might accept the expertise of the subordinate.

Arguably, the level of acceptance and respect is a matter of continued adjustment. The converts must use the appropriate language and cultural knowledge of the influential group to explain and teach without fear of ridicule, shame or judgement. Simultaneously, the converts must maintain their position in their pre-conversion cultural community as a member who is attempting to bridge the gap. Without becoming isolated, marginalised or considered the sole expert, the convert must function within and between both groups and recognise the limitations of their own positions and capacity to represent.

# Conclusion

In this chapter, I have given some insight into MGT and used it to analyse a specific aspect of the practical issues experienced by Hindus in Britain who convert to Christianity. I have provided an example of attempts to broaden the cultural knowledge and experience from within the Evangelical context. The result of the endeavour has demonstrated the challenges of the dominant group in drawing upon what they perceive to be the pertinent issues of British Gujarati culture while maintaining the structural belief system of Evangelical Christianity based upon the Bebbington Quadrilateral.

By way of comparison, I provided an alternative approach that relied upon British Gujarati Christians broadening the interaction between Evangelical Christian culture and the British Gujarati Hindu culture. The second attempt was within the dominant setting of the Evangelical Christian community and provided a creative tension between British Gujarati religio-cultural tradition and the Bebbington Quadrilateral. By using the image of light overcoming darkness and using the Gujarati language for singing and reading the Bible, aspects of conversion, activism, crucicentrism and biblicism were satisfied. Simultaneously, the idea of a festive celebration with food, friendship, music and dance satisfied the British Gujarati religio-cultural tradition.

A specific culture may be identified and defined differently depending on positional perspective in relation to dominance. The subordinate who is a part of the dominant culture is constantly adjusting and, if appropriately engaged in overlapping communities, may be able to contribute to the overall culture in both groups. Definitions and identifications may rely on categorisation, but it is the individual's deliberated actions from within that form and reform the culture. It is the recurring question within MGT of the subordinate group. They must resolve how to use the dominant language or what speaks for whom and how that affects personal practices in multifaceted living (Barkman 2018:6).

The problem of representation by the dominant on behalf of the subordinate is that it is based on verification of a fixed position of expertise that is sometimes based upon a hierarchical level based upon those within the same group. Therefore, misrepresentation is far more likely to occur, but less likely to be addressed and becomes fixed, thus leading to the development of a structured subculture that becomes harder to adjust even though the motive and the end result are less than desired.

What mutes Majority World converts from other faiths are its members' claims to participate in social life considered irrelevant by the dominant group. The subordinate groups that accept the dominant voice affirm their disengagement and support the belief that they are not entitled nor qualified to choose to interpret and define their Evangelical Christian practices for themselves. This results in a diminished sense of Christian identity and self-esteem that results in individuals who struggle to have a positive social identity as a subordinate group member while surrounded by the dominant power structures who then have the positional power to represent the subordinate group.

The purpose of MGT in the Evangelical Christian context is not to identify victims and perpetrators and therefore stifle any attempts to change. Rather, the purpose of applying MGT within the Western Evangelical Christian contexts is to discuss and resolve power disparities that lead to marginalisation. Opening discussions between dominant and subordinate groups provides opportunities for ongoing interactions that bring ongoing corrective action, thus fostering a flexibility of cultural belonging for all concerned.

# 12

# Reverse mission and climate justice: unmuting an African theological response

ISRAEL OLUWOLE OLOFINJANA

We have become used to hearing of extreme weather conditions in the Majority World. Extreme weather incidents in Britain make the news more and more often and the conversation has become more prevalent in recent years. There is no doubt the issue of climate change is global. There is now a general acceptance in media reports on the devastation of communities in extreme weather incidents in the Caribbean, Asia and Africa. However, despite this, African voices are still silent or muted in climate discussions.

This chapter will therefore focus on climate justice from an African perspective, offering two theological concepts that can develop African agency on climate justice. It will discuss reverse mission and whether concerns around climate justice are an integral part of the mission strategy of African reverse missionaries. We have so many flavours of African churches planted across the UK. Many of these churches have an aspiration to reach out to multicultural British society, but despite this ambition, the reality is that due to lack of engagement with the public about concerns such as the climate crisis, African reverse mission is limited.

Reverse mission is limited because it is very strong on church planting, evangelism, discipleship, renewal, and the provisions of social welfare and the meeting of needs, but it is still weak on tackling structural issues such as racial injustice and climate injustice. If reverse mission is going to engage these structural issues, it has to develop a public theology that can unmute African voices, thereby enabling African Christians in the diaspora to contribute uniquely to the climate conversation. What theological perspectives can African public theology contribute to the discourse on climate justice? This is the crucial question of this essay.

Before proceeding, here is a clarification on how I am using the term, 'reverse mission'. Reverse mission is one of the mission strategies that Africans have employed in carrying out God's mission in the West; therefore, it is understood as a divine strategy to establish or usher in God's kingdom in the West. This is not to say that God's kingdom is not already present, but that the migration of Majority World Christians brings a missiological significance in terms of God's multi-ethnic kingdom (Olofinjana 2022). Another term I am using in this chapter is 'climate justice', as opposed to creation care. This is because, as shall be made clearer in the discussions below, creation care lends itself to care for the planet only. However, climate justice thinks about the people, especially people of colour. The language of creation care panders to green theology, while climate justice engages Brown theology.

## Reverse mission and public theology

The idea of reverse mission lends itself to reconceiving Britain and the Western hemisphere as a mission field. Formerly, this was not the case because missionaries went from Europe to the rest of the world because the Majority World (Asia, Africa, Latin America and Oceania) was defined as the mission field. The shift in the heart of Christianity from the North to the South in terms of the accelerated growth in the South while declining in the North, has also facilitated the sending of missionaries from the Majority World into Europe and North America. But is reverse mission problematic because of the name or because it is not really happening in reality? In addition, what is or should be the goal of reverse mission?

There are different ways that African scholars have spoken about reverse mission. For example, Dr Harvey Kwiyani will talk about reverse mission in the context of 'Blessed Reflex', that is, an idea and vision that mission thinkers in the West have about a time when Africans and other

Christians from the so-called young churches will be a blessing one day to global mission (Kwiyani 2014:11–12). Kwiyani altogether prefers that we label what the African mission enterprise does as mission because of our current understanding of mission as polycentric.

Polycentric missiology is usually expressed in terms of mission now from everyone to everywhere (Yeh 2016). Another friend of mine, Professor Babatunde Adedibu, who leads the Redeemed Christian Church of God (RCCG) theological institution in Nigeria, describes reverse mission as putting religion back in the public square in a postmodern, secular British society that somehow relegates faith to a private affair (Adedibu 2012). In essence, reverse mission is conceived of in terms of religious presence that challenges aggressive secularism. Lastly, my friend, Dr Girma Bishaw, who leads the Gratitude Initiative, believes that in order to have a constructive conversation around difficult issues in society such as racism, we need to start or enter the conversation from a positive context. He therefore promotes gratitude as a helpful framework to aid mission and societal transformation (Gratitude Initiative n.d.). Gratitude therefore offers us another unique way of constructing African mission in Britain.

Returning to some of the problems attached to reverse mission, some found the term problematic because it could sound as though the original mission is European, but reversing it – which sounds inferior – is African, Asian or Latin American. Also, how do we assess the role of African Caribbean and African American missionaries who were part of the modern missionary movement who went to Africa and other parts of the world? How do we define the work and contributions of people like Thomas Lewis Johnson (1836–1921) who went to serve as a Baptist Missionary Society (BMS) missionary in Cameroon? Or that of his contemporaries, Joseph Jackson Fuller (1825–1908), a missionary to the island of Fernando Po on the coast of West Africa and Dr Theophilus Scholes (c. 1858–c. 1940), a medical missionary in the Congo? To make this even more complicated, how do we define the theological contributions of St Hadrian who migrated as a refugee from north Africa first to Italy and then to Canterbury (AD 637–710) and who reformed the liturgy and rites of the English Church? His ministry was at the start of the medieval period!

All of these examples attest to the fact that people of African ancestry have been involved in mission for more than a few years. I have not even mentioned the fact that many of the early Church Fathers were Africans and Asians and that their theological output has shaped the contours of both Western and Eastern Christianity for centuries. But despite this, I think reverse mission brings a postcolonial critique to our mission enterprise because it probes who are today's missionaries and questions the centre of power in mission activity. One-way reverse mission displaces mission thinking in that refugees and asylum seekers from the Majority World are some of the missionaries in Europe. This disrupts our traditional thinking of who a missionary is, that is, someone who is well trained, equipped and sent by a respectable Church. But God in his wisdom through people on the move is using people from the Majority World as missionaries.

But my central concern, as stated in the introduction, is what types of reverse missionaries do we currently have and what new ones do we need to realise the goal of reverse mission? Is the goal of reverse mission to evangelise British people or it is to plant as many churches as possible all across the UK? I think the goal of reverse mission should be societal transformation that sees the gospel penetrating different spheres of our community. If this is going to happen, we have to engage public theology, which will enable us to better engage the public square. Currently, we have reverse missionaries who are evangelists. These reverse missionaries are those who variously proclaim the gospel on street corners, plant churches and engage in other evangelistic activities. There are also reverse missionaries who are prayer missionaries. They intercede for the nation with regard to renewal and change in the nation. These missionaries are very keen about revival. There are reverse missionaries who are marketplace workers. These are some of the Africans, Asians and Latin Americans in our churches who have their secular jobs, but who have a sense of calling to serve in our churches or through their vocations. Some of them are medical doctors, nurses, cleaners, clerks, administrators, and so on. There are also reverse missionaries who are theologians. These are the ones who teach in theological colleges, trying to diversify the curriculum and injecting into the curriculum subjects such as African Christianity, diaspora mission, the historical development of Black Majority Churches (BMCs) and World Christianity.

A major part of this work is developing theological training resourced by Majority World theologians who are resident in the UK. This is important in centring a polyphonic voice within British theological education. This is why the formation of Christ Theological College as an alternative college, with the majority of its faculty drawn from the Majority World,[1] is significant in the process of bringing a distinctively ministerial formation that can adapt to the changes in context. But are all these types of reverse missionaries enough to bring societal transformation or do we need new ones? I want to suggest that we need an additional kind of reverse missionaries who can help us imagine an integrated, just society, as well as help us address global issues such as the climate crisis. In order to do this, we need reverse missionaries who are public thinkers and theologians who can answer the public's questions on key cultural issues.

Public theology will enable the public witness of African reverse missionaries in this contested, postmodern, secular, post-secular British society. We therefore need African public theologians with prophetic imaginations and action who can engage with the public on issues such as racial injustice, climate crisis, mental health, the immigration system and the criminal justice system, to name a few. One important reason why we need reverse missionaries who can think publicly and actively lead on some of these issues is because some of these issues disproportionately affect people from the Majority World. For example, as will be discussed in this chapter, the climate crisis that we face, while it affects us all, impacts more countries in the Majority World. The floods in Pakistan and Nigeria in the early 2020s are examples of these.

Another reason why we need reverse missionaries who are public theologians is that God's mission has to be lived, proclaimed and demonstrated. We incarnate the gospel with our lifestyle, we proclaim the gospel through evangelism and social action, we demonstrate the gospel through signs and wonders, and political action. Reverse missionaries are very good in incarnating, proclaiming and demonstrating the gospel through signs and wonders, but are still lacking in terms of political action. Having African Christians in Britain who are public thinkers and theologians could help address this deficiency.

1  www.ctcollege.org.

# Reverse mission and the muteness of African voices

It is fair to say that African voices in Britain are muted with regard to discussions on climate justice; therefore, my own application of Muted Group Theory (MGT) is first to Africans, but in particular regarding how some of these voices are muted when it comes to the climate conversation. This chapter will therefore explore the reasons why their voices are muted and ask: When African voices are unmuted, what significant contributions can they make to the climate discourse?

What are the African theological perspectives that we can glean and learn from that can enrich this conversation on climate justice? The Majority World, including the Caribbean and African countries, are disproportionately impacted by the climate crisis, and they are usually the victims of the environmental crisis because they are in the Global South. There are other factors such as poverty, but there is also a legacy to this that we can see in the historical connection. There is a disproportionality in terms of how this affects and impacts the Majority World. Despite the fact that the Majority World is disproportionately impacted, the ambassadors and the voices that we hear when it comes to climate campaigns are usually White Westerners.

To give an example, there is a story of five young women activists, including Greta Thunberg, at a particular climate conference in Davos in 2020. All of them participated in a photo shoot. Four of the young climate activists were White and one was Black. The Black girl was Vanessa Nakate from Uganda, whose face was cropped out of the picture that was published by the Associated Press. Initially, when this hit the news, Vanessa's face was cropped out until there was an outcry from Vanessa and others. This incident is symbolic and illustrates how African voices are muted when it comes to the climate conversation. The question is, why was her face cropped out of this particular picture? The media responsible for the picture was putting it out into the public arena, but they didn't want the image of Vanessa to be seen. They only wanted the four white faces, not the black face!

The missiological significance in terms of unmuting the African reverse mission is to empower African Christians in the British context so that their voices can be heard in the eco-theological conversation. While Vanessa Nakate is not a British African, the story above sheds light on how Majority World voices are curated in climate campaigns and advocacy, not just for the Western world, but for the very people who are most impacted by the decisions that are made. Reverse missionaries can therefore bring the discussion into their networks that overlap geographically and culturally, thus reverberating between Africa and the Majority World to Europe and Europe back to the Majority World, and so on. But before I explore what theological perspectives Africans can contribute to the climate discourse, it is important to consider why their voices are muted. I want to consider four reasons why African Christian voices are muted in climate conversations. These are: the focus on evangelism and renewal, an eschatology from above, colonial approaches to the climate crisis and disintegrated historical narratives.

## Focus on evangelism and renewal

As discussed above, one of the strong emphases of reverse mission is that it focuses on evangelism and renewal as a key strategy to carrying out God's mission in the West. African churches are not short of evangelists who daily go out and preach on the streets of Britain. African churches also have many evangelists who are serving as church planters planting churches across the UK. While this is a good thing and reminds British Christians of the need to regain a confidence in articulating the gospel boldly, an understanding that the gospel is primarily expressed only through evangelism is problematic and mutes African voices when it comes to advocating for climate concerns.

A faulty hermeneutic that sees the gospel expressed through evangelism will consider climate justice concerns as political issues that the Church does not need to engage with or be involved in. If African Christian voices in the British diaspora are going to be unmuted, we therefore need African public theologians who can empower the African Church to read the biblical text in the light of a holistic understanding of the gospel. African political theology with a liberative hermeneutic will be relevant in this discussion. As articulated earlier, the gospel must be incarnated, expressed and demonstrated.

## An eschatology from above

A second reason why African Christians in Britain are silent on this subject is a continuation of the first in that it is another hermeneutical problem. This is in reading the biblical text in the light of a heavy pre-millennial thinking that focuses on the second coming of Jesus through the rapture theories. African Christians focus on eschatology and by consequence, evangelism placing more emphasis upon eternal life in heaven. In this respect, the theological understanding of one of the purposes of Christ's return was to create a new earth. The expectation of the Messiah's second coming to judge the world and in that discarding the old earth and creating a new version has somehow lent itself to some African Christians thinking why bother to care for this earth if it is going to be destroyed? If the coming judgement of this world also means the destruction of the cosmos and the recreation of the heavens and earth and a new Jerusalem, then what is all the fuss about creation care or the planet?

To unmute African Christian voices, we therefore need distinctly African public theologians. These are African thought leaders who are bringing practical theological reflection on public issues that impact Africans and other minorities on the continent of Africa, as well as in the diasporic contexts. They have the unique capacity to empower the African Church on the need for a responsible eschatology that holds together in tension the present reality of God's kingdom that focuses on lament and stewardship and the future dimension of God's kingdom that helps us to live in expectation and hope of the parousia. We must hold in tension the idea of God's future kingdom and that of his present kingdom. His present kingdom means we must continue to lament and fight for racial justice and climate justice, but also know that his future kingdom will be a reality one day.

## Colonial approaches to the climate crisis

The first two factors considered in the muteness of African Christian voices could be described as self-muteness because they relate to how the African Church hermeneutic has influenced and shaped how African Christians respond to the issue of climate justice. In this third factor, that is not the case because colonial approaches to the climate crisis have silenced African Christian voices on the subject. For example, one of the common terms used in the Western Church is the language of creation care. While this language is helpful to the Church and an average Christian in connecting the doctrine of creation to how this should shape and influence our activism on issues to do with the environment, it could also obscure some issues pertaining to how racial injustice intersects with climate injustice. As clarified in the introduction, this is why I am using the term climate justice. We must therefore recognise that our language for issues on the climate is filtered through a particular lens or, in this case, theology. Specifically, the prevailing language among the Western Christian population undergirds the term creation care with responsibility for God's people to take care of 'creation' as God's directive given in the book of Genesis. It is hard for some of us then not to gravitate toward distant reminiscences of ancient pictures of Adam and Eve deeply embedded in the mind as a White man and woman who care for all of creation. The prevailing image in our minds of creation care is therefore to return to those misty and mysterious memories of the perfection of creation carefully tended by White people.

If we are going to deconstruct this image, we need to consider other perspectives that can elucidate the creation story with new insights. This looking at creation theology from a Western perspective is different from a Christian who is from a Hindu background. For example, Usha Reifsnider's personal Hindu diaspora background contains a theology of ecology, expressed perhaps through the most well-known spiritual ideas in Jainism. The Jainism tradition of vegetarianism is furthered by their non-consumption of root vegetables where life forms invisible to the naked eye may inadvertently be killed. In the pre-colonial era, Jain migrants were known to travel with migrant merchants from India to the African continent, where they set up care systems for animals and insects, lest their trade with other nations led to exploitation of the inhabitants of the land. Nonetheless, the current discussions about preserving the planet are held within a particular language that favours the voice from the West, with the inclusion of the Majority World perspectives seemingly determined by others.

What could African cosmology and indigenous culture teach us about creation care, and how can African reverse missionaries harness this indigenous wisdom in a way that engages with the present significant theological discussions in Britain? In order to do this, African Christians have to bring along with them their African world views such that, while strongly diluted by Western interference due to their theological education and use of English as *lingua franca*, also include their various African and diaspora expressions of Christianity. In essence, African Christians must rediscover some of the indigenous wisdom in their culture and how that can help them to speak and advocate for concerns on climate justice.

Another problem with colonial approaches to climate justice is the current crisis around colonial conservation that sees some Western organisations moving indigenous people away from their inherited ancestral land all in the name of preserving wildlife species. Colonial conservation is the need to preserve land for animals on the verge of extinction, thereby taking land from the indigenous people in the name of conservation. This is one way in which the voices of Majority World people are silenced because conservationists with a Western perspective determine which area of land needs to be preserved for nature and wildlife. This is often done without considering the outcome of decisions upon the local populations. Decisions regarding their livelihood and economy are made by others. By comparison, what if a group of conservationists from Africa decided that areas of England should be set aside for the preservation of nature and wildlife, perhaps to increase the population of foxes that are a nuisance in some parts of Britain? African conservationists then displace people from their homes. They may even purchase the land, but they do not consider the residents who may have their own reasons to keep the land under the control of the indigenous English people.

## Disintegrated historical narratives

If colonial approaches to the climate conversations have muted African voices, dichotomised historical narratives have further alienated Africans from clearly seeing that this issue is one that has impacted them historically. Some Western schools of thought, in order to cascade the global contributions of the Industrial Revolution and empire, tend to separate this history from that of enslavement of Africans and their colonisation. These disintegrated historical narratives consider the history of the Industrial Revolution as a single entity. But today, there is more awareness that it is not possible to look at the history of the Industrial Revolution in isolation as it has to be viewed synoptically with the history of the slave trade and colonisation in Africa and elsewhere.

The transatlantic slave trade as a global economic system and institution prospered because of racial ideology that conceived Africans as objects and properties that needed to be dominated because they were inferior and not intelligent. Sometimes, Christian mission with its understanding that Africans were heathens and pagans that needed saving, colluded with colonial authorities to propagate the gospel. The transatlantic slave trade was also an integral part of the Industrial Revolution from the 1750s onwards. One of the first scholars to identify the links between racism and capitalism was Eric Williams (1911–81), the first prime minister of Trinidad and Tobago. Williams uncovered slavery's role at the heart of the Industrial Revolution. He states in his published doctoral thesis *Capitalism and Slavery* (2022:48):

> The triangular **trade** thereby gave a triple stimulus to British industry. The **enslaved** (my emphases) were purchased with British manufacturers; transported to the plantations, they produced sugar, cotton, indigo, molasses and other tropical products, the processing of which created new industries in England; while the maintenance of the Negroes and their owners on the plantations provided another market for British industry, New England agriculture and the Newfoundland fisheries. By 1750, there was hardly a trading or a manufacturing town in England which was not in some way connected with the triangular or direct colonial trade. The profits obtained provided one of the mainstreams of that accumulation of capital in England which financed the Industrial Revolution.

Williams's groundbreaking work was one of the first to integrate our thinking on slavery, colonialism and the Industrial Revolution. A further step I am identifying in this chapter is the link between racial injustice and climate injustice that is historically rooted in slavery, colonialism and the Industrial Revolution and which continues to shape current injustices around climate conversations.

# Reverse mission and the unmuting of African voices

If African Christian voices have been muted partly due to self-muteness and others silencing them, how can those voices be unmuted? First, African Christians must realise that they have a lot to contribute through African theological perspectives that can enable them to enter the conversation on climate justice. I want to propose two African theological frameworks that can empower the agency of African Christians in tackling the climate crisis. They are: the traditional African notion of God as the Creator and the sustainer of all things. The second is, an integrated world view of land, people, forest, sea and animals.

## Traditional African notion of God as Creator and sustainer

The first theological framework is seeking to infuse our understanding of creation care through an African understanding of God as Creator and sustainer of all things. The different West African names of God demonstrate and reveal that God is interested in his creation and has never abandoned it. This notion of God as the one who sustains creation challenges a Western rationalistic understanding of God abandoning his creation as articulated in Deism. This notion of God can also help us to develop a theology of creation that encourages our participation in caring for the environment. One of the striking features about African names for God is that several of them demonstrate God as the Creator of heaven and earth, but more importantly they evidence that he is involved in such a way that he continues to care for his creation. Biblical theology of creation affirms this as well because Scripture says, 'The earth is the LORD's, and everything in it, the world, and all who live in it' (Ps. 24:1). Some of the names take a further step to assert that God cares and sustains his creation. Take for example, the Edo name for God, *Osanobuwa*. This means, 'the Source Being who carries and sustains the universe'. Other African names for God, such as *Olodumare* (Yoruba),

*Ngewo* (Mendes), *Nyame* (Akan) and *Odomankoma* (Akan), all reveal that God really cares and is interested in maintaining the universe (Mbiti 1969; Awolalu and Dopamu 1979).

While African cosmology and world view is rich in an understanding that sees God as the Creator and carer of his creation, African Churches are somewhat disconnected from this narrative because of the colonial residue that sees everything to do with African religions and spirituality as evil. In looking at the African understanding of nature, the richness of the world view has been replaced by colonisation as it was considered animistic. Thus, Africans now hold the dominant influence of being saved from that by Western education and theology. The misconception is how Africans view their own world view. They have been told they are pagan. To be a Christian is to leave that. One of the consequences of this mental colonisation is the lack of engagement with climate justice issues. African Churches, in order to be unmuted, must therefore connect with their rich theological roots to give them the language to enter this conversation with a unique perspective.

## An integrated world view

The second theological framework is an integrated world view of land, people, forest, sea and animals. While there are specific geographic, ethnic, linguistic and spiritual characteristics among peoples in Africa, African religion in general is the indigenous faith and practice of African peoples, which is the product of their perception, encounter, reflection upon and experiences of the universe in which they live. Generally, the African world exists in two spheres – the visible, tangible, and concrete world of humans, animals, vegetation and other natural elements; and the invisible world of the spirits, ancestors, divinities and the supreme Deity. Yet it is one world, indivisible, with one sphere touching on the other (Tarusarira 2017:400). This shows that African religious beliefs are a prime source of guidance and support for most African people. African reverse missionaries therefore have the benefit of sifting through the gems of African world views and religions that speak about the vital union of all things. There are multiple variations of this holistic world view across Africa. For example, in traditional times in some parts of Ghana, people were forbidden from going fishing on Tuesdays, but the importance was the ecological impact. It is a way of preserving resources, similar to God instructing the people of Israel as part of their Jubilee celebrations to farm for six years and then let the land lie fallow in the seventh. Some of the African indigenous wisdom has now been lost due to colonisation and some being considered devil worship. There is an ongoing discussion on whether indigenous wisdom contributes to sustainable development, but that is beyond the scope of our present discussion.

We need African theologies that can help us sift through religious customs and world views to see what is applicable to caring for the environment. We need African public theologians to help unearth that. Brown theology therefore provides an opportunity to create a more integrated world view as theologians in the Majority World further discuss these issues. In making this case, it is important to start with a comparison between green and Brown theologies. Using the term 'Brown theology' sounds somewhat problematic. One could easily argue that theology does not have a colour. However, to unmute the African Christian context is to hear what is contained in the term 'Brown theology' and then determine its validity to those for whom the term holds meaning.

Brown theology is a postcolonial theology, in that it recognises the impact of colonialism and post-colonialism that contains within it a perceived objective theological perspective that does not recognise the relevance of the Majority World standpoint. Brown theology explicitly and implicitly offers a perspective from a proportion of the world that, though large, has little ability to influence mainstream Western theology. Brown eco-theology will further look at climate discussions and decisions that ought to also include the voices of those who are affected by the decisions made regarding ways to protect the most vulnerable communities and the resources of the planet.

On the other hand, green theology as defined by Button, is

A set of beliefs and concomitant lifestyle that stresses the importance of respect for the earth and all its inhabitants, using only what resources are necessary and appropriate, acknowledging the rights of all forms of life, and recognising that all that exists is part of one interconnected whole.
(Button 1988:190)

The terminology and structure of green theology may be broadly agreed upon by experts whose position is justified by others, the others being those who share the same physical, cultural and academic characteristics. However small this group may be, their influence permits them jurisdiction over the interpretation of theology for the vast majority of people without alternate ideas, experiences, culture or location being taken into consideration. The discussion is from a position that claims to represent a universalised structure of understanding and implementation of theology. Using this definition of green theology one might ask, who decides what resources are necessary or how they are appropriated? While stating that green theology is aware and considerate of all the inhabitants, what would the term 'respect' as used in the definition look like within the Brown eco-theological perspective? One of the main contentions with green theology today is the overemphasis on the conservation and preservation of green spaces, deserts and wildlife extinction almost at the exclusion of ecological degradation and exploitative economies of the West and its impact on people from the Majority World. Therefore, the way green theology is appropriated and practised by the Western world puts those who live in the Majority World at a disadvantage.

Another argument I have advanced in this respect in another article (Olofinjana 2022) highlights the gaps within the climate crisis structures that marginalise not just the voices of the subordinate groups, but also their lived experiences and their choices in how their future is realised. While a green theology from the West focuses on their perspective of what sustainability looks like, once again, it focuses on what is best for the planet from the Western perspective. In terms of sustainability, does the debate leave room for the right of sustenance for the Majority World? Are the Africans offered the same opportunities of access to education, personal fulfilment, social mobility and accumulation of wealth as the West?

While Brown theology does not claim objectivity, it brings to the forefront issues of sustainability, development and climate care that affect those groups who are living with the decisions made by those whose voices have dominance.

Care for the planet demands justice for all creation, without one perspective holding dominance. If people from the Majority World are going to experience justice, our language of creation care, which favours and incorporates a green theology, must be balanced with a Brown theology that integrates climate justice. This is why I prefer the language of climate justice and have attempted to foreground it here. On the one hand, creation care is not just for Christians. Those who are involved in the conversations include Christians, atheists, agnostics, scientists and politicians. However, it does seem that the dominant voices in these conversations come from the West. The anthropogenic nature of climate justice is undeniable, the impact of climate change and the decisions around solutions have a greater impact on those in the Majority World, but their voices are muted. Climate activists who campaign for justice are not only those who are scientists, politicians and businesspeople, but ordinary youngsters such as the Swedish activist, Greta Thunberg. So, while it seems the impact on the Majority World is greater, the response and ambassadors appear to be from the West. The problem is brown, but the solutions are white!

The response gets louder and louder from political leaders, NGOs and Christian organisations. But we must ask, who are the dominant voices in this public conversation?

# Engagement with secular Brown agenda: the case of Rose Musito

Having discussed climate justice from an African theological perspective, we now turn our attention to challenges from multiple geographical locations, but without the Christian theological lens, which perhaps has a tendency to position those of the Majority World through a Western hierarchical lens.

Rose M. Musito is a Kenyan energy researcher. Musito acknowledges the data-driven international plans to achieve the goal of zero carbon emissions. However, there is a massive gap in the data as it does not include the voices, needs, experiences, research or concerns of 1 billion African residents. 'Africa lacks good data, appropriate models and local technical expertise that are necessary to develop credible, actionable and equitable energy transition plans' (Musito 2022). I would argue that the global research community also reveals a lack of data as they have overlooked, dehumanised and chosen to ignore Brown ecology.

Musito gives a simple perspective that requires the attention and engagement of the dominant groups. She reveals that the combination of forty-eight nations in the continent of Africa produce less than 1% of carbon emissions. She states that the entire nation of Senegal uses less electricity than the residents of the state of California use playing video games. Additionally, while only 3% of Nigerians have air conditioners, gym users in New York are known to keep temperatures at 10 degrees, as exercising in cooler temperatures is believed to burn more fat.

Arguably, these disparities are grossly unjust, but the whole discussion of climate justice must be reframed. Energy-poor countries produce far fewer emissions per capita and also have unreliable power supplies, which limit the energy supporting the infrastructure. In other words, daily life, medical needs, business activities, and the production of food and other resources vastly compromise access to basic necessities.

Energy poverty as part of the subordinate group's reality is rarely discussed within dominant group language that includes 'environmental justice', but it suggests a limited perspective for whom or what benefits from the term. For the people of Africa, access to energy is directly related to the reduction of every aspect of poverty. However, the highest stakeholders do not fully comprehend or consider those who require access to energy.

While the wide disparities are not unknown by those who suffer the most, Africans do not have equal access to data within their own continent. This is due to the cost involved in accessing such information. Africans need access to energy for the purposes of development of their infrastructure. Billions of Africans struggle to access this. In summary, Musito's argument as an energy scientist reveals the disparity that still exists with regard to the collection of data on energy consumption and therefore highlights how African voices are muted.

# Concluding reflections

This chapter has sought to position the discourse on reverse mission with that of climate justice asking why African reverse missionaries are muted in climate conversations. While African reverse missionaries have a hermeneutical problem, such as their narrow interpretation of the gospel and eschatology, their voices are nevertheless muted because of Western colonial approaches to climate justice and how history has been viewed.

To unmute African voices in this conversation therefore means a rethinking of the African world view and religions and how it can help us to elucidate the biblical text in the light of climate justice. This can empower and develop African agency needed to combat the climate crisis that disproportionately affects the Majority World. I have offered two theological frameworks that can facilitate this; they are: the African view of God as Creator and the sustaining one. The second is a holistic African world view on the union of life that can help to develop a Brown theology that connects racial injustice and climate injustice. Lastly, in this enquiry, I have engaged the voice of Rose Musito, an energy scientist from Kenya who offers an interdisciplinary perspective on the subject, demonstrating how Africans are muted with regard to energy poverty.

# 13

# Unmuting voices in a congregational conflict

## GUICHUN JUN

'Pastor, our church building is on fire.' Receiving an urgent call from a church member, pastor Mike hurriedly drove to the church building located twenty minutes away from his home. Fortunately, fire engines arrived early and extinguished the fire. However, the interior of the church building was burned and the ceiling collapsed. The reaction of the church members who arrived at the scene was divided into two. One group of members fell to the ground, either weeping or stunned, looking at the burned church building in silence. Another group were smiling lightly, saying that God's will was accomplished through the fire. Why did individuals, bonded by faith and belonging to the same congregation, exhibit such opposing responses in the face of a shared loss?

This true story informs the degree of intergroup conflict in a merged urban congregation in Britain. Initially, the merger of two small congregations brought several positive consequences, such as increased church membership and finance, which contributed to the stability and capability of ministry. However, before long, the two congregations got involved in a power struggle to take the initiative to lead the merged congregation to fulfil their desired ministry vision and to realise their theological understanding of local church ministry. The fierce power struggle created a power asymmetry in which one group became dominant and the other group became subordinate. The dominant group changed the leadership structure and management systems to reinforce their dominance. The subordinate group deliberately chose avoidance as a coping mechanism to ignore or withdraw from the conflict because they realised that resistance did not work effectively, and their voices were systematically muted.

This narrative poses profound questions in the attempt to give voices to the voiceless and building peace in the unequal intergroup conflict: How can the voices of the oppressed be unmuted again? How can the intergroup conflict be transformed so that harmony is restored in the divided congregation? These two questions provide a theoretical intersection between Muted Group Theory (MGT) and Conflict Transformation Theory (CTT). Despite MGT's extensive application across academic realms such as feminism, communication and racial studies, its potential in conflict studies remains largely untapped. This chapter aims to propose the theoretical possibility of integrating MGT and CTT in an intergroup conflict situation of a local congregation, and how the integration practically contributes to transforming that conflict situation by building peace, as well as unmuting the voices of the oppressed. Moreover, the integrative approach will be reflected through a theological lens. This theological reflection will draw inspiration from the biblical concept of unity from 1 Corinthians because the apostle Paul's metaphor of the church as the body of Christ offers a useful framework for understanding the gravity of this intergroup conflict situation.

# Setting the contextual scene
## Contextual background

Understanding the processes of transforming the intergroup conflict and the muting of the voices of the oppressed requires an appropriate investigation into the political, economic, cultural and institutional context (Wall and Gannon-Leary 1999:27). The context of the narrative and lived experiences of the muted in this chapter is an urban local congregation called Grace Community Church (GCC) in a metropolitan city in the UK. GCC used to be called Grace Evangelical Church (GEC) before it was merged with Hope Community Church (HCC) in 1998. GEC was founded as a City Medical Mission (CMM) in 1875 to provide free medical care and to share the gospel with the poor in the city. However, as state-led medical services took precedence in 1948, CMM metamorphosed into the local church entity known as GEC. In the early days of GEC, the leaders tried to create a sense of unity by emphasising the remarkable social and spiritual legacies of CMM as a collective identity marker. One of their efforts was to fill the church's interior with furniture, artefacts and photographs that symbolise CMM's historicity and identity. The most symbolic object of all was the wooden pulpit that had been used since the early days of CMM. These symbolic items had the effect of uniting congregations of various backgrounds.

Despite its successful ministry for a long period, several years after commemorating the centenary anniversary of the foundation of CMM, GEC experienced a serious numerical decline. Moreover, most of the congregants were in their sixties or older. Finances were significantly reduced, so it was no longer possible to hire a pastor, and even the maintenance of the church building became difficult. Due to the deprived socioeconomic environment of the area where GEC had been located for more than a century, the remaining congregants were a small group of people who were socially marginalised, professionally lesser-educated working class, economically underprivileged and theologically following the Reformed tradition. Confronted by these stark realities, the small number of remaining congregants of GEC opted for a strategic merger with Hope Community Church (HCC), a younger assembly situated a few miles away. HCC sprouted from the house church movement in the 1970s, burgeoned numerically and sought a permanent sanctuary as they held Sunday services in rented school premises. Unlike the GEC congregants, HCC comprised individuals entrenched in middle-class societal strata, adorned with professional occupations, steeped in education and espousing Pentecostal and charismatic theological tenets. This merger between GEC and HCC formed a crucible where diverse demographics converged, forging a new entity marked by contrasting backgrounds, socioeconomic statuses and theological orientations. The merger not only promised vitality and a fresh narrative, but also birthed an undercurrent of conflict – emerging from the clash between established traditions, divergent theological perspectives and distinct social demographics.

## Intergroup conflict and mutedness

In general, a merger of two congregations can be a challenging process, and it is crucial to ensure that the core elements of the new church's vision and ecclesiology are agreed upon by all parties involved. Unfortunately, in the case of the merger that took place between GEC and HCC, a consensus was not reached, and the decision was made primarily to meet practical needs. As a result, the differences in social, educational, cultural and doctrinal backgrounds of the members of the two congregations emerged as various aspects of conflict. These differences soon began to manifest in the forms of disagreement, dissonance and competition, not only in practical church governance and mission engagements, but also in fundamental doctrinal stances and ecclesiological traditions. Ultimately, these initial struggles triggered excessive competition between them. While the superficial factors for the competition were to secure limited ministry resources and to occupy more and higher positions in the leadership structure, the fundamental underlying factor was the power struggle to become the dominant group.

Halverstadt (1991:63) argues that conflicts are kept in a chronic stage of submerged latency when one or both groups discover that their behaviour is enmeshed around differences in the initial period of the merger. Power can then be used manipulatively to control the differences. However, intergroup conflict at GCC did not seem to be in a state of submerged latency, but was manifested viciously in various forms and at different levels. The differences between the two congregations were too significant to be resolved easily, and the situation worsened with time. Unexpectedly, the merger failed to achieve its intended goals and resulted in a situation where both groups suffered.

The HCC leaders began to exert every effort to seize power to subdue the leaders and congregants from GEC and to mute their voices. First, they eliminated GEC people from their ministry positions. People from GEC, who had served in various ministry and leadership positions such as Sunday school teacher, worship coordinator, caretaker, bursar or deacon were replaced with people from HCC for dominance in all the ministry departments, including committees where important decisions were made. This deprived the people of GEC of any opportunity to express their views and opinions officially. This was the first step of muting the voices of people from GEC by creating power asymmetry. Second, the HCC leaders removed all the traditional artefacts, photos and furniture that imbued people from GEC with a sense of belonging to CMM, which reinforced their historical legacy and spiritual identity. The worst incident was when two HCC leaders came to the church building with an axe at night and smashed the wooden pulpit in the name of church reformation. As I mentioned in the section on contextual background, the wooden pulpit was the most important symbolic item for people from GEC. This was the second step in muting the voices of people from GEC by disconnecting them from their historical legacy and spiritual identity. Finally, the HCC leaders modified the church constitution and other policy documents to revise the purpose and vision of the church, the statement of faith and the regulations on membership and discipline, not only to concretise their dominance, but also to indoctrinate the subordinates with their theological stances. This third step of muting the voices of the subordinates was to create a dominant governance structure, a result of which caused systemic inequality and unfairness in opportunities and discipline.

## Setting the theoretical scene

Mutedness and silence are not synonyms in social science. According to MGT, mutedness implies an absence of perspectives and voices of the subordinate groups as the dominant group controls the various avenues of communication in society (Miller 2005). This understanding of mutedness addresses three areas of inquiry in social science: human behaviours, systemic inequality and transforming power structure. MGT was originated by Edwin and Shirley Ardener, who tried to understand the reasons why the opinions and experiences of women were devalued in cultural anthropology. Ardener (1975) discovered that men, as the dominant group, developed the communication system and world view of society and behaved in such a way as to perpetuate them to take advantage over women. MGT was further developed by scholars such as Cheris Kramarae (1981) in feminism and Mark Orbe (1998a; 1998b) in racial and ethnic studies, who not only focused on the cultural behaviours of the dominant group and the non-dominant groups, but also on the dominant socio-cultural system fostering systemic structural problems that mute and oppress the marginalised. In this light, MGT is a critical theory that not only discloses the power imbalance and its negative impact on behaviours of the dominant group and the dominant social structure, but also actively seeks to find ways to both unmute the voices of the oppressed group and transform the social structure (Dainton and Zelley 2005:97).

The aforementioned basic understanding of MGT provides the theoretical possibility of applying MGT in order to analyse and transform an intergroup conflict situation at GCC. In particular, the nature and characteristics of MGT provide a framework to integrate MGT and CTT, not only to unmute and empower the oppressed groups, but also to build peace and foster a culture of equality by transforming the unequal power structure. John Paul Lederach originated the first holistic and revolutionary approach to handle deep-rooted and protracted conflicts caused by social structural issues. Lederach explains conflict transformation as a revolutionary approach that is not only involved in understanding the nature and identifying structural problems of conflict, but also in transforming them to bring peace and unity (Lederach 1995:11). Understanding the nature and characteristics of CTT, Jun (2020:145–6) proposed four steps of conflict transformation in his thesis as follows: conscientisation (or education), individual advocacy, systems advocacy and mediation to establish new institutions.

With the intention of theoretical and practical integration between MGT and CTT, conscientisation and advocacy are essential strategies to help the subordinate group realise the unequal and unfair structural issues and to be empowered to unmute their voices without fear. As far as education is concerned, it will serve both the dominant and subordinate groups in developing their critical understanding of reality. Conscientisation and the two advocacy strategies will show the collaborative integration of MGT and CTT. MGT will help to disclose the imbalance in power or unfairness in the conflict situation, which will become significant preconditions for CTT to take practical actions to liberate and empower the oppressed and unmute their voices. Mediation for establishing new institutions will be a transformative engagement between the dominant and the oppressed in understanding the structural issues and in changing them by creating fair third spaces for better policies and institutions.

The practical demonstration below showcases the seamless integration of MGT and CTT in employing the systematic approach comprising the four conflict transformation steps. In other words, this demonstration serves as a tangible manifestation of the theoretical integration of MGT and CTT in practice. It offers a comprehensive insight into the efficacy of this integrated framework in not only unmuting the voices of the voiceless, but also in effectively transforming the entrenched intergroup conflicts prevalent within GCC. One general contribution of this synergistic integration between GMT and CTT is to propose a way of fostering meaningful change and facilitating constructive transformation within complex societal dynamics in which the voices of the oppressed and the marginalised are muted.

# Transformative approaches for unmuting the voices

## Conscientisation as a form of education

Bell Hooks (1994:59) states an inspirational scholarly motivation in terms of looking to theory for healing as follows:

> I came to theory because I was hurting – the pain within me was so intense that I could not go on living. I came to theory desperate, wanting to comprehend – to grasp what was happening around and within me. Most importantly, I wanted to make the hurt go away. I saw in theory then a location for healing.

This personal experience described by Hooks eloquently expresses the profound impact of personal anguish as the impetus for delving into theory, driven by an urgent need to comprehend and alleviate the profound distress within herself and the surrounding environment. By integrating MGT's exploration of muted voices and CTT's approach to conflict transformation, this convergence aspires to address the profound wounds inflicted by the destructive power struggle and provide healing from the anguish that pervades both individuals and groups.

In particular, MGT has the capacity not only to analyse the factors of muting the voices of the oppressed, but also to transform the hurting community into the location of healing for both the dominant and the oppressed. Orbe (2005) stresses that MGT is useful as a theory in providing a lens to understand the reality of the unfairness and pain felt by the non-dominant groups from the margins. In other words, MGT helps the oppressed cultivate their consciousness to eliminate ignorance and increase awareness of mutedness. Paul Freire (1970:27) describes this function as conscientisation, which is an emancipatory pedagogical process to help the marginalised develop a critical awareness of their social reality through reflective education to uncover real problems and actual needs for transformation. I argue that this conscientisation needs to be inclusive and to also educate members of the dominant group who intend to maintain the status quo because they have a false perception of reality. There will be no authentic transformation in the community if those in the dominant group continually uphold their prevailing mythology and ideology for their dominance.

I had the opportunity to organise and lead several workshops where I presented significant findings from my research to both groups as a method of conscientisation. The focus of the workshops was on the intergroup conflict between the dominant HCC and subordinate GEC. I presented several critical incidents to disclose how HCC had been obsessively involved in the power struggle, using all necessary means for dominance, and how GEC had been oppressed and muted, losing their ministry positions and historical and spiritual legacies from CMM. As expected, there were disputes and an initial rejection of my findings and analysis by both groups. HCC was defensive and reluctant to acknowledge its role in the conflict, while GEC was hesitant to speak up due to fear of retaliation. However, as the workshops continued, both groups gradually began to reflect on their collective behaviours in the intergroup conflict. They began to understand the power dynamics at play and the harm caused by their actions.

People from GEC began to realise that they were powerless and vulnerable in terms of perceiving the situation correctly and taking appropriate action. They realised that their voices had been muted by the dominant group, and they needed to speak up to be heard. This led to a greater sense of confidence among the GEC members, who began to express their opinions and views more freely. It was also a challenging moment for people from HCC as they confronted blind conformity and collective moral desensitisation in the power struggle. They began to realise that their actions were causing harm to others and that they needed to work towards a more equitable and just environment. This led to a greater sense of empathy and understanding among the HCC members, who began to listen to the views and opinions of the GEC members. Overall, the workshops were a valuable opportunity for both groups to reflect on their actions and behaviours. They learned to understand each other's perspectives and work towards a more inclusive and equitable environment. Through these workshops, they were able to cultivate their consciousness and reflect on their collective behaviours in the intergroup conflict. The workshops helped to create a safe space where both groups could express their opinions and views and work towards resolving their differences.

## Individual advocacy: emancipation and empowerment

Conscientisation helps both groups to confront reality and take action for positive changes. However, it is often found that the subordinate groups do not have enough courage to unmute and raise their voices due to the existing dominance and fear of retaliation based on their past experiences. Therefore, first, the oppressed group needs to be liberated from the wounds and trauma caused by the dominant group's hostility and heavy tactics in the power struggle. Second, the oppressed group needs to be empowered to raise their level of confidence for fearless confrontation with the dominant group and the situation of power asymmetry. In an intergroup conflict situation, members of the oppressed group usually do not have a capacity for both emancipation and empowerment as they suffer greatly from a victim mentality and traumatisation. In other words, individuals in the oppressed group do not have the capability for self-advocacy to communicate and assert their views, thoughts and emotions with confidence. This is why individual advocacy is essential as a significant precondition in both MGT and CTT for the oppressed or victimised in incidents such as human trafficking (Matzke-Fawcett 2019) or sexual violence (Paul Baer 2017), not only to protect and promote their rights and desires, but also to find and unmute their voices.

Individual advocacy in an intergroup conflict situation is to stand beside and take action for a person or individuals within the oppressed group who have experienced injustice or unfairness to provide care and support for emancipation and empowerment. The advocate must be an independent and neutral third party who can offer impartial support for the oppressed. The steering group I had formed for peacebuilding at GCC with equal numbers of leaders from GEC and HCC requested local church leaders to be voluntary advocates for those who were traumatised psychologically and spiritually in the intergroup conflict. The voluntary advocates from various churches provided Christian counselling for healing for individuals who suffered from victim mentality and empowered them to increase their motivation to find their voices. They also conducted prayer meetings and Bible studies to help the victims to be restored from their spiritual depression and to increase their confidence to embrace their painful experiences of losses.

Based on the data collected through in-depth interviews of the individuals from GEC, this individual advocacy at the micro-level was useful for the victims to be released from psychological pain, encouraged and empowered so that they had motivation and confidence to change their approach to the intergroup conflict from avoidance to collaboration. The steering group also invited these local church leaders to share biblical perspectives on forgiveness and reconciliation and lead workshops on Sundays for the entire congregation. This independent collective advocacy created a supportive environment in which both the dominant and subordinate groups began to share their experiences and emotions, even confessing their mistakes and sins in public.

## Systems advocacy

While individual advocacy takes place at the micro-level to support the victims, systems advocacy involves changing policies and rules at the macro-level to resolve structural and systemic issues (Lopez-Baez and Paylo 2009). Individual advocacy directs the non-dominant group to emancipate and empower individuals to initiate structural changes. The steering group and the advocates then needed to focus on working with the same oppressed group to change the unequal systems to make them non-oppressive through systems advocacy (Lopez-Baez and Paylo 2009:277). Both MGT and CTT are critical theories that aim to give voices to those whose voices have been muted by changing oppressive and unequal systems. In other words, MGT and CTT are to develop the critical sense for the oppressed to analyse the factors and features of social structural issues such as power asymmetry, unequal opportunities, systemic barriers and injustice, not only to resist their oppressors, but also to find better alternatives (Forte 2014:55).

Systems advocacy plays a crucial role in intergroup conflicts to empower the non-dominant group and amplify their muted voices and limited power. In other words, the goal of systems advocacy is to invite the non-dominant group to see the areas of change at the structural level and provide them with analytical information on the factors and features of the conflict situation. In this light, advocates involved in systems advocacy act as consultants, providing convincing recommendations, rather than as facilitators who lead a value-free and objective group discussion. Due to the nature and characteristics of systems advocacy, advocates focus on assisting the oppressed group in realising the inequality and unfairness in policies, regulations and statements in the conflict context. By analysing the policies and regulations, advocates provide the oppressed group with the necessary information to identify the systemic problems and work towards their resolution. Advocates also assist the oppressed group in developing strategies and approaches to challenging and changing these deep-rooted systemic problems.

Through systems advocacy, people from GEC began to identify elements of unfairness and inequality in any written documents and unwritten customs that had been practised since the merger. One of the examples of unfairness from the GEC members' viewpoint was that all the ministry positions had been appointed by the senior ministry team without consultation with or recommendation by the majority of church members. The real problem in this case was that the majority of the senior ministry team were leaders from HCC so people from HCC had been given more opportunities to get involved in various ministries in the merged congregation. It is a typical example of how power asymmetry at the strategic level system manipulates the decisions of appointing workers to cause more imbalance in ministry positions at the management-level systems. This manipulation eventually reinforces the situation of power asymmetry and unfairness so that the mutedness of the oppressed is perpetuated. The advocates assisted the GEC members in developing their understanding of the power dynamics at play and provided them with the necessary tools and strategies to address these issues. Through their efforts, the advocates helped the GEC members to amplify their voices and work towards creating a more equitable and just environment.

# Mediation: a dialectical process

The final step for transforming intergroup conflict is mediation, which brings both groups together for constructive communication and to seek better alternatives for the current systemic problems. Different from arbitration, which is directive in terms of making decisions and proposing solutions to the groups, mediation is a non-directive approach that helps the parties to transform the conflict situation by establishing better institutions and policies through negotiating their views and perspectives. People from GEC have experienced emancipation and empowerment through individual advocacy, as well as remotivation through systems advocacy to volitionally move from avoidance and victim mentality to collaboration and unmuting their voices to transform the conflict situation. People from HCC have also been educated by the various means introduced by the advocates, enabling them to perceive reality from a more objective perspective by demolishing their prevailing myth or ideology. Nevertheless, it was not easy for both parties to negotiate their views and give up their vested rights to establish better institutions and impartial policies through the dialectical process for various systemic issues. Both parties continuously struggled to find a more neutral and fairer third space for each structural problem that they discussed.

One remarkable change observed in the dialectical discourse was that their behaviours and attitudes became non-aggressive and respectful towards their opponents. Although they could not reach a consensus on various issues, it was observed that the dialectical mediation process contributed to fostering a culture of peace, openness and equality that they had never experienced before in the merged congregation. Most of all, it was observed that the voices of the oppressed were unmuted, enabling them to express their opinions and views without limitation and fear in the discourses.

Experiencing mutual respect in the dialectical mediation discourse enabled both parties to be more willing to analyse the underlying structural problems causing the intergroup conflict and become more flexible towards changing their stances and finding fairer and more impartial institutions. One of the examples proposed in the discourse was to change the clause in the constitution stating that the elders have the highest authority on ministry matters, and in matters of finance and property, the board of trustees is the highest decision-making body. They found a healthy third alternative in which the annual general meeting has the highest authority to approve all suggestions and decisions including matters of personnel, finance and property proposed by various committees, the senior leadership team and the board of trustees.

Both groups believed that this change in the constitution would be a much fairer system, not only in preventing a few leaders from making arbitrary decisions, but also in promoting healthy ways of accommodating diverse opinions and creating unity in diversity. This new change in the constitution triggered another change in the personnel management system at GCC concerning the composition of the senior leadership team and the board of trustees as there had been an imbalance in the numbers of representatives from both groups. Through the dialectical discourse, it was agreed that there should be equal numbers of representatives from both groups in the senior leadership team. In particular, as far as the composition of the board of trustees was concerned, it was agreed that there should be equal numbers of representatives from GEC, HCC and advocates who are local church leaders. To have equal numbers of advocates on the board of trustees was an innovative change because it allowed for a check-and-balance system, not only for monitoring the situation, but also for participating in important decision-making processes as an objective third party.

As a result of this transformative mediation process, not only were the voices of the voiceless heard, but also several problematic institutions were dismantled so that the congregation could flourish with biblical and democratic values such as justice, trust, equality, dignity, respect and fairness.

# Theological reflection: from a perspective of unity (1 Corinthians)

To engage in a theological reflection on the nature and characteristics of the intergroup conflict and the transformative integration of MGT and CTT and its practical application at GCC from the perspective of unity in a local church context, it is imperative to revisit the profound questions posed in the introduction: How can the voices of the oppressed be unmuted again? How can the intergroup conflict be transformed so that harmony is restored in the divided congregation? The tangible expressions of disunity within the congregation, exemplified by divergent responses to the fire incident, destruction of symbolic artefacts and intense power struggles between merged congregations, vividly illustrate the fractured nature within the body of believers. This disunity stems from a power imbalance in the merged congregation, where the dominant group suppresses the perspectives, concerns and contributions of the oppressed group, ultimately muting their voices. This imbalance creates an environment where the oppressed feel disenfranchised, unable to voice their opinions, and, as a result, are marginalised in decision-making processes.

Additionally, the disunity contributes to a breakdown in communication, further silencing the voices of the oppressed in a local church context. Therefore, it is crucial to approach the resolution of disunity and power dynamics both theologically and through the lens of social science. This dual perspective is vital, not just for fostering harmony, but also to ensure that every member, especially the oppressed, has a platform to express their viewpoints and make substantial contributions to the congregation's vitality. This approach seeks to establish an environment in which everyone feels acknowledged, equal, respected and treated fairly.

This theological reflection, centred on unmuting the voices of the oppressed and transforming intergroup conflict for peacebuilding, is grounded in the concept of unity as portrayed in 1 Corinthians 12, viewing the local congregation as the body of Christ. The aforementioned disunity contrasts starkly with Paul's exhortation for harmony and mutual support among the diverse members of the church body (1 Cor. 12:12–27). The apostle Paul underscores the interdependence of different members within the body of Christ, emphasising the essential nature of each part (1 Cor. 12:14–20).

Similarly, the conflicted GCC congregation must recognise the significance of every member, acknowledging the unique contributions and perspectives of both GEC and HCC. The intergroup conflict within GCC exposes a disparity in power dynamics, akin to the power struggles described in 1 Corinthians 12:21–6. The dominant group, represented by HCC, seeks to exert control and suppress the voices of the oppressed. This mirrors the imbalance Paul addresses in the Corinthian church, emphasising that the weaker members should be treated with special honour (1 Cor. 12:22–4). The call for unity in 1 Corinthians becomes a mandate for the GCC congregation to rectify the power asymmetry, restoring a balance that honours the diverse contributions of both congregations.

The contextual background of GCC, marked by the merger rooted in practical needs rather than a shared vision, reflects the challenges faced by the church in Corinth. Paul admonished the Corinthians for their divisions and urged them to be of the same mind and judgement (1 Cor. 1:10). The lack of consensus during the merger of GEC and HCC parallels the Corinthian situation, necessitating a theological response grounded in unity. The proposed integration of MGT and CTT offers a theoretical framework for comprehensively addressing the conflict within GCC, combining various lenses to critically and holistically analyse the conflict reality. Applying these theories synthetically to the biblical concept of unity underscores the need for conscientisation and advocacy to unmute the voices of the oppressed, alongside mediation to transform the unfair and unjust systemic problems to bring about peace, which removes the factors hindering unity and builds an authentic body of Christ.

In this light, the integration of MGT and CTT aligns with the transformative approach advocated by the apostle Paul in 1 Corinthians, emphasising the renewal of minds and the pursuit of peace (Rom. 12:2; 1 Cor. 14:33) for unity among believers in a local congregation. The practical demonstration of transformative approaches also aligns with Paul's exhortation to pursue love and to build up the body of Christ (1 Cor. 14:1–5). Conscientisation, individual advocacy, systems advocacy and mediation become avenues through which the GCC congregation can embody the principles of love, justice and reconciliation outlined in 1 Corinthians. These transformative steps mirror Paul's call for GCC to function harmoniously, recognising the diversity within the body for continuous peacebuilding, as well as unmuting the voices of the oppressed and weak.

# Conclusion: more than unmuting the voices

Both MGT and CTT emphasise the ongoing reformative engagements through the dialectical process to continually develop the structure and systems in the congregation because unmuted voices may be muted again if the structure and systems do not become relevant and fair to all of the members of the congregation. In other words, the ultimate goal of MGT and CTT is not only to unmute the voices of the voiceless, but to maintain a culture of peace, equality and trust by being critical of the current organisational structure and systems. The steering group with the help of the local advocates have been continually working hard for the last several years to achieve higher outcomes than just unmuting the voices of the oppressed. All the steps of the transformative approaches mentioned above have achieved more than the steering group initially expected. They educated both groups by enabling them to confront the reality of intergroup conflict. They liberated and empowered the oppressed to overcome their psychological and spiritual traumas and to motivate them to change their approach towards the conflict situation from avoidance to collaboration. They helped both groups to actively engage in the dialectical process to establish new policies and institutions.

However, the culture of peace and the level of collaboration that they experienced at the macro-level is still superficial and temporary, even fragile and vulnerable, so there is a certain level of latent risk that the power balance may be broken again. What GCC needs to focus on in order to move continually forward is to restore individuals' broken relationships at the micro-level. Lepchitz (2012:50) says MGT is about power dynamics, but it is relationships, not merely situations, that are responsible for muting voices. The four transformative approaches mentioned above focused on handling conflict situations in the broken congregation at the macro-level. This means that the individuals' broken relationships at the micro-level have not been properly dealt with yet. The greatest synergy effect expected through the combination of MGT and CTT is to enable individuals from both the dominant and the oppressed to experience biblically authentic forgiveness, reconciliation and reintegration in the broken congregation. To accomplish this, it is crucial to focus on the aforementioned theological reflection, which underscores the necessity of addressing intergroup conflict at GCC through the lens of unity as portrayed in 1 Corinthians. The metaphor of the body of Christ becomes a guiding principle, urging the congregation to recognise the interconnectedness of its diverse members at the micro-level and rectify power imbalances at the macro-level. The proposed integration of MGT and CTT aligns with Paul's emphasis on transformative approaches, offering a pathway to unmute voices, foster genuine reconciliation and build a unified body that reflects the love and justice exemplified by Christ.

# Afterword

As this book draws to a close, I recognise that the unmuting process in terms of speaking out and listening differently is at different stages of practice and expectation. Each of the contributors in this volume has chosen to reflect on parts of their life experience using Muted Group Theory (MGT) as a tool to unmute and also to engage in mutual listening. While being able to speak for oneself should be possible for all, the spaces that welcome those voices may often be restricted. Readers may be disappointed that this has been a book of different voices or delighted with the breadth of the kingdom described.

As the editor and, in a sense, initiator of the discussion on the relevance of MGT in our lived Christian experiences, it has been my pleasure to bring together a group of people whose life experiences were examined through MGT. It really is not sufficient to have read this book and limit it to the realm of cerebral knowledge. Through this book the authors hope that the stories of real people will help the reader to listen more and to act appropriately among those marginalised. There will always be dominant and subordinate perspectives; this is why our capacity to build and strengthen our beliefs will continue to be challenged. The task before us is not to destroy all structures of thought, but to carefully and sensitively allow life experiences of the muted and marginalised to gently manoeuvre others to interact as alongsiders. Deconstruction is not destruction. It is about creating careful, considerate places where we handle one another as part of the extraordinary body of Christ. Collectively, we live to embody God while here on earth.

All the authors except for Donna Jennings were able to gather online to meet one another, some meeting each other for the very first time. Looking at the screen, I recognised the broad range of geographical spaces that were represented. As each person on the screen spoke about their writing and life experiences with 'virtual' strangers, we found the internet space became our place. Our life experiences found meaning beyond our geographical spaces; in a place of relationships, brought together because of our capacity to speak and be heard.

I want to acknowledge the particularly relevant connection made by French philosopher and Jesuit priest, Michel De Certeau (1925–86). De Certeau analysed everyday practices, which focused on unconscious ways that determine patterns of beliefs and behaviours, and how places of belonging are created. MGT became a place where we found a means of belonging together.

I hold the remarkable privilege to have the final say in this Afterword. Included are some quotes and thoughts from that final online video call, as well as additional comments from Donna Jennings as each author contributed to the closing conversation. In some cases, the authors, perhaps unknowingly, revealed a deeper connection between their writing and their life experiences.

Speaking from Portugal, Elsa Correia Pereira began, 'I'm in a public space. I'm sorry for the noise in the background.' Her background noise is not just the male voice in the Portuguese church spaces, but also the noise of the wide range of voices coming from diverse directions and perspectives. It is telling that she spoke from a carved-out private space in a public setting. The Western voices on the subject of the role of women within the Church in some ways resound further because of the privilege of expertise coming from the English-speaking world. The people of Portugal have their own way of speaking to be heard and may find other Western European Christian feminist voices muting their own cultural feminist journey, and thereby imposing voices that may create a form of muting in itself.

Paul Woods found his contribution to this book as 'an unmuting, re-muting and then unmuting again'. I requested that his original idea of unmuting aspects of leadership should be replaced by providing a theological connection to MGT. A theological perspective to MGT to provide a background might make the journey to unmuting perhaps a little less onerous for those who have not encountered it before. For better or worse, though the balance of Christianity is currently in the Majority World, the transitions of the theological voices will always have room for everyone. The voice of the Western world is still welcome, but it is not the only voice. 'We could write a whole book on MGT and the Bible.' The dominant power of Almighty God becoming the subordinate sacrifice of Jesus unmutes humanity with all its failings and frailties.

What would it be to favour the voices and life experiences of the Other as we look at the biblical texts beyond our previously held structures? This concept remains pertinent to David Wise as he reflected on his experience of engaging with MGT. As a pastor, Wise grew a multi-ethnic church into an intercultural community group that took their expression of Christianity beyond the church walls to contribute to the moral and ethical treatment of migrants in their lived experiences.

While MGT was new to Wise, enabling others' voices to be heard became a key intentional part of developing Greenford Baptist Church beyond the four walls of their building. Wise recognises that his very presence as an educated White male changes the way people express their thoughts; therefore, he chooses to remain vigilant in his ongoing journey, to listen well and resist the temptation to control the subordinate voices in subject areas where expertise is considered from traditional Western specialists. The possibilities for an alongsider unmuting theologies would be an exciting next step in research and publication.

Limiting unmuting to the voice is the challenge taken up by Donna Jennings. The pressing question in the discussion on disability is to ask, 'What is voice?' How can those who live with profound disability contribute prophetically as humans and image-bearers of Christ to a discourse that assumes and operates in the mode of self-defining, self-agency, self-expression. The humanity of those with profound disability may require the rest of us to be silent, and to slow down in order for the prophetic voice of the disabled to be received. It is in this way that the fragility of the socio-cultural models of justice is exposed, and through which the Evangelical Church can learn a new way of being, of 'speaking'. We would be as a church of brothers and sisters in Christ, like Tabitha, who have always been alongside, whose lives have been infused from the inside out and who have adopted another way of perceiving everyday life. Language and speech may not necessarily be the foremost method of communication.

How could the Evangelical Church, having the privilege to be able to give, shift their posture from only giving to include receiving from those in the margins? Ironically, during the final online call, Ethiopian Lemma

Desta was on a bus in Norway. The moment served as a metaphor for the constant sense of motion of many first-generation migrants as they hold the multiple tensions of voice and the sense of belonging. What is it to be heard and to have a voice of influence in a new home country? The migratory experience is transitory, fluid and flexible.

It is no stretch of the imagination to listen carefully to the challenge of being heard from a Roma perspective. Melody Wachsmuth and Raphael Năstase, by functioning as alongsiders, take the lead in this book by working to unmute themselves and each other beautifully. As an American theologian and academic, Wachsmuth displays the rare gift of favouring the subordinate above her own cultural position as a Western woman within many traditional Roma settings. Năstase noted in our final online conversation that working with Wachsmuth went a long way to establishing a voice; and as the subordinate identity as a connection to the eternal body of Christ, rather than focusing only on prejudicial identifications. Wachsmuth takes the slower road to listen, speak and learn alongside Năstase as the Roma and scholar.

The physically, culturally and spiritually marginalised as walking among us in the blurred spaces was clearly articulated by Ashleigh Gibb as she spoke to the rest of the authors on her chapter on unmuting the female body. She boldly unmuted her experience as a survivor of sexual trauma who found her healing and unmuting through physical fitness and unmuting the female body post-trauma. Among our online group of authors, she articulated her life experience and the power of personal unmuting that enables her to see the physical and spiritual redemption to be lived, researched and taught with boldness.

I believe the use of MGT could address the way we think about the boundary between the spiritual and physical aspects of a person. The spiritual aspects of repentance, redemption and reconciliation is carefully curated by the cultural dominance of male leadership within the church, which shows in the way the Evangelical Church responds to physical sexual acts. In terms of lived cultural acceptance, the conditions of repentance, redemption and reconciliation are different for men and women, most specifically in relation to sexual behaviour. A historical case in point is the name, David. It is commonly found among Christianised nations around the world. While in the lineage of Christ, David's sin of adultery and murder are not held against him. However, Rahab while also in the lineage of Christ, is remembered only as a prostitute and her name is associated only with her role as a sex worker.

Ashleigh Gibb spoke openly about the trauma of sexual abuse and the ongoing attitudes within the Church that reflect our treatment of survivors. Our discomfort of recurring issues and emotions surrounding sexual trauma are understood and are forgiven by God. However, as the body of Christ, our physical and spiritual responsibilities to one another in cultural spaces deserve our ongoing attention.

Claire Chong's bold voice as a Southeast Asian theologian discusses the cultural realities of how bodies carry cultural practices into the lived experiences of faith. The practices of Majority World communities to display respect, honour and venerate elders has been at best restricted and at worst, it has prohibited any possibility for billions of Asians to engage with the message of the gospel. The theological expression of the fourth of the Ten Commandments appears firmly fixed within a Western translation of family values and honour. Claire Chong's wisdom unmutes the interpretation of context that occurred due to the limitation of a Western lens in a Majority World location.

Israel Olofinjana commented on his contribution during our online video call. Olofinjana has been involved in the unmuting process in multiple fields from different perspectives during his twenty-year career as a missionary to the West from the Majority World. He has raised awareness and contributes to discussions on many issues of race within the Church and beyond. The challenges of creation care, climate justice and reverse mission are determined through his understanding of indigenous cultural wisdom. While, arguably, Western theology has recognised the need to include Majority World theologies, the influence of Majority World culture in the Evangelical Church context is limited to the confines of the congregational gatherings. Creation care with a foundation of Brown theology is better understood through climate justice. Cultural wisdom has the propensity to influence practised faith in a diversity of situations.

The scope of MGT in challenging acceptable Christian culture through dealing with church conflict was expertly articulated by Guichun Jun. As a soft-spoken Korean missionary to Britain, Jun was able to simultaneously step into a pastoral role and researcher to help facilitate long-term change in the way in which church disagreements are resolved. The value of contributing a chapter on Christian conflict resolution and MGT, along with theology, was in drawing attention to real-life situations in the context of congregational gatherings.

As our online meeting drew to a close, Rafael Năstase, while sitting in his car in Serbia, spoke of feeling moved by the opportunity to hear the other authors all offer their growth in understanding of the application of MGT and the sense of awareness of changes in terminology and comprehension as part of the conversation. Throughout all our discussions, the sense of personal identity is within the body of Christ. However, self-identity is challenged by external identification; speaking and being heard is not the whole of the story.

Gigi Khanyezi commented that, while this book has brought so many incredible voices into this space speaking from unique contexts around the world, our lenses of understanding the Scriptures have been from a historically dominant perspective. Cultural understanding is often claimed to be firmly situated in the oft-quoted verses: Galatians 3:28–9. The suggested interpretation is that differences are not differences, but that we are all one. Diversities of race, gender and social status are irrelevant among followers of Jesus as we become equal heirs of Abraham's promise. However, she proposes an alternate interpretation of this scripture. Is it possible that the author of this scripture is not suggesting that differences cease to exist? Rather, the author is listing the dominant and subordinate groups. Greeks oppressed the Jews; men oppressed the women; the free oppressed the slave. The author suggests a dismantling of power dynamics once we are in Christ. The divisions were created by humanity.

The core of the gospel is clearly demonstrated through the life of Jesus. Khanyezi cites Philippians 2 as one of the highest Christological chapters. Humility replaces hierarchy. Jesus dismantled unjust power structures that had been created by humankind. He brings full liberation and freedom with equal love for all of humanity. Jesus is the unmuter of the silenced. The separation between the social and spiritual contexts is false. The gospel in its entirety is the gospel of social justice and the gospel of proclamation as exhibited through the life of Christ.

Khanyezi further observes that, according to Genesis 1, every one of us is made in the image of God. The call and capacity to exercise dominion does not favour any one people group. No people group is designed to have more dominion than another. Humanity did that to itself. None of us bears more of God's image than another. The image of God is found in all of humanity. While physical characteristics are used to identify and recognise one another, our identities are multifaceted. Our ultimate identity is not in appearance. It not held within a categorisation created by a hierarchical structure. Humanity has created power structures to keep others in and maintain control and influence through a small group who dominate and become gatekeepers of authority and belonging.

It seems that the topic of unmuting goes far beyond one individual pushing themselves out of the margins with an exhausted desperation. Unmuting is to collectively believe and pray, 'on earth as is in heaven' (Matthew 6:10b), while simultaneously believing and praying that we will see, '... a great multitude that no one could count, from every nation, tribe, people, and language, standing in front of the throne ...' (Revelation 7:9b).

Unmuting is about silence and speaking, hearing and acting, trying and failing, but trying again and again because the body of Christ should always be a place for the voices of the subordinate to be heard carefully and judged fairly.

# Bibliography

Achim, V. (2005). 'Statistica țiganilor în Principatele Române în perioada 1830–1860', *Revista istorică* 14 (5–6):97–122.

Acton, T. A. (1998). *Authenticity, Expertise, Scholarship and Politics: Conflicting Goals in Romani Studies: An Inaugural Lecture Delivered at the University of Greenwich*, 11 June 1998 (London: Greenwich University Press).

Addison, James T. (1925). 'Chinese Ancestor-Worship and Protestant Christianity', *Journal of Religion* 5 (2): 140–9.

Adedibu, B. A. (2012). *Coat of Many Colours: The Origin, Growth, Distinctiveness and Contributions of Black Majority Churches to British Christianity* (Gloucester: Wisdom Summit).

Anderson, G. A. (2013). *Charity: The Place of the Poor in the Biblical Tradition* (New Haven, CT: Yale University Press).

APM (1890). *Records of the General Conference of the Protestant Missionaries of China Held at Shanghai, May 7–20, 1890*. Shanghai: American Presbyterian Mission Press, http://archive.org/details/recordsofthegene00unknuoft (accessed 17 June 2024).

Ardener, Edwin (1972). 'Belief and the Problem of Women', in J. S. La Fontaine (ed.), *The Interpretation of Ritual* (Abingdon: Routledge), pp. 135–58.

———. (1978). 'Some Outstanding Problems in the Analysis of Events', in G. Schwinner (ed.), *The Yearbook of Symbolic Anthropology* (London: Hurst), pp. 103–21.

Ardener, Shirley (1975). *Perceiving Women* (New York: Wiley).

———. (1993). 'Introduction: The Nature of Women in Society', in S. Ardener (ed.), *Defining Females: The Nature of Women in Society* (Oxford: Berg), pp. 1–33.

Arén, G. (1978). *Evangelical Pioneers in Ethiopia: Origins of the Ethiopian Evangelical Church Mekane Yesus. Studia Missionalia Upsaliensia XXXII* (Stockholm: EFS förlaget).

———. (1999). *Envoys of the Gospel in Ethiopia: In the Steps of the Evangelical Pioneers, 1898–1936, Studia Missionalia Upsaliensia LXXV* (Stockholm: EFS Förlaget).

Atanasov, M. (2010). *Gypsy Pentecostals: The Growth of the Pentecostal Movement among the Roma in Bulgaria and Its Revitalization of Their Communities* (Lexington, KY: Emeth Press).

Awolalu, Omosade and Dopamu, Adelumo (1979). *West African Traditional Religion* (Ibadan, Nigeria: Onibonoje).

Bae, Choon Sup (2008). 'Ancestor Worship and the Challenges It Poses to the Christian Mission and Ministry', PhD, University of Pretoria.

Bailey, Stephen and Dwight Martin (2020). 'The FJCCA Church Planting Movement', *Mission Frontiers*, July–August: 43–5.

Bakke, J. (1987). *Christian Ministry: Patterns and Functions within the Ethiopian Evangelical Church Mekane Yesus* (Oslo: Solum Forlag A.S).

Barkman, L. (2018). 'Muted Group Theory: A Tool for Hearing Marginalized Voices', *Priscilla Papers* 32 (4):3–7.

Barram, M. (2007). 'The Bible, Mission, and Social Location: Toward a Missional Hermeneutic', *Interpretation: A Journal of Bible and Theology* 61 (1):42–58.

Bauckham, Richard (1996). 'James and the Gentiles (Acts 15.13–21)', in Ben Witherington III (ed.), *History, Literature, and Society in the Book of Acts* (Cambridge: Cambridge University Press), pp. 154–84.

Beale, G. (2004). *The Temple and the Church's Mission, NSBT 17* (Nottingham/Downers Grove, IL: Apollos/IVP Academic).

Bebbington, David W. (1989). *Evangelicalism in Modern Britain: A History from the 1730s to the 1980s* (London: Unwin Hyman).

———. (2021). *The Evangelical Quadrilateral: Characterizing the British Gospel Movement* (Waco, TX: Baylor University Press).

Beck, S. and Ivasiuc, A. (2020). *Roma Activism: Reimagining Power and Knowledge*, Romani Studies 1 (New York: Berghahn Books, 2020).

Benti, Solomon, Terefe, Heyaw and Callo-Concha, Daniel (2022). 'Implications of Overlooked Drivers in Ethiopia's Urbanization: Curbing the Curse of Spontaneous Urban Development for Future Emerging Towns', *Heliyon* 8 (10):1–15.

The Bible for Normal People (2016). *When God Is Unfaithful: Reclaiming the Theology of Lament*, https://thebiblefornormalpeople.com/when-god-is-unfaithful-reclaiming-a-theology-of-lament/ (accessed 29 October 2023).

Bourdieu, Pierre (1977). 'The Economics of Linguistic Exchanges', *Social Science Information* 16:645–68.

———. (2010). *Distinction* (Coimbra, Portugal: Edições 70).

Bourdieu, Pierre and Wacquant, Loïc J. D. (1992). *An Invitation to Reflexive Sociology* (Cambridge: University of Chicago Press).

Broomhall, A. J. (1981a). *Hudson Taylor and China's Open Century (Book 6): Assault of the Nine* (Sevenoaks: Hodder & Stoughton and OMF).

———. (1981b). *Hudson Taylor and China's Open Century (Book 7): It Is Not Death to Die* (Sevenoaks: Hodder & Stoughton and OMF).

Brown, B. (2019). *Braving the Wilderness: The Quest for True Belonging and the Courage to Stand Alone* (New York: Random House).

Brueggemann, W. (2011). *Disruptive Grace: Reflections on God, Scripture and the Church* (London: SCM Press).

Button, John (1988). *A Dictionary of Green Ideas* (Abingdon: Routledge).

*Cambridge Dictionary* (2023). Definition of harassment, https://dictionary. cambridge.org/us/dictionary/english/harassment#:~:text=illegal%20 behaviour%20towards%20a%20person,workplace%20harassment%20 and%20racial%20discrimination (accessed 1 October 2023).

Chang, Eunhye, Rupert Morgan, J., Nyasulu, Timothy and Priest, Robert J. (2009). 'Paul G. Hiebert and Critical Contextualization', *Trinity Journal* 30 (2):199–207.

Charlton, J. I. (1998). *Nothing About Us Without Us, Disability, Oppression and Empowerment* (London: University of California Press).

Christ Theological College, https://www.ctcollege.org/ (accessed 31 July 2023).

Christian Union (2023). https://monitor.civicus.org/globalfindings_2023/ (accessed 11 June 2024).

Cohen, G. (2022). *Belonging: The Science of Creating Connection and Bridging Divides* (New York: W.W. Norton & Company).

Collins, Paul M. (2007). *Christian Inculturation in India* (Abingdon: Routledge).

Collinson (1988). *The Birthpangs of Protestant England: Religious and Cultural Change in the Sixteenth and Seventeenth Centuries* (London: Macmillan).

Conner, B. (2015). 'Enabling Witness: Disabling Witness in Missiological Perspective', *Journal of Disability and Religion* 19 (1):15–29.

Constantineanu, Corneliu and Renner, Peter (eds) (2023). *Eastern European Bible Commentary* (Carlisle: Langham Global Library).

Crenshaw, K. (1989). 'Demarginalizing the Intersection of Race and Sex: A Black Feminist Critique of Antidiscrimination Doctrine, Feminist Theory and Antiracist Politics', *University of Chicago Legal Forum*, 1 (8):139–67.

———. (2020). '"Difference" through Intersectionality', in Sunaina Arya and Aakash Singh Rathore (eds), *Dalit Feminist Theory: A Reader* (New York: Routledge).

Cross, K. and O'Donnell, K. (eds) (2020). *Feminist Trauma Theologians: Body Scripture and Church in Critical Perspective* (London: SCM Press).

Cummings, Brian (2012). 'The Problem of Protestant Culture: Biblical Literalism and Literary Biblicism', *Reformation* 17 (1):177–98.

Dainton, M. and Zelley, E. D. (2005). *Applying Communication Theory for Professional Life: A Practical Introduction* (Thousand Oaks, CA: Sage).

Dawson, N. (2024). *She Needs: Women Flourishing in the Church* (London: Inter-Varsity Press).

De La Torre, M. (2011). *Genesis, Belief: A Theological Commentary on the Bible* (Louisville, KY: Westminster John Knox Press).

Desta, L. (2014). *An Invitation to the Pilgrimage of Justice and Peace*, World Council of Churches, https://www.oikoumene.org/resources/documents/an-invitation-to-the-pilgrimage-of-justice-and-peace (accessed 11 June 2024).

———. (2018). *What Could the World Council of Churches Do Regarding Global Migration?* World Council of Churches, https://www.oikoumene.org/blog/what-could-the-world-council-of-churches-do-regarding-global-migration (accessed 11 June 2024).

Desta, L. and Reifsnider, U. (2021). 'Decolonizing Mission' Seminar, Video, Lausanne Europe Gathering, https://www.lausanneeurope.org/le2021-gathering/decolonizing-mission/ (accessed 11 June 2024).

Dirksen, A. H. (1932). *The New Testament Concept of Metanoia* (Washington, DC: Catholic University of America).

Dubar, E. (2021). *Trafficking Hadassah: Collective Trauma, Cultural*

*Memory and Identity in the Book of Esther and in the African Diaspora* (New York: Routledge).

Duerksen, Darren T. and Dyrness, William A. (2019). *Seeking Church: Emerging Witnesses to the Kingdom* (Downers Grove, IL: InterVarsity Press).

Dunbar-Ortiz, R. (2014). *An Indigenous Peoples' History of the United States* (Boston, MA: Beacon Press).

Dunn, J. D. G. (2016). *The Acts of the Apostles* (Grand Rapids, MI: Eerdmans).

Eiesland, N. L. (1994). *The Disabled God: Toward a Liberatory Theology of Disability* (Nashville, TN: Abingdon Press).

Enns, Pete (2016). 'When God Is Unfaithful: Reclaiming a Theology of Lament', *The Bible for Normal People*, https://thebiblefornormalpeople.com/when-god-is-unfaithful-reclaiming-a-theology-of-lament/ (accessed 17 June 2024).

Eshete, T. (2009). *The Evangelical Movement in Ethiopia. Resistance and Resilience* (Waco, TX: Baylor University Press).

European Union (2014). *Romania: Funding, Strategy, Facts and Figures*, Council of Europe, https://commission.europa.eu/strategy-and-policy/policies/justice-and-fundamental-rights/combatting-discrimination/roma-eu/roma-equality-inclusion-and-participation-eu-country/romania_en (accessed 11 June 2024).

Fagerli, B., Jørgensen, K., Olsen, R. and Storstein Haug, K. (2012). *A Learning Missional Church: Reflections from Young Missiologists* (Augsburg: Fortress Publishers).

Fairclough, N. (1992). *Discourse and Social Change* (Cambridge: Polity Press).

Fineman, M. (2008). 'The Vulnerable Subject: Anchoring Equality in the Human Condition', *Yale Journal of Law and Feminism* 20:1–24.

Flood, A. (2021). https://www.theguardian.com/books/2021/nov/26/robot-artist-to-perform-ai-generated-poetry-in-response-to-dante (accessed 1 November 2022).

Forte, J. A. (2014). *Skills for Using Theory in Social Work: 32 Lessons for Evidence-informed Practice* (London and New York: Routledge).

Fosztó, L. (2007). 'Born Again in Postsocialist Romania: Ritual, Personhood, and Conversion among the Roma in a Transylvanian

Village', PhD Thesis, der Martin-Luther-Universität, 2007, 83. DOI:10.13140/2.1.2866.4641.

Freire, P. (1970). *Cultural Action for Freedom* (Cambridge, MA: Harvard Education Review).

———. (1972). *Pedagogy of the Oppressed* (Harmondsworth: Penguin).

———. (2000). *The Pedagogy of the Oppressed (30th Anniversary Edition)* (New York: Continuum Press).

———. (2018). *Pedagogy of the Oppressed* (London: Bloomsbury Publishing).

Furtună, Adrian-Nicolae (2020). *Sclavia romilor în Ţara Românească / Roma Slavery în Wallachia, Centrul de cultură a romilor* (Bucureşti: Romano Kher).

Gadamer, Hans-Georg (1975). *Truth and Method* (London: Sheed & Ward).

Genocide of European Roma (Gypsies) 1939–1945, *Holocaust Encyclopedia*, https://encyclopedia.ushmm.org/content/en/article/genocide-of-european-roma-gypsies-1939-1945 (accessed 15 October 2023).

Global Findings (2023). https://monitor.civicus.org/globalfindings_2023/ (accessed 11 June 2024).

Gorman, M. (2006). *Becoming the Gospel: Paul, Participation, and Mission* (The Gospel and Our Culture Series, GOCS) (Grand Rapids, MI: Eerdmans).

Gratitude Initiative (n.d.). https://gratitudeinitiative.org.uk/ (accessed 31 July 2023).

Gunton, C. E. (1993). *The One, the Three, and the Many: God, Creation, and the Culture of Modernity* (New York: Cambridge University Press).

———. (1998). *The Triune Creator: A Historical and Systematic Study*, Edinburgh Studies in Constructive Theology (Grand Rapids, MI: Eerdmans).

Guy-Evans, Olivia (2023). 'Fight, Flight, Freeze, or Fawn: How We Respond to Threats,' *Simply Psychology*, https://www.simplypsychology.org/fight-flight-freeze-fawn.html#What-Is-Fight-Flight-or-Freeze (accessed 1st October 2023).

Halverstadt, H. R. (1991). *Managing Church Conflict* (Louisville, KY: Westminster/John Knox Press).

Hancock, I. (2007). 'The Struggle for the Control of Identity', *Transitions* 4 (4):36–44.

Harper, L. S. (2016). *The Very Good Gospel: How Everything Wrong Can Be Made Right* (Colorado Springs, CO: Waterbrook).

Hauerwas, S. (2005). 'Suffering the Retarded: Should We Prevent Retardation' in J. Swinton (ed.), *Critical Reflections on Stanley Hauerwas' Essays on Disability: Disabling Society, Enabling Theology* (New York: Haworth Press), pp. 86–106.

Hiebert, Paul G. (2008). *Transforming Worldviews: An Anthropological Understanding of How People Change* (Grand Rapids, MI: Baker Academic).

Hiebert, Paul G. and Meneses, Eloise H. (1995). *Incarnational Ministry: Planting Churches in Band, Tribal, Peasant, and Urban Societies* (Grand Rapids, MI: Baker Books).

Hooks, B. (1994). *Teaching to Transgress: Education as the Practice of Freedom* (New York: Routledge).

Houston, Marsha and Kramarae, Cheris (1991). 'Speaking from Silence: Methods of Silencing and of Resistance', *Discourse & Society* 2 (4):387–99.

Hsia, Ronnie Po-chia (2018). 'Chinese Voices in the Rites Controversy: From China to Rome', in Ines G. Županov and Pierre Antoine Fabre (eds), *The Rites Controversies in the Early Modern World* (Leiden: Brill), pp. 29–49.

Immerwahr, D. (2019). *How to Hide an Empire: A History of the Greater United States* (New York: Farrar, Straus and Giroux).

Jackson, Darrell and Passarelli, Alessia (2021). Mapping Migration, Mapping Churches' Responses in Europe: 'Being Church Together', Churches' Commission for Migrants in Europe and World Council of Churches, https://ccme.eu/wp-content/uploads/2021/05/2021-05-20_Mapping-Migration3-2020-PDF-FINAL.pdf (accessed 11 June 2024).

John Paul II, Pope (1985). *Encyclical Epistle Slavorum Apostoli of His Holiness John Paul II* (Strathfield, Australia: St Pauls Publications).

Jones, S. (2019). *Trauma and Grace* (2nd edn) (Louisville, KY: Westminster/John Knox Press).

Jun, G. (2020). *A Holistic Model of Handling Conflicts: Lessons from a Multicultural Congregation in Britain* (Oxford: Regnum).

Jupiter, J. L. (2017). *Basic Etiquette with Monks and in the Khmer*

*Temple by Venerable Prenz*, YouTube, https://www.youtube.com/watch?v=wOkUCXNQuGs (accessed: 5 August 2023).

Kenrick, D. (2007). *Historical Dictionary of the Gypsies (Romanies), Historical Dictionaries of Peoples and Cultures Series* (Lanham, MD: Scarecrow Press).

Khmer Online Dictionary (2017). http://www.khmer-dictionary.appspot.com/?q=ផ្កាយបុរាណ&btnG=Search&dic=headley&criteria =word and http://www.khmer-dictionary.appspot.com/?q=បុរាណ&btnG=Search&dic=headley&criteria =word.

Kóczé, A. (2015). '"Speaking from the Margins", Roma Rights, Roma Rights 2: Nothing About Us Without Us?' *Roma Participation in Policy Making and Knowledge Production*: 83–6.

Kogălniceanu, M. (1908). *Desrobirea țiganilor. Ștergerea privilegiilor boierești* (București: Emanciparea țăranilor).

Kool, A.-M. (2016). 'Eastern European Churches Engaging Roma People: Historical and Missiological Perspectives,' in Corneliu Constantineanu et. al. (eds), *Mission in Central and Eastern Europe: Realities, Perspectives, Trends*, Regnum Edinburgh Centenary Series 34 (Oxford: Regnum), pp. 520–43.

Kovats, M. (2002). 'The European Roma Question', The Royal Institute of International Affairs, March 2002, https://www.chathamhouse.org/sites/default/files/public/Research/Europe/roma.pdf (accessed 19 April 2024).

Kramarae, Cheris (1981). *Women and Men Speaking: Frameworks for Analysis* (Rowley, MA: Newbury House Publishers).

Kramarae, C. and Spender, D. (eds) (2000). *Routledge International Encyclopedia of Women: Global Women's Issues and Knowledge* (New York: Routledge).

Kretsedemas, Philip, Capetillo-Ponce, Jorge and Jacobs, Glenn (eds) (2013). *Migrant Marginality: A Transnational Perspective* (London: Routledge).

Kwiyani, Harvey (2014). *Sent Forth: African Missionary Work in the West* (New York: Maryknoll).

Larsen, Timothy (2021). *Every Leaf, Line, and Letter: Evangelicals and the Bible from the 1730s to the Present* (Downers Grove, IL: IVP Academic).

Lederach, J. P. (1995). *Preparing for Peace: Conflict Transformation Accultures* (Syracuse, NY: Syracuse University Press).

Lee, Jung Young (1995). *Marginality: The Key to Multicultural Theology* (Minneapolis, MN: Augsburg Fortress Press).

Lepchitz, R. (2012). 'Perceived Muted Voice and Its Impact on Female Communication Techniques in the Workplace', MA thesis, Gongaza University, Washington.

Lin, Chi Ping (1985). 'Ancestor Worship: The Reactions of Chinese Churches', in Bong Rin Ro (ed.), *Christian Alternatives to Ancestor Practices* (Taoyuan, Taiwan: Asia Theological Association), pp. 147–61.

Lin, Jin Shui (1994). 'Chinese Literati and the Rites Controversy', in David E. Mungello (ed.), *The Chinese Rites Controversy: Its History and Meaning* (Nettetal: Steyler Verlag), pp. 65–82.

Lopez-Baez, S. I. and Paylo, M. J. (2009). 'Social Justice Advocacy: Community Collaboration and Systems Advocacy', *Journal of Counselling & Development* 87:276–83.

McBride, H. L. (2021). *The Wisdom of Your Body: Finding Healing, Wholeness, and Connection through Embodied Living* (Ada, MI: Baker Publishing Group).

McGarry, Aidan (2013). 'Romophobia: The Last Acceptable Form of Racism', opendemocracy.net, https://www.opendemocracy.net/en/can-europe-make-it/romaphobia-last-acceptable-form-of-racism/ (accessed 19 April 2024).

Mahrukh, S., Ahmad, A. and Iqbal, L. (2017). 'Silencing the Silence: A Study of Women at Workplace', *Global Social Sciences Review* 2 (2):162–76.

Malley, Brian (2004). *How the Bible Works: An Anthropological Study of Evangelical Biblicism* (Walnut Creek, CA: AltaMira Press).

Martin, F. (2001). 'Spirit and Flesh in the Doing of Theology', *Journal of Pentecostal Theology* 9 (8):5–31, https://doi.org/10.1177/096673690100901802 (accessed 18 June 2023).

Martin, William A. P. (1896). *A Cycle of Cathay: Or, China, South and North with Personal Reminiscences* (Edinburgh: Oliphant Anderson and Ferrier).

———. (1903). 'The Worship of Confucius: Is it Idolatry?', *The Chinese Recorder*, February: 92–4.

———. (1904). 'The Worship of Ancestors: How Shall We Deal With it?', *The Chinese Recorder*, June: 301–8.

———. (1912). *The Lore of Cathay: Or, the Intellect of China* (New York: Fleming H. Revell).

Maschler, Y. (2009). *Metalanguage in Interaction: Hebrew Discourse Markers* (Amsterdam: John Benjamins).

Matzke-Fawcett, A. (2019). *Muted Groups Theory in Human Trafficking*, College of Arts and Letters Posters, 6, https://digitalcommons.odu.edu/arts_and_letters/6 (accessed 17 June 2024).

Mbiti, John (1969). *African Religions and Philosophy* (London: Heinemann Educational).

Meares, Mary M. (2002). '"People Need to Be Heard": Perceptions of Voice from Employees from Traditionally Muted Groups', PhD, University of New Mexico.

———. (2017). 'Muted Group Theory', in *The International Encyclopedia of Intercultural Communication* (London: Wiley-Blackwell), pp. 1–8.

Meares, M., Torres, A., Derkacs, D., Oetzel, J. and Ginossar, T. (2004). 'Employee Mistreatment and Muted Voices in the Culturally Diverse Workplace', *Journal of Applied Communication Research* 32 (1):4–27.

Meier, V. (2018). 'Neither Bloody Persecution nor Well Intended Civilizing Missions Changed Their Nature or Their Number', *Critical Romani Studies* 1 (1): 86–126, https://doi.org/10.29098/crs.v1i1.7 (accessed 19 April 2024).

Memory, J. and Reifsnider, U. (2023). 'Are We Really Listening to what God Is Saying to the Church in Europe Today?', Lausanne European Movement, https://evangelicalfocus.com/europe/24349/lausanne-europe-2023-are-we-really-listening-to-what-god-is-saying-to-the-church-in-europe-today (accessed 11 June 2024).

Middleton, J. Richard (2005). *The Liberating Image* (Grand Rapids, MI: Brazos Press).

Miller, K. (2005). *Communication Theories: Perspectives, Processes, and Contexts* (New York: McGraw Hill).

Mills, J. (2006). 'Talking about Silence: Gender and the Construction of Multilingual Identities', *International Journal of Bilingualism* 10 (1):1–16.

Mirga-Kruszelnicka, A. (2018). 'Challenging Anti-Gypsyism in Academia',

*Critical Romani Studies* 1 (1): 8–28, https://doi.org/10.29098/crs.v1i1.5, 11 (accessed 17 June 2024).

Moder, A. (2020). 'The Changing Self: Forming and Reforming the *imago Dei* in Survivors of Domestic Abuse', in K. O' Donnell and K. Cross (eds), *Feminist Trauma Theologies: Body, Scripture and Church in Critical Perspective* (London: SCM Press).

Mullins, Mark R. (1998). *Christianity Made in Japan: A Study of Indigenous Movements*, Nanzan Library of Asian Religion and Culture (Honolulu, HI: University of Hawaii Press).

Mungello, David E. (ed.) (1994). *The Chinese Rites Controversy: Its History and Meaning* (Nettetal: Steyler Verlag).

Musito, Rose M. (2022). 'Net-Zero Plans Exclude Africa', *Nature*, https://www.nature.com/articles/d41586-022-03475-0 (accessed 7 June 2023).

Năstase, George Rafael (2023). 'Conversion – the Path to Roma Individual and Community Transformation: A Theological Perspective of the Transformation of Roma Communities in Romania through the Lens of Black and Liberation Theology', in *Jurnal Teologic* 22 (2):143–63.

National Center for Roma Culture (2023). *Dukhake lila / Scrisorile Durerii* (Letters of Sorrow), YouTube, https://www.youtube.com/watch?v=gBu6Tea0ivQ (accessed 11 June 2024).

Negash, Tekeste (1996). *Rethinking Education in Ethiopia* (Uppsala: Nordiska Afrikainstitutet).

Nguyen, T. T., Bellehumeur, C. R. and Malette, J. (2014). 'Women Survivors of Sex Trafficking: A Trauma and Recovery Model Integrating Spirituality', *Counselling and Spirituality* 33 (1):111–133, https://doi.org/10.2143/CS.33.1.3044833 (accessed 13 January 2023).

Nowakowski, E. S., Rooney, M., Vogue, D. and Woods, S. (2023). 'A Grounded Theory of Weightlifting as a Healing Strategy for Trauma', *Mental Health and Physical Activity* 25, https://www.sciencedirect.com/science/article/abs/pii/S1755296623000194 (accessed 4 October 2023).

O'Donnell, K. (ed.) (2020). *Feminist Trauma Theologians: Body Scripture and Church in Critical Perspective* (London: SCM Press).

Olivera, M. (2012). *Romanes, tradinția integrarii la romii gabori din Transilvania* (Editura Institutului pentru Studierea Problemelor Minorităților Naționale).

Olofinjana, Israel (2022). 'Sustainability, African Identity and Climate

Justice: Reframing the Climate Conversation', *ANVIL Journal of Theology and Mission* 38:2, https://churchmissionsociety.org/anvil/sustainability-african-identity-and-climate-justice-israel-olofinjana-anvil-vol-38-issue-2/ (accessed 17 June 2024).

Orbe, Mark P. (1998a). *Constructing Co-cultural Theory: An Explication of Culture, Power, and Communication* (Thousand Oaks, CA: Sage).

———. (1998b). 'From the Standpoint(s) of Traditionally Muted Groups: Explicating a Co-cultural Communication Theoretical Model', *Communication Theory* 8 (1):1–26.

———. (2005). 'Continuing the Legacy of Theorizing from the Margins: Conceptualizations of Co-cultural Theory', *Women and Language* 28 (2):65–72.

Oxford Centre for Mission Studies (2024). https://www.ocms.ac.uk/regnum-centenary-free-downloads/ (accessed 11 June 2024).

Paul Baer, A. (2017). 'Muted Groups and Public Discourses: The Web of Sexual Violence and Social Media', Doctor of Education thesis, Frostburg State University.

Perez, C. (2019). *Invisible Women: Data Bias in a World Designed for Men* (New York: Abrams Press).

Peterson, David G. (2009). *The Acts of the Apostles* (Chicago, IL: Eerdmans).

Polaris Project (2023). *Love and Trafficking*, https://polarisproject.org/love-and-trafficking/ (accessed 27 October 2023).

Poluha, Eva (2004). *The Power of Continuity: Ethiopia through the Eyes of Its Children* (Uppsala: Nordiska Afrikainstitutet).

Population and Housing Census (2011). https://www.recensamantromania.ro/rpl-2011/rezultate-2011/ (accessed 8 March 2021).

Quijano, Aníbal (2007). 'Coloniality and Modernity/Rationality', *Cultural Studies* 21 (2/3):168–78, https://doi.org/10.1080/09502380601164353 (accessed 17 June 2024).

Raheb, M. (2014). *Faith in the Face of Empire: The Bible through Palestinian Eyes* (New York: Orbis Books).

Rahmato, D. (1984). *Agrarian Reform in Ethiopia* (Uppsala: Scandinavian Institute of African Studies).

Rambo, S. (2010). *Spirit and Trauma: A Theology of Remaining* (Louisville, KY: John Knox Press).

Redie, B. (2013). *The Horn of Africa: Intra-State and Inter-State Conflicts and Security* (London and New York: Pluto Press).

Reifsnider, Usha (2022). 'Reclaiming British Gujarati Hindu Culture after Conversion to Evangelical Christianity', PhD, Oxford Centre for Mission Studies, Middlesex University.

Reis, L. (1997). 'The Role of Women in the Ministry', *Novas de Alegria Magazine* 648, January 1997, 7–8.

Reuter, L. (2000). 'Human Is What Is Born of a Human: Personhood, Rationality, and a European Convention', *Journal of Medicine and Philosophy* 25 (2):181–94.

Reynolds, T. (2008). *Vulnerable Communion: A Theology of Disability and Hospitality* (Grand Rapids, MI: Brazos Press).

Rieser, R. (2006). 'Disability Equality: Confronting the Oppression of the Past', in M. Cole (ed.), *Education, Equality and Human Rights* (London: Routledge), pp. 118–40.

Ritskes, C. (2018). 'A Defense of Penal Substitutionary Atonement and Divine Justice', *Churchman* 132 (4):311–18, churchsociety.org/churchman/archive/ (accessed 17 June 2024).

Ro, Bong Rin (1985). *Christian Alternatives to Ancestor Practices* (Taichung: Asia Theological Association).

Roma Archive (n.d.). https://www.romarchive.eu/en/ (accessed 18 June 2024).

Rose, D. (2019). *Stop Trying to Heal Me*, https://www.bbc.co.uk/news/uk-48054113/ (accessed 20 October 2022).

Rostas, I. (2020). *O muncă de Sisif: de ce eşuează politicile europene pentru romi* (Bucureşti: Editura Centrului Naţional de Cultură a Romilor).

Rumbaut, Ruben G. (2004). 'Ages, Life Stages, and Generational Cohorts: Decomposing the Immigrant First and Second Generations in the United States', *International Migration Review* 38 (3):1160–205.

Ryder, A. R., Rostas, I. and Taba, M. (2014). '"Nothing About Us Without Us": The Role of Inclusive Community Development in School Desegregation for Roma Communities', *Race, Ethnicity and Education* 17 (4):18–39, https://doi.org/10.1080/13613324.2014.885426 (accessed 19 April 2024).

Sanyal, Mithu (2019). *Rape from Lucretia to #Me Too* (London: Verso).

Selling, J. (2018). 'Assessing the Historical Irresponsibility of the Gypsy

Lore Society in Light of Romani Subaltern Challenges', *Critical Romani Studies* 1 (1):44–61, https://doi.org/10.29098/crs.v1i1.15. 48 (accessed 17 June 2024).

Shaw, R. Daniel (2010). 'Beyond Contextualization: Toward a Twenty-first Century Model for Enabling Mission', *International Bulletin of Missionary Research* 34 (4):208–15.

Shaw, R. Daniel, DeLoach, Danny, Grimes, Jonathan, Herrmann, Simon and Bailey, Stephen (2016). 'Contextualization, Conceptualization, and Communication: The Development of Contextualization at Fuller's Graduate School of World Mission/Intercultural Studies', *Missiology* 44 (1):95–111.

Shiloh Project (2017). *For Such a Time as This? #UsToo: Sexual Trafficking, Silence, and Secrecy in the Book of Esther*, https://www.shilohproject.blog/for-such-a-time-as-this-ustoo-sexual-trafficking-silence-secrecy-in-the-book-of-esther/ (accessed 3 October 2023).

Silverman, C. (2018). 'From Reflexivity to Collaboration', *Critical Romani Studies* 1 (2):76–97, https://doi.org/10.29098/crs.v1i2.16 (accessed 19 April 2024).

Singer, A. (2022). *It's Time to Embrace Profound Autism*, https://www.spectrumnews.org/opinion/viewpoint/its-time-to-embrace-profound-autism (accessed 1 November 2022).

Smith, Christian (2011). *The Bible Made Impossible: Why Biblicism Is Not a Truly Evangelical Reading of Scripture* (Grand Rapids, MI: Brazos).

Snodgrass, Klyne R. (2018). *Who God Says You Are: A Christian Understanding of Identity* (Grand Rapids, MI: Eerdmans).

Stanback, M. H. and Pearce, W. B. (1981). 'Talking to "the Man": Some Communication Strategies Used by Members of "Subordinate" Social Groups', *Quarterly Journal of Speech* 67:21–30.

Standaert, Nicolas (2018). 'Chinese Voices in the Rites Controversy: The Role of Christian Communities', in Ines G. Županov and Pierre Antoine Fabre (eds), *The Rites Controversies in the Early Modern World* (Leiden: Brill), pp. 50–67.

Steffaniak, Jordan L. (2020). 'The God of All Creation: A Critique of Evangelical Biblicism and Recovery of Perfect Being Theology', *Journal of Reformed Theology* 14 (4): 358–80.

Stewart, M. S. (2017). 'Nothing About Us Without Us, or the Dangers of a Closed-Society Research Paradigm', https://discovery.ucl.ac.uk/id/eprint/10040006 (accessed 19 April 2024).

Strömbom, L. (2013). *Israeli Identity, Thick Recognition and Conflict Transformation* (Basingstoke: Palgrave Macmillan).

Swinton, J. (2010). 'Disability Theology', in I. McFarland, D. Fergusson, K. Kilby and I. Torrance (eds), *Cambridge Dictionary of Christian Theology* (London: Cambridge University Press), pp. 140–1.

———. (2011). 'Who Is the God We Worship? Theologies of Disability; Challenges and New Possibilities', *International Journal of Practical Theology* 14 (2):273–307.

———. (2012a). 'From Inclusion to Belonging: A Practical Theology of Community, Disability and Humanness', *Journal of Religion, Disability & Health* 16 (2):172–90.

———. (2012b). 'Many Bodies, Many Worlds', in *Disability*, pp. 18–24, https://www.baylor.edu/content/services/document.php/188190.pdf (accessed 12 October 2022).

Tam, C. (2002). 'Faithful Presence: A Practice of Belonging with People Experiencing Profound Autism', *International Journal for the Study of the Christian Church* 22 (1):21–34.

Tarusarira, J. (2017). 'African Religion, Climate Change and Knowledge Systems', *The Ecumenical Review* 69 (3):398–410, https://doi.org/10.1111/erev.12302.

Thurfjell, D. (2013). *Revivalism in a Nordic Romani Community: Pentecostalism amongst the Kaale Roma of Sweden and Finland*, Library of Modern Religion, v. 21 (London: I.B. Tauris).

Tong, Daniel (1993). *Ancestral Veneration: A Handbook for Christians* (Singapore: The Christian Library).

Turner, L. H. and Turner, R. W. (2020). *Introducing Communication Theory: Analysis and Application* (London: McGraw Hill).

Union of the Physically Impaired Against Segregation (1976). Fundamental Principles of Disability (London: UPIAS).

United Nations Women (2017). *Religion and Gender Equality*, New York, Religion_and_Gender_Equality_UNWOMEN.pdf (partner-religion-development.org) (accessed 17 June 2024).

US Department of State (2020). *About Human Trafficking*, www.state.gov/humantrafficking-about-human-trafficking/ (accessed 2 October 2023).

Van Baar, Huub (2020). 'Neoliberalism and the Spirit of Nongovernmentalism', in Sam Beck and Ana Ivasiuc (eds), *Roma Activism: Reimagining Power and Knowledge*, Romani Studies 1 (New York: Berghahn Books, 2020), pp. 25–44.

Van der Kolk, B. (2014). *The Body Keeps the Score: Brain, Mind, and Body in the Healing of Trauma* (New York: Penguin Random House).

Vest, N. (2000). *Still Listening: New Horizons in Spiritual Direction* (New York: Morehouse Publishing).

Volf, M. (1996). *Exclusion and Embrace: A Theological Exploration of Identity, Otherness, and Reconciliation* (Nashville, TN: Abingdon Press).

Wall, C. J. and Gannon-Leary, P. (1999). 'A Sentence Made by Men: Muted Group Theory Revisited', *European Journal of Women's Studies* 6 (1):21–9.

Walls, A. F. (1996). *The Missionary Movement in Christian History: Studies in the Transmission of Faith* (Maryknoll, NY: Orbis).

Walton, J. (ed.) (2019). *Cultural Backgrounds Study Bible: New Revised Standard Version* (Grand Rapids, MI: Zondervan).

Walton, J. R. (2000). *Feminist Liturgy: A Matter of Justice* (Collegeville, MN: Liturgical Press).

Wang, Xue Ying (2022). '"The Ancient Rites of China": Yan Mo on Ancestral Rites During the Chinese Rites Controversy, *Journal of World Christianity* 12 (1):90–112.

Weber, M. (2022). *Economy and Society* (Coimbra, Portugal: Edições 70).

West, Richard L. and Turner, Lynn H. (2017) (6th edn). *Introducing Communication Theory: Analysis and Application* (New York: McGraw Hill).

Wilkerson, I. (2020). *Caste: The Origins of Our Discontents* (New York: Random House).

Willard, Dallas (2015). *The Allure of Gentleness: Defending the Faith in the Manner of Jesus* (New York: HarperCollins).

Williams, Eric (2022). *Capitalism and Slavery* (Milton Keynes: Penguin Classics).

Wise, D. (2022). Developing a Genuinely Multi-ethnic Local Church Congregation: An Auto-ethnographic Investigation into Greenford Baptist Church 1987–2014, https://pure.roehampton.ac.uk/portal/

en/studentTheses/developing-a-genuinely-multi-ethnic-local-church-congregation (accessed 19 April 2024).

Wolde-Mariam, M. (1986). *Rural Vulnerability to Famine in Ethiopia* (London: Intermediate Technology Publications Ltd).

World Council of Churches (2012). *Together Towards Life: Mission and Evangelism in Changing Landscapes*, https://www.oikoumene.org/resources/documents/together-towards-life-mission-and-evangelism-in-changing-landscapes (accessed 11 June 2024).

———. (2018). *The Arusha Call to Discipleship*, https://www.oikoumene.org/resources/documents/the-arusha-call-to-discipleship (accessed 11 June 2024).

World Missionary Conference (1910). *Reports of Commission I to VIII and The History and Records of the Conference Together with Addresses Delivered at the Evening Meetings* (Edinburgh and London: WCC).

Wrogemann, Henning and Böhmer, Karl E., *Intercultural Theology*, vol. 1, *Intercultural Hermeneutics*, vol. 1, Missiological Engagements (Downers Grove, IL: InterVarsity Press, 2016).

Yeh, Allen (2016). *Polycentric Missiology: Twenty-First-Century Mission from Everyone to Everywhere* (Downers Grove, IL: IVP Academic).

Young, F. (2014). *Arthur's Call: A Journey of Faith in the Face of Severe Learning Disability* (London: SPCK).

Zeng, Zhen Yu (2011). 'Semantic Criticism: The "Westernization" of the Concepts in Ancient Chinese Philosophy: A Discussion of Yan Fu's Theory of Qi', *Frontiers of Philosophy in China* 6 (1):100–13.

Zurlo, G. (2023). *Women in World Christianity, Building and Sustaining a Global Movement* (Hoboken, NJ: Wiley-Blackwell).